Frozen Tears

The Blockade and Battle of Leningrad

Albert Pleysier

UNIVERSITY PRESS OF AMERICA, ® INC.
Lanham • Boulder • New York • Toronto • Plymouth, UK

Copyright © 2008 by
University Press of America,® Inc.
4501 Forbes Boulevard
Suite 200
Lanham, Maryland 20706
UPA Acquisitions Department (301) 459-3366

Estover Road
Plymouth PL6 7PY
United Kingdom

Library of Congress Control Number: 2008927919
ISBN-13: 978-0-7618-4125-8 (clothbound : alk. paper)
ISBN-10: 0-7618-4125-3 (clothbound : alk. paper)
ISBN-13: 978-0-7618-4126-5 (paperback : alk. paper)
ISBN-10: 0-7618-4126-1 (paperback : alk. paper)
eISBN-13: 978-0-7618-4172-2
eISBN-10: 0-7618-4172-5

The book is dedicated to Leon Goure (1922–2007)

Contents

Preface

In June 1941, Germany's military forces invaded the Soviet Union from the west and in the following month Finland's troops advanced into Soviet territory from the north. By the end of September the Germans and Finns had established a blockade against the city of Leningrad. Thereafter, the Germans struck the besieged city with incessant aerial bombing and with artillery fire from long-range guns. The bombs and the artillery shells caused the pipes of Leningrad's water system to burst, and the rivers that flowed through Leningrad and the city's canals became the people's sources of water. A shortage of fuel in the city reduced the power supply, adversely affecting heating, lighting and cooking. But what was most devastating was the shortage of food. Supplies were airlifted into Leningrad and delivered on barges across Lake Ladoga located east of the city, but they were insufficient to feed the people. During the last days of November and throughout most of December the daily ration of bread was 250 grams for workers in factories and 125 grams for office workers, dependents and children. People ate whatever they could find to stay alive. The winter of 1941-1942 was particularly severe and one of the coldest in many years. The freezing temperatures, however, deepened the ice that covered Lake Ladoga and made it possible to create ice roads across the lake. Food and other supplies were brought from the Russian mainland to the east shore of the lake, transported across the lake on ice roads and then taken into Leningrad. The Road of Life, as it was called, saved the city. Yet hundreds of thousands of its people would die from starvation during the first winter of the siege. The blockade around the city finally came to an end in early 1944. By that time more than a million Leningraders had lost their lives.

Acknowledgments

The picture on the cover of the book is based on a photograph that was made in Leningrad during the blockade. The man is holding his daily ration of bread. He is suffering from starvation which is evident in his hollow cheeks, his sharp-featured nose and his protruding eyes. The picture was done in oil pastels by Jane Pleysier and the author wishes to thank the artist for giving him permission to use it.

The author also wishes to thank Aron Pleysier for creating the maps that are included in the text and Elena Martilla for giving permission to use one of her sketches.

Finally, the author is indebted to Dr. Alexey Vinogradov, a friend and colleague, for helping the author translate the letters of Robert Pershitz.

Introduction

History, as an academic discipline, possesses an inherent tension. It is a study of the recorded past which consists of data and facts. At times the record of past events is uninspiring and even boring. At others times it is interesting and captivating. History also involves a search for the meaning of events that have been recorded. It is the interpretation of data, an exploration of the significance of the facts, and it is the effort to explain which distinguishes the historian from the storyteller. However, the author believes that too often historians ignore the role as storyteller. If historians wish to address an audience beyond the academic world and communicate with a larger society they must record the events of the past as a story. The author has tried to do this by telling the account of Leningrad's epic struggle during World War Two. It is a chronological approach that starts with the events that would bring about Germany's military invasion of the Soviet Union in 1941. It continues with Germany's advance on Leningrad and concentrates on the blockade that was established against the city and the consequences from which its people suffered. The story ends with the city's liberation in 1944.

The lives of public figures, people that society regards as important men and women, are often used by historians to record the events of the past. The events are seen through their eyes. The decisions that they made and the actions that they took and the influence that those decisions and actions had on future developments are described and explained. Political leaders such as Joseph Stalin, military leaders like Marshal Georgy Zhukov, a composer and musician such as Dmitry Shostakovich and literary figures such as Olga Berggoltz hold prominent places in the histories written about the siege of Leningrad. Yet the experiences of the so-called lesser figures, men, women and children who are not mentioned by name in textbooks, often illustrate better the events that occurred. Believing this to be true, the author has taken the contents of diaries, letters, essays and interviews that were written or given by persons who lived in Leningrad during the siege and placed the experiences of these people within their historical setting. It is the hope of the author that the importance of these people's decisions and the significance of their actions become evident to the reader.

Map 1 - The Advance on Leningrad

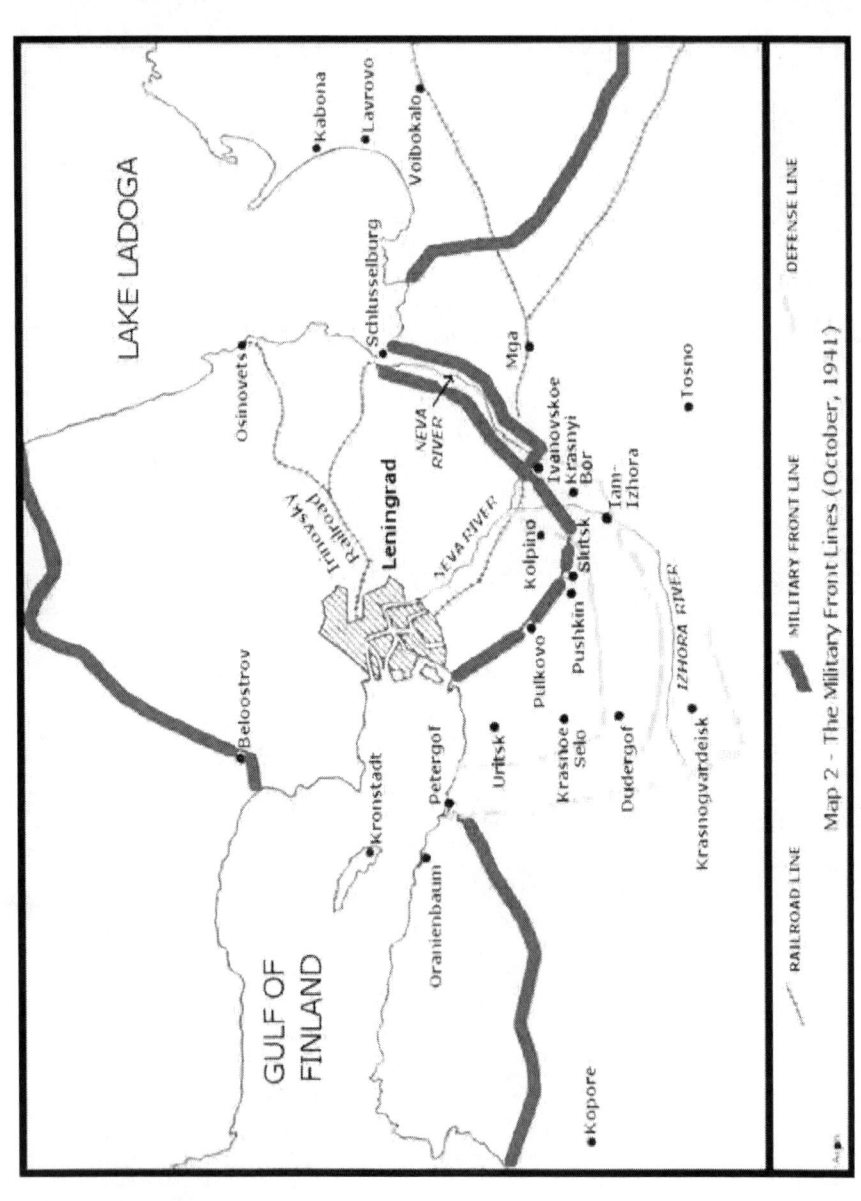

Map 2 - The Military Front Lines (October, 1941)

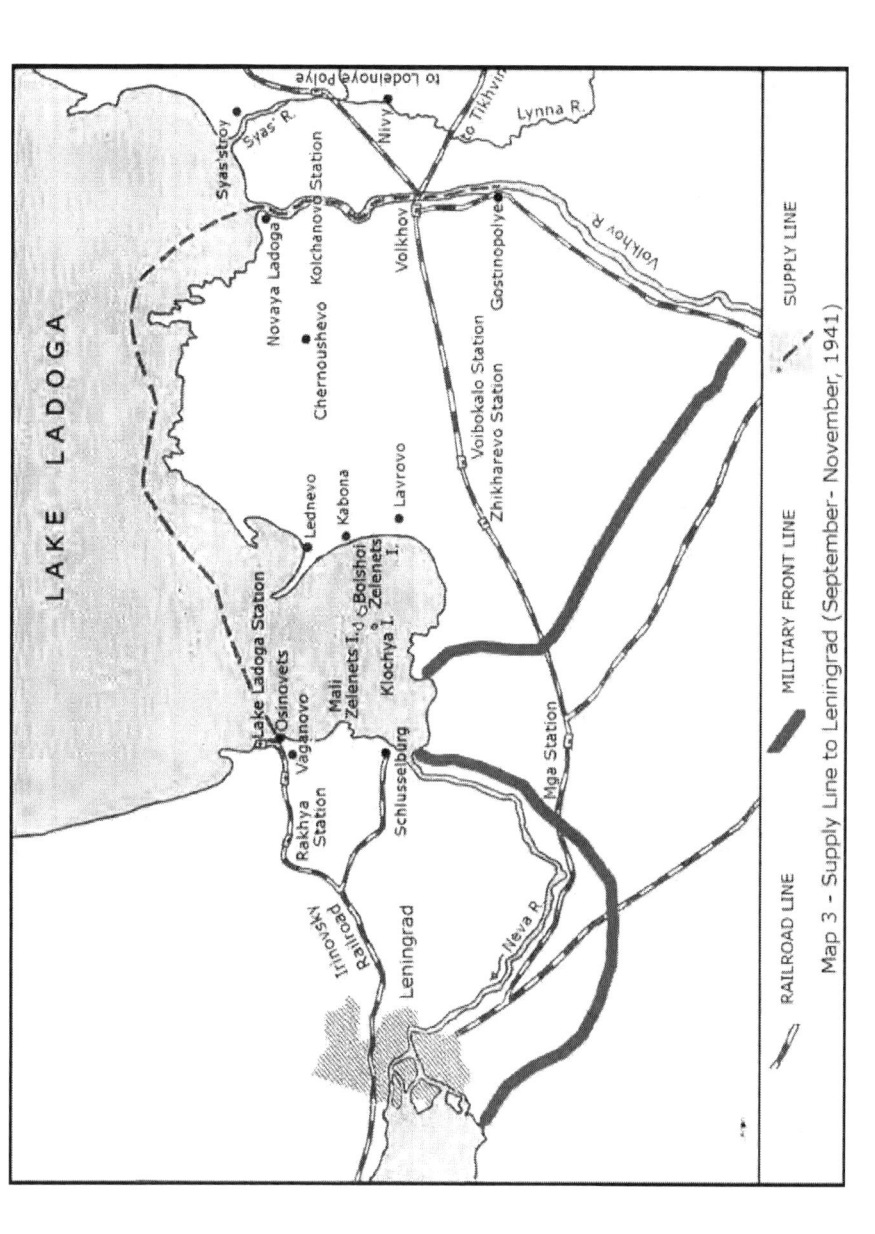

Map 3 - Supply Line to Leningrad (September- November, 1941)

RAILROAD LINE

MILITARY FRONT LINE

SUPPLY LINE

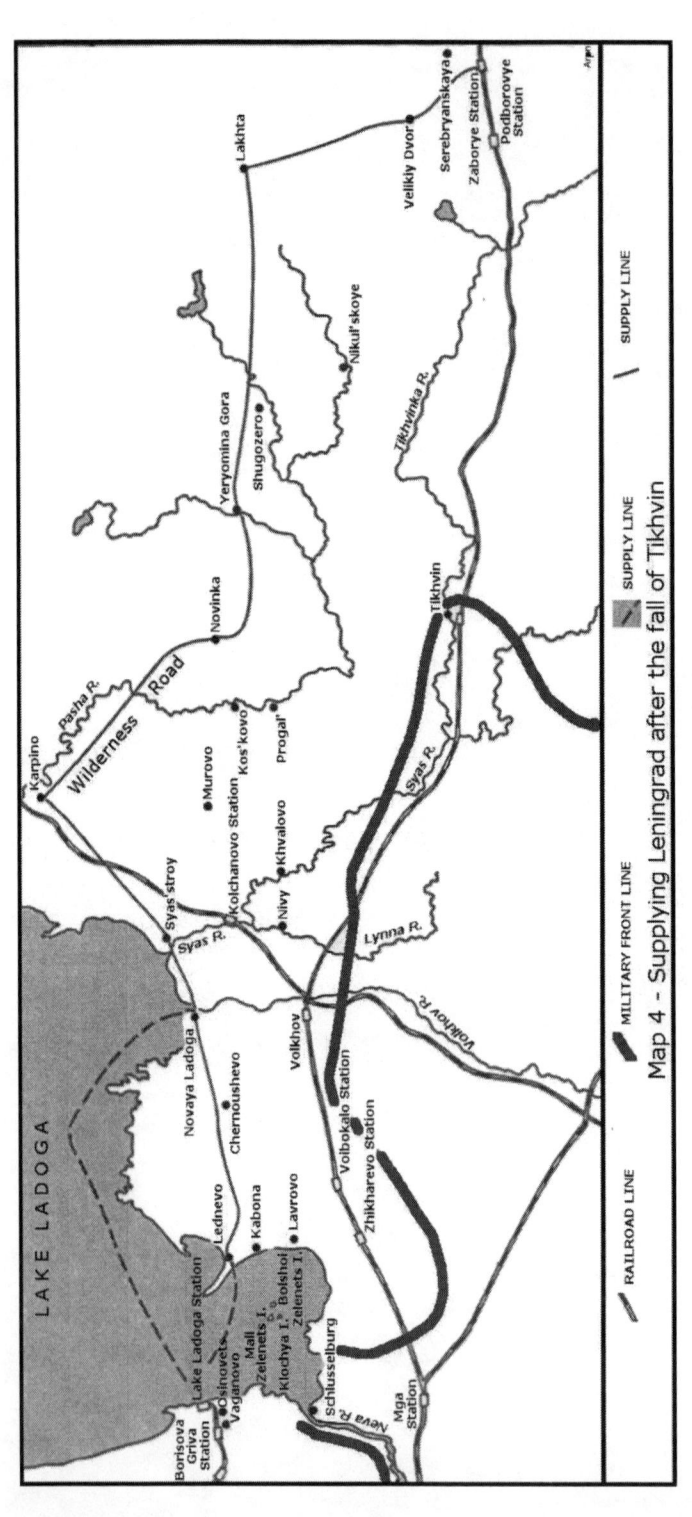

Map 4 – Supplying Leningrad after the fall of Tikhvin

RAILROAD LINE

MILITARY FRONT LINE

SUPPLY LINE

SUPPLY LINE

LAKE LADOGA

Borisova Griva Station
Osinovets
Vaganovo
Mall Zelenets I.
Klodya I. Bolshoi Zelenets I.
Lednevo
Kabona
Lavrovo
Schlusselburg
Neva R.
Mga Station
Zhikharevo Station
Volbokalo Station
Volkhov
Volkhov R.
Chernoushevo
Novaya Ladoga
Lynna R.
Nivy
Kilvalovo
Kolchanovo Station
Progal'
Kos'kovo
Murovo
Syas R.
Syas'stroy
Syas R.
Karpino
Pasha R.
Wilderness Road
Novinka
Yeryomina Gora
Shugozero
Nikul'skoye
Tikhvin
Syas R.
Tikhvinka R.
Lakhta
Velikiy Dvor
Serebryanskaya
Zaborye Station
Podborovye Station

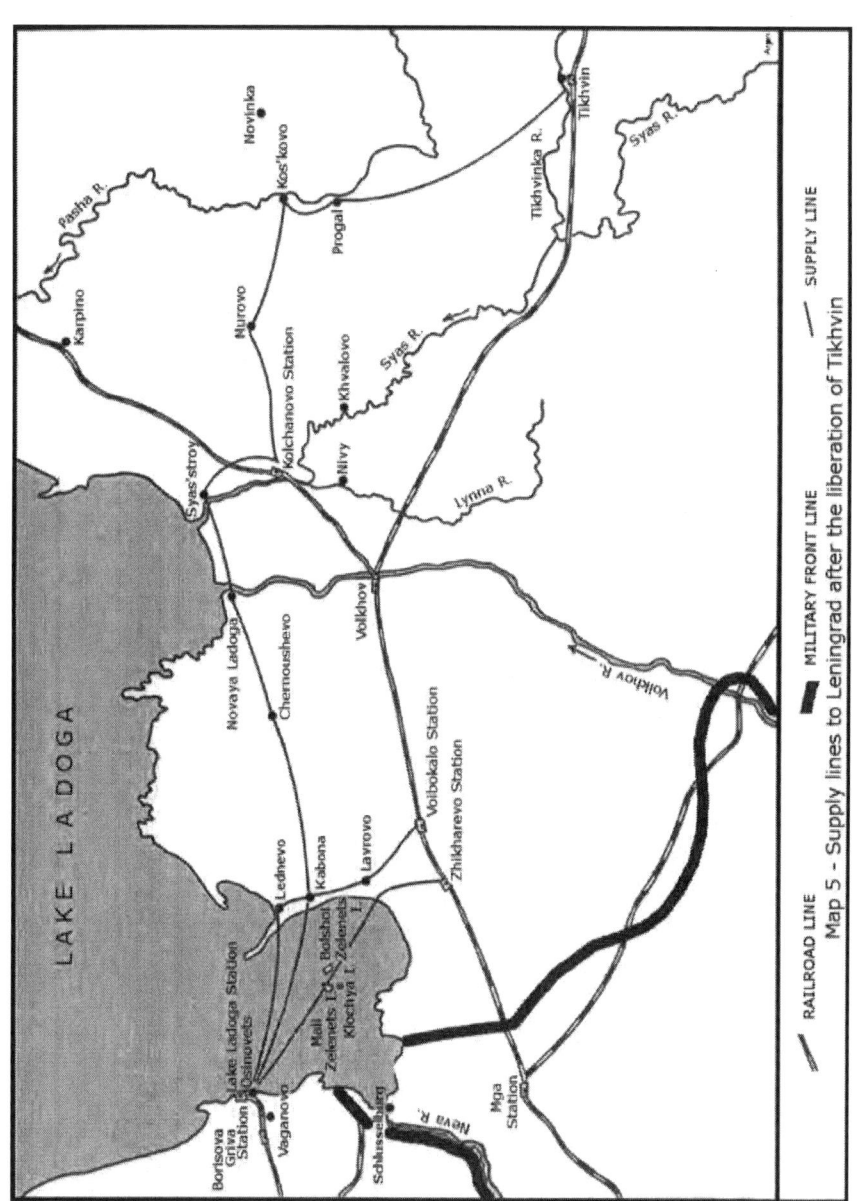

Map 5 - Supply lines to Leningrad after the liberation of Tikhvin

RAILROAD LINE   MILITARY FRONT LINE   SUPPLY LINE

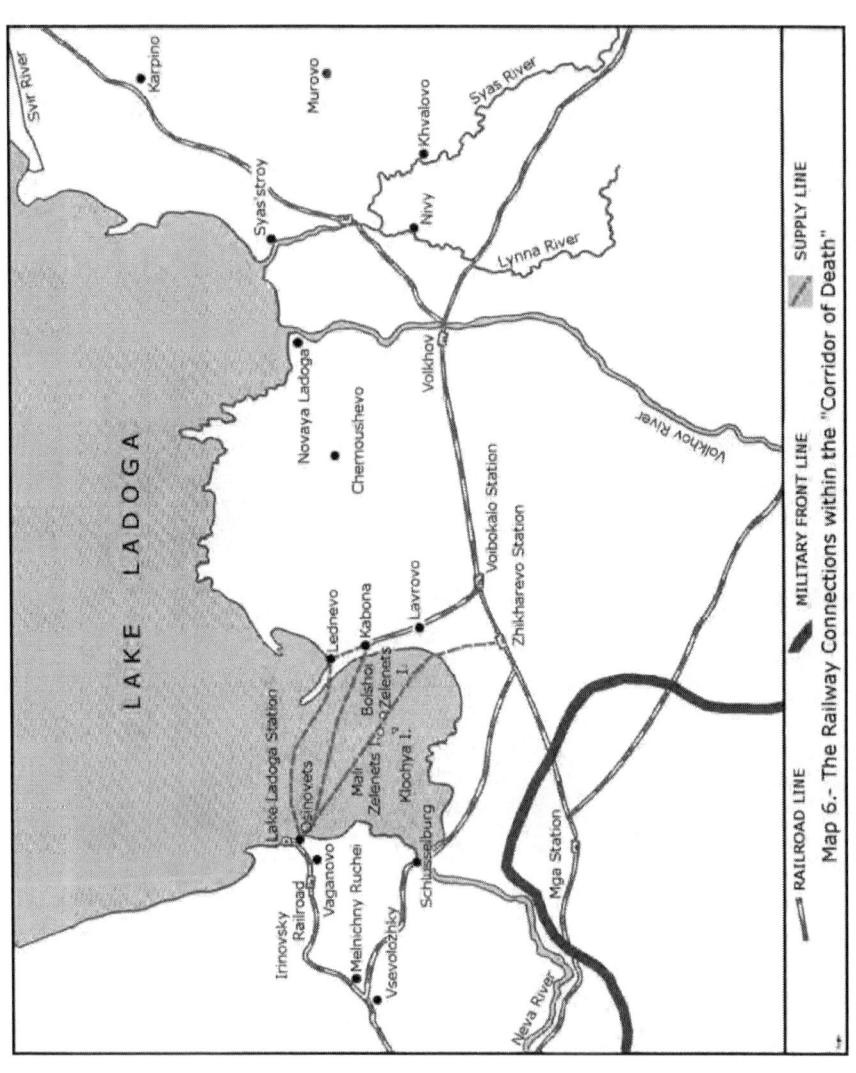

Map 6.- The Railway Connections within the "Corridor of Death"

RAILROAD LINE — — MILITARY FRONT LINE — — SUPPLY LINE

Chapter One

Prelude to the Invasion

The attack on Leningrad was the culmination of a series of events that began in 1933. In that year the National Socialist German Workers' Party became the largest political party in the Reichstag, the lower house of Germany's Parliament, and the party's leader, Adolph Hitler, was appointed Chancellor of the Weimar Republic. Shortly thereafter, the deputies in the Reichstag passed the Enabling Act, which gave the new Chancellor dictatorial power. Hitler hated the German Communists and their Marxist socialist ideology and would use his newly acquired political power to destroy the Communist movement in Germany. He also told the German citizenry that Germany needed "lebensraum" and that this living space would be acquired from Czechoslovakia, Poland and the Soviet Union.

Hitler's actions against the German Communists and the fear that the Soviet Union might become a victim of Hitler's designs caused Joseph Stalin to try and protect communist Russia through collective security. In September 1934, the Soviet Union entered the League of Nations. The Soviet delegate to the League of Nations, Maxim Litvinov, quickly became a proponent of universal disarmament and an advocate for punishing nations that carried out acts of aggression. In 1935 the Soviet Union signed pacts with France and Czechoslovakia. These treaties stated that if the League of Nations certified that Czechoslovakia had become a victim of German acts of aggression, the Soviet Union would come to the aid of the Czechs. Soviet aid would be forthcoming only after the French, who were bound to the Czechs by a long-standing alliance, honored their obligations first. But the French along with the British failed to support Czechoslovakia when Hitler demanded Czech lands at the Munich Conference held in September of 1938. The two western powers had also failed to stand up to Germany's violations of the Versailles Treaty ever since 1934. Stalin decided that he could not rely on the French and British to stop Hitler's Germany.

Convinced that collective security was no longer an option, Stalin worked at improving relations with Hitler hoping to postpone a German invasion of the Soviet Union. In May 1939, Stalin, knowing that Hitler was strongly anti-Semitic, replaced Litvinov who was Jewish with Vyacheslav Molotov as People's Commissar for Foreign Affairs. Stalin also ordered Molotov to remove all Jews from his ministry. The changes forecasted a new direction in Soviet foreign policy. In June, a Soviet diplomat in Berlin informed the German government that his country was willing to enter into a non-aggression pact with Germany. The proposal was welcomed in Germany. Hitler was eager to join the Soviets in such an agreement. He was ready to start a war with Poland and hoped to prevent French and British intervention by depriving the two western democracies of any assistance from the Soviet Union.

A non-aggression pact was signed between Germany and the Soviet Union on August 23, 1939. The two powers agreed not to attack each other and to remain neutral should either be attacked by a third party. A secret territorial protocol in the pact marked out Lithuania and western Poland as German spheres of interest. Eastern Poland, Latvia, Estonia, Finland and Bessarabia—still a part of Rumania—were marked as the Soviet Union spheres of interest. Stalin was pleased with the pact. The secret territorial protocol gave the Soviet Union the opportunity to recover lands that Russia had lost during World War One and its aftermath. At the same time, the pact gave Stalin the time he needed to build up his country's military and industrial strengths in case the Soviet Union should find itself in a military conflict with Germany.

In September German and Soviet military forces invaded Poland with the understanding that upon Poland's defeat Germany would take control of the western half of that nation and the Soviet Union would take the eastern half. The war against Poland began on the first day of September when the Germans invaded from the west. The initial phase of the attack was conducted from the air as the German Luftwaffe destroyed Poland's small air force, and German dive-bombers demolished rear guard communications and spread terror among the civilian population. The next phase of the attack was initiated by heavy tanks that were followed by lighter armored divisions. After tearing through the Polish lines, the German motorized columns streaked across Poland's flat lands, often several days ahead of the main body of German infantry. On September 17, two weeks after France and Great Britain had declared war on Germany for its invasion of Poland, Stalin sent Soviet forces into eastern Poland. By the end of the month Polish resistance had collapsed.

Stalin feared that Hitler would next order his forces against the Soviet Union and felt that measures needed to be taken to secure Russia's western borders from a military attack. He quickly forced Estonia, Latvia and Lithuania to agree to mutual assistance pacts under which the Soviet Union was given military, air and naval bases in the Baltic States. (The secret territorial protocol in the Soviet-German non-aggression pact, signed back in August 1939, marked Lithuania as a German sphere of interest; however, following Poland's defeat Lithuania was made a Soviet sphere of interest). In June 1940, the Soviet leadership accused the Baltic States of violating their mutual assistance pacts with the Soviet Union. They demanded that new governments must be established in the Baltic States, governments that would respect the mutual assistance pacts and permit Soviet troops free access to the Baltic territories. Elections were held in all three countries in July, and immediately thereafter the newly elected governments agreed to incorporate their states in the Soviet Union. Estonia, Latvia and Lithuania, which had been created out of Russian provinces at the close of World War One, were now made republics in the Union of Soviet Socialist Republics

In an attempt to further secure Russia's western borders, Stalin invited neighboring Finland to discuss "concrete political questions." In the negotiations that followed, Stalin requested that Finland cede to the Soviet Union small parcels of territory, including the naval base of Hango on the northern shore of the Gulf of Finland. From the naval base the Soviet Union would be able to block off the Gulf of Finland from German naval forces and protect Leningrad. In exchange for his requests, Stalin offered to give to Finland about eight thousand eight hundred square kilometers (5,456 square miles) of Karelia along the Finnish border; it was an area of land that was twice the size that Stalin was requesting from Finland. The talks were reported to Finland's population and they, like their government, were opposed to the Soviet Union's proposals. The Finns felt that Stalin's offer was merely a first step in subjugating Finland. The Soviet leadership believed that Finland's rejection of their offer indicated that the Finns planned to assist Hitler's Germany in a future war against the Soviet Union.

On November 30, 1939, the Soviet forces attacked Finland by land, sea and air. The leadership of the Soviet Union claimed that previous to the attack the Finns had shelled the Soviet border killing several Russian soldiers. Thereafter, the Soviet Union had demanded that the Finnish army be withdrawn some twenty-five kilometers (16 miles) from Finland's southern border. When the government of Finland refused to comply, the Soviet forces were ordered to attack. Soviet ground forces, about 600,000, were assigned to break through the Mannerheim Line, a strongly fortified zone, some thirty-two kilometers (20 miles) deep, running diagonally across the Karelian Isthmus. It was the basis of the Finnish defense system, and here much of the Finnish artillery and infantry, numbering some 300,000, were concentrated.

In December the Soviet assault was stopped on the Mannerheim Line, and by the end of the month the Finns had dealt the Soviets a series of humiliating military defeats.

By the beginning of January the Soviet military command had been reorganized, and intensive preparations for a new military offensive against the Finns were being made. Masses of tanks and heavy field guns and more than a million men were assembled. Throughout the month of January the Soviet air force and artillery bombarded the Mannerheim fortifications. On February 11, the Soviet ground forces were ordered to advance, and five days later they breached the Mannerheim Line. The breach led to a series of Finnish retreats, and by early March the Finnish army was on the verge of collapse.

The war came to end officially with the Moscow Peace Treaty which was signed on March 12, 1940. By the terms of the peace agreement, Finland was forced to give the Soviet Union land along Finland's southeastern border including its second largest city, Viipuri (Vyborg). It ceded to the Soviet Union islands in the Gulf of Finland; plus the base of Hango was to be leased to the Soviet Union for thirty years. Finland also ceded land in the Salla sector in northeastern Finland and a part of the Rybachiy Peninsula in the Petsamo area. The territories that Finland was forced to relinquish were one-tenth of the country's land mass, and they contained its best agricultural soil. Twelve percent of Finland's population lived there, and only a few hundred decided to stay. The other more than 400,000 people gave up their homes and property and moved to Finnish held territory. Through the treaty and the war against Finland that preceded it, Stalin attained his immediate objectives; the Soviet Union acquired naval bases in the Gulf of Finland and took possession of Finnish lands that were located close to and north of Leningrad.

In June 1940 Stalin demanded from Romania the province of Bessarabia and northern Bukovina. The province of Bessarabia had been taken from Russia after World War One. Bukovina was not a Russian territory, but it had a large Ukrainian population and was strategically valuable. Hitler had expected the Soviet Union to seize Bessarabia but not Bukovina because it had not been mentioned in the Soviet-German non-aggression pact. Germany permitted the seizure, but this was as far as Hitler was willing to cooperate with Stalin in eastern Europe. Hitler had found it expedient to sign a non-aggression pact with Stalin, but he never abandoned his plans for an eventual attack on the Soviet Union.

As early as July 1940, Hitler decided to invade the Soviet Union in a military operation that would be code-named Barbarossa. The invasion was to be carried out by three German armies. German Army Group South was to capture Kiev, the Donets industrial region and the Crimean Peninsula. German Army Group Center was to be directed against Minsk, Smolensk and Moscow.

German Army Group North was to invade and take control of the Soviet Baltic Republics, Kronstadt and the city of Leningrad and their ports in order to deprive the Soviet Baltic Fleet of its naval bases. German Army Group North included the Fourth Panzer Group which was to spearhead the drive to Leningrad. Flanked on the left was the Eighteenth Army which was to capture the Soviet Baltic Republics. The Sixteenth Army was on the right flank and was responsible for making contact with German Army Group Center thereby securing the latter's left flank. To achieve these objectives, General Field Marshal Wilhelm von Leeb, who was given command of German Army Group North, was to be provided with support from the air by Germany's First Air Fleet. On June 22, 1941, Operation Barbarossa was launched as German troops crossed the Soviet frontier on a front that extended from the Baltic Sea to the Black Sea. The unprovoked attack began what the Russians would call the Great Patriotic War.

Chapter Two

Invasion and Response

Operation Barbarossa began at 4:00 A.M. Moscow time, and the first official news of the invasion was heard in Leningrad eight hours later. Vyacheslav Molotov, the People's Commissar for Foreign Affairs, announced on the radio that the Soviet Union was at war:

> Citizens of the Soviet Union! The Soviet Government and its head, Comrade Stalin, have instructed me to make the following announcement:
>
> Today, at 4:00 A.M., without presenting any claims against the Soviet Union or issuing a declaration of war, German troops have attacked our country, assaulting our borders in many places and subjecting our cities of Zhitomir, Kiev, Sebastopol, Kaunas and other of our towns to bombing by their aircraft. Air raids by enemy planes and artillery bombardment were also made from bases in Rumania and Finland.
>
> This perfidious aggression against our country is a treachery without precedent in the history of civilized nations. The attack on our country has been made despite the fact of the non-aggression pact between the USSR and Germany and despite the conscientious fulfillment of the Soviet Government of all the terms of this pact. The attack on our country has been made despite the fact that the German Government had not submitted a single claim against the USSR regarding the observance of the pact during the entire time it was in force.[1]

Molotov went on to express the conviction that the Soviet military and naval forces would carry out their duty to their country with honor. He called upon the people of the Soviet Union to rally closer around the Communist Party and the government. He finished with the words:

> Our cause is just. The enemy will be defeated. Victory will be ours.[2]

Molotov's announcement left most of the city's population stunned. They had been told only a week earlier that Germany was a good friend and had no designs on Soviet territory. One Communist Party member was reported to have said that the news surprised him and his associates so much that they did not at first believe what they had heard. Many women wept, aware of the horrors that the city might be forced to endure. There were people who became indignant that the Soviet Union was under attack despite the Soviet-German non-aggression pact. A response common to the great majority of the people was to rush to the nearest banks and stores to withdraw personal savings and to purchase food and other necessities.

The local standing orders in case of war went into effect immediately. A number of schools were requisitioned and turned into hospitals. All civil defense organizations and teams were alerted and mobilized. District medical aid stations were placed on round-the-clock duty. Blackout and civil defense instructions were broadcasted throughout the city. At the same time certain security measures were carried out. The authorities ordered that all privately owned radio receivers be turned into the militia (the police). It was a step taken to prevent the population from hearing news from abroad and to shield them from exposure to enemy propaganda. To avoid this confiscation was very difficult. The owner of a private radio had been required upon purchase of the instrument to register his name, and he was required each year to pay a nominal tax. Thus, the names of the owners of radios were known by the authorities.

The population was permitted and encouraged to use their small loudspeakers which were connected by wire to the local broadcasting station. A large-scale installation of wired radio units had been launched back in 1927, and at the outbreak of the war there were some 460,000 household units. There were also some 1,700 large loud-speakers mounted on the sides of buildings in the city's streets and in parks and city squares. Through the small and large loud-speakers the Radio Committee of the Leningrad City Radio Broadcast Network would bring to the people during the war the State approved news, speeches of Party leaders, work orders issued by the leadership, words of encouragement from front-line soldiers and others, readings by writers and musical performances. The Radio Committee would work twenty-four hours a day transmitting air-raid warnings, instructions and all clear signals. Therefore, the people were urged to keep their wired radio units switched on at all times. In between the announcements, speeches, programs and air-raid warnings, the listening audience would hear the ticking of a metronome. Its beat represented the pulsating heart of the city. The ticking of the metronome assured Leningraders that their city was still alive and independent of enemy control.

Mass meetings were held by almost all organizations and in almost all the city's enterprises, offices and institutions. They were designed to inspire the people's loyalty toward their city and the Soviet leadership. The Leningradskaya Pravda, the city's most important newspaper, printed an issue on June 22 which was filled with resolutions that had been passed by factories and various institutions and organizations. They described Germany's aggression as unprovoked and treacherous, a description that mirrored Molotov's announcement, and pledged that they would work harder, produce more and contribute to the destruction of the enemy. In a resolution passed in the Krasnyi Vyborzhets Plant, the workers stated that "All of us to a man consider ourselves mobilized to carry out any work and are ready at the first call of the Party and the Soviet Government to rise in defense of our beloved Motherland and defend its inviolability to the last drop of our blood."[3]

Thousands of Leningraders rushed to volunteer for the armed services. Women, elderly men and adolescents went to the enlistment offices. Many members of the Komsomol organization also expressed their desire to volunteer (see Glossary—Komsomol). The turnout was so great that at the mobilization centers many volunteers waited for two to three days before they were transported to join the Soviet forces along one of the fronts. The Communist leadership assigned thousands of Komsomols and Party members to the mobilization centers to help the officials and workers there. Helpers were also sent to the city's railroad stations to assist in directing traffic.[4]

There were several fronts and the plan of action for each was determined by the People's Commissariat which was closely supervised by Joseph Stalin and the Soviet Union's Communist Party Politburo and Central Committee. In the Baltic Military District the Soviet forces were ordered to stop the Germans who had entered Soviet territory from East Prussia. Their chief commanding officer was General F. Kuznetsov, and they became the Northwestern Front. The Soviet Baltic Fleet, commanded by Vice-Admiral Vladimir Tributs, was ordered to prevent enemy ships from entering the Gulf of Finland as well as the Gulf of Riga and to prevent enemy landings on the Soviet coastline. The Soviet Baltic Fleet had more than 119,000 men stationed at the Tallin, Hango, Kronstadt and Libau navel bases. The Fleet included more than 220 combat ships, more than 600 aircraft and more than 2,000 guns and mortars.[5] Air defense over the northern areas of the Soviet Union including the Leningrad region was to be provided by the men of the Northern Air Defense Zone. These forces were equipped with more than 900 anti-aircraft guns, more than 200 anti-aircraft machine guns, 300 searchlights, 360 aerial obstacle balloons, more than 300 early warning posts and 300 fighter airplanes.[6] The Soviet forces stationed in the Leningrad Military District became the Northern Front. They were commanded by Lieutenant-General Markian

Popov and were ordered to stop any enemy from approaching Leningrad through the Karelian Peninsula.

On June 27, 1941, Lieutenant-General Popov placed Leningrad under martial law when he issued Order No. 1. It said that work in offices in the city and throughout the Leningrad region was to begin at 8:30 A.M. Places of entertainment, restaurants and places of public gathering were ordered to be closed by 10:45 P.M. The order established a curfew from midnight to 4:00 A.M. It closed the city to all people who were not authorized to reside in Leningrad or did not have special passes issued by their place of employment. The order provided for a complete black out of the city and described both the alert and all clear signals. It ordered a twenty-four-hour watch on all buildings. It required that flammable materials be removed from the vicinity of buildings and from attics, that attic floors be covered with a ten centimeter (4 inch) layer of sand and that boxes of sand and barrels of water, used to douse fires, be stored in attics. The order authorized the administrators of enterprises, offices and housing buildings to recruit a sufficient number of people to fight fires in their locality and do salvage work. The order was to go into effect on June 29, and from that time forward the civilian population was subjected to tighter control by Leningrad's administrators.[7]

On June 30, 1941, the State Defense Committee under Joseph Stalin's chairmanship was created. The members of the committee were Stalin, Vyacheslav Molotov, Marshal Kliment Voroshilov and two more trusted aides of Stalin, Georgi Malenkov and Lavrenti Beria. The Committee was given the authority to coordinate all of the country's military efforts both at the battle and home fronts. Its decisions were binding on "all citizens" and on all "Party, Soviet, Komsomol and military organs." [8] It organized and controlled the country's armed forces and defense, the distribution of supplies to the military and civilian populations, transportation, agriculture, the stockpiling of all types of fuels and heating materials, new construction, labor reserves and the allocation of labor and materials. The State Defense Committee maintained close control over the administration of Leningrad.

The execution of orders and directives issued by the State Defense Committee was the responsibility of Leningrad's Communist Party organs. The chief of the Leningrad Communist Party organization was Andrei Zhdanov. His official title was First Secretary of the Leningrad Communist Party. Aleksei Kuznetsov was the Secretary of the Leningrad Regional Party Committee and Peter Popkov headed the Executive Committee of the Leningrad City Soviet. Popkov, when interviewed by western reporters, would identify himself as the mayor of the city. Together Zhdanov, Kuznetsov and Popkov presided over and directed a hierarchy of city, district and regional Party committees, each headed by a Party member. All had the authority to mobilize for the defense of Leningrad

the material resources and the inhabitants that and who were under their jurisdiction.

On June 27 the Executive Committee of the Leningrad City Soviet issued
the Compulsory Labor Decree in order to mobilize the city's population for
defense work. The decree stated that all men between the ages of sixteen and
fifty and all women between sixteen and forty-five residing in Leningrad or
in the city's suburbs could be recruited to work on defense projects. The decree excluded people employed in defense industries, people who were ill,
women who were pregnant or women who were caretakers of children. Unemployed people were required to work eight hours a day; people who were
employed as well as students were required to work three hours after their
regular work or following their classes. Every seven days of required work
was to be followed by a four-day rest period. District executive committees
were assigned to enforce the decree and directors of factories, enterprises and
institutions and managers of housing buildings were to register within
twenty-four hours all persons subject to the decree. Anyone that failed to perform the required work could be penalized with "loss of freedom by administrative decision for a period of up to six months or . . . a fine of up to 3,000
rubles." [9] The people recruited under the decree were assigned a variety of
tasks. Many dug slit trenches, built air-raid shelters and sandbagged vital installations. Others worked in factories as replacements for the people who had
joined the armed services.

The expected enemy air strikes against Leningrad concerned the city's parents, and many wanted their children out of harms way. In late June it was decided that 392,000 children were to be evacuated and brought to the rural areas in the Leningrad, Kalinin and Yaroslavl regions. The children were to be
sent off under the supervision of the personnel from the school, the orphanage or the children's home with which the children were associated. On June
29 the first of ten trains carrying 15,192 children left Leningrad for the countryside. Some of the children were brought to vacation spots near towns such
as Gatchina and Luga and around cities such as Pskov and Novgorod (see
Map 1). At the same time the German forces, in their drive toward Leningrad,
were approaching the communities to which the children had been brought.
Thus, shortly after the children arrived at their destinations they were hurried
away and transported back to Leningrad in order to avoid their capture by the
enemy.[10]

Along the Northwestern Front the soldiers of the Red Army fought stubbornly but were unable to stop the advance of the enemy. By June 26 the
Fourth Panzer Group of German Army Group North had captured Kovno
and reached the Dvina River crossing it at Dvinsk. By July 1 the Eighteenth
Army on the left flank had captured Yelgava and the ports of Liepaya and

Riga (see Map 1). Meanwhile, from twelve to fifteen Red Army divisions were destroyed. On Hitler's order, German Army Group North then halted to regroup. The Red Army took advantage of the respite to bring up fresh forces. The Soviet leadership hoped to stop the enemy at the Pskov Defense Line (also known as the Stalin Line) which extended from Pskov to the Dvina River. On July 4 forces of the Fourth Panzer Group captured Ostrov, and four days later the Panzers broke through the Soviet defenses along the Stalin Line and captured Pskov (see Map 1). The Germans had entered the Leningrad region. Shortly thereafter, the Sixteenth Army on the right flank captured Opochka and the Eighteenth Army penetrated deep into the republic of Estonia (see Map 1). In less than three weeks, German Army Group North had reached a position from which it could launch an attack on Leningrad.

It was evident already during the first week of fighting that the Soviet forces of the Northwestern Front would need assistance to stop the enemy. On June 27 Leningrad's highest military and Party leaders decided to organize a people's volunteer army consisting of 200,000 men. On June 29–30 the Military Council of the People's Volunteer Army was formed along with its staff. The executive committee of each district Soviet in Leningrad was assigned to requisition schools and other buildings to house the volunteers, to provide facilities for feeding the volunteers and to acquire military instructors and supervisory personnel. Recruiting commissions were organized in every factory and large economic or municipal institution, as well as in all large offices. The actual recruiting drive was the responsibility of the Party organizations which included the Komsomol.[11]

The drive to recruit volunteers began on June 30 and was given great impetus after Joseph Stalin spoke by radio to the Soviet citizens on July 3. Stalin's speech reads in part as follows:

Comrades! Citizens! Brothers and sisters! Men of our army and navy! I am addressing you my friends!

The perfidious military attack on our fatherland, begun on June 22nd by Hitler's Germany, is continuing.

In spite of the heroic resistance of the Red Army, and although the enemy's finest divisions and finest air force units have already been smashed and have met their doom on the field of battle, the enemy continues to push forward, hurling fresh forces into the attack.

Hitler's troops have succeeded in capturing Lithuania, a considerable part of Latvia, the western part of Byelo-Russia and part of the western Ukraine. The fascist air force is extending the range of operations of its bombers and is bombing Murmansk, Orsha, Mogilev, Smolensk, Kiev, Odessa and Sebastopol.

A grave danger hangs over our country.[12]

At meetings in factories, institutions and places of public gathering, Party agitators appealed for volunteers. The official propaganda line reiterated the statements that had been made by Stalin in his radio address:

The Red Army, the Red Fleet and all the citizens of the Soviet Union must be ready to defend each foot of Soviet soil, fight to the last drop of blood for our cities and villages, and demonstrate the courage, initiative and enterprise characteristic of our people. [13]

The recruiting drive was a great success. Entire families volunteered. In factories and institutions nearly all the employees and managerial personnel rushed to register. It is reported that 80 writers, 40 percent of the Union of Leningrad Painters and 2,500 university students volunteered. Some schools and institutes lost up to 90 percent of their male students. In the forefront of the volunteers were members of the Party and the Komsomol organization. Soviet sources report that from 20,000 to 30,000 Party members and some 18,000 Komsomols joined the People's Volunteer Army and other military units. [14]

The response to the recruiting drive threatened to hamper the workings of the Party, the city's administrative machinery, public services and industry. It was necessary therefore that the directors of the Party organizations, factories and institutions, prevent their most important people from joining the People's Volunteer Army. In the Kirov Works, according to its director, "everybody without exception volunteered." The director claimed, "we could have sent 25,000 people if we had wanted to; we let only 9,000 or 10,000 go." [15] When the Elektrosila Works decided to form a regiment for the People's Volunteer Army, everyone who was able to bear arms volunteered. Thus, a selection had to be made or else the factory would not have been able to continue its operations.

On July 4 it was decided to organize immediately three People's Volunteer Army divisions. The initial plan to form fifteen divisions was abandoned when it became evident that the Red Army along the Northwestern Front was in desperate need of assistance. Each division had about 10,000 men, and the volunteers were organized into three infantry regiments, an artillery regiment and a tank battalion. Each division was provided with a few light artillery pieces and some machine guns. A majority of the men in the infantry regiments were issued rifles and the others were armed with hand grenades or Molotov cocktails (see Glossary—Molotov cocktail). In all three divisions nearly half of the men had no previous military training. Less than 5 percent of the officers had infantry training and the others were political appointees or reservists with technical specialization. Although the volunteers were untrained, the emergency was too great to allow sufficient time to prepare them for combat.[16]

As soon as the divisions were formed, they were sent into battle. The volunteers of the First Division, formed on July 10, arrived at the military front on July 14. The Second Division, formed July 12, departed for the front on July 13. The Third Division made its way to the front on the day the division was formed, July 15. Each division was created around large groups of workers from major factories. Thus, the First Division which was primarily recruited from the Kirov Works became known as the Kirov Division. All three divisions upon their arrival at the military front became involved in heavy fighting.[17]

In order to protect Leningrad from attack it was decided that lines of fortifications needed to be constructed at various locations from the city. The defense line farthest from Leningrad was to be built along the Luga River. Construction on the Luga Line began on June 29, and it was to run from the town of Narva, located near the southern shore of the Gulf of Finland, southeast to the town of Kingisepp and then along the Luga River through the town of Luga to a town named Shimsk at Lake Il'men (see Map 1). Three rings of fortifications were to be constructed closer to the city. These were to be used by the Soviet forces defending the Luga Line, should they be forced to retreat. The outermost ring was to extend from the Gulf of Finland at a location east of Petergof, run south around Krasnogvardeisk and end a distance east of that community. The second ring was to begin on the Neva River in the area of Ust-Tosno and to extend southwest by way of Iam-Izhora to the Izhora River and follow the river west. The innermost ring was to extend from the Neva River going southwest to protect Kolpino, Slutsk and Pushkin and then curve north to cover Krasnoe Selo and end along the southern shore of the Gulf of Finland (see Map 2). Along the southern outskirts of the city, barricades were to be built across streets, and buildings were to be fortified.

Large numbers of workers were needed to construct the fortifications, and it was decided that the Compulsory Labor Decree of June 27 was to be used to mobilize the population. Later, on July 11 and on August 9, two more decrees were issued. The decree of August 9 would extend the age range of persons liable to compulsory labor from fifteen to fifty-five for men and from sixteen to fifty for women. The decree also changed the work schedule to seven days of work followed by one day of rest for work performed within the city and fourteen days of work followed by two days of rest for work done on distant fortifications.[18]

The Communist Party organizations took an active role in the mobilization of the people. Draft orders were often issued by the secretary of a Party cell in an enterprise or an institution. At one medical school, for example, the secretary of the school's Komsomol organization made the following announcement to the assembled students:

> Comrades! Despite firm resistance by our troops, the enemy has succeeded in moving forward. Our city is in imminent danger. Leningrad, the cradle of the Revolution, is threatened. Therefore, after discussing the situation with the military authorities, the Leningrad Soviet and the Party organization in the city have issued the following orders:
>
> 1. All studies at institutions of higher learning, with the exception of several technical courses and the last two years of medical school, are suspended.
> 2. All students and part of the faculty will be sent to dig trenches.
> 3. Upper-class students of high schools will be sent to dig trenches.
> 4. It is suggested that factory directors allot part of their workers and administrative personnel to dig trenches.
>
> In accordance with this order, Comrades, all first, second and third year students will report to the institute at eight tomorrow morning with the following equipment: a blanket, a change of underwear, some personal belongings, a plate, a spoon and a cup as well as a two-day supply of food. I warn you now that anyone not appearing at the designated time will be expelled from the institute. The only valid excuse will be a certificate from the institute clinic. No student having outside work will be exempted from digging trenches.[19]

There are no precise figures on the number of people who were drafted for defense construction. Administrators, people in important public services, workers in defense plants and other essential persons were exempted. The great majority of the draftees were older men, women and adolescents. According to Soviet sources between a half million and a million people were drafted. In addition, the populations of the villages and towns located in the Leningrad region were mobilized to work on the defense fortifications.[20]

The draftees in Leningrad assembled at assigned places in the city. Each group was placed under the leadership of someone representing the district authorities and this was usually a member of the Communist Party. The groups were then marched or transported to a construction site. When the workers arrived at a construction site they were divided into labor brigades and given tools to carry out their assignments. An assignment, which in most instances consisted of constructing tank traps, trench systems and fortified positions, had to be completed within a prescribed time and according to the specifications established by military authorities. Upon the completion of an assignment, the workers were immediately marched or brought to another construction site.

The draftees suffered considerable hardships. Often they were forced to work twelve to fifteen hours with just a few breaks. Fortunately, it was summer for many of the people were not properly dressed. Girls and women arrived at the construction sites wearing light summer dresses and shoes that were not designed for marching, outdoor living and hard physical labor. Most of the girls were not accustomed to digging with a shovel or using a crowbar to break up the dry, clay soil. The supply of food was another problem. Many of the draftees had been told that they would be digging from two to five days and were instructed to bring enough food for that period of time, but in practice the people were required to stay longer. There were also disagreements as to which authorities were supposed to feed the draftees, the civilian authorities or the military. As a consequence, draftees sometimes went hungry. Finally, there were many mothers who became worried for their children at home when they were forced to remain longer than they had anticipated.[21]

The efforts put forth by the workers won the admiration of the city's leaders. Peter Popkov, head of the Executive Committee of the Leningrad City Soviet (Mayor of Leningrad), told a foreign correspondent in 1943 that whenever he refers to the people of his city he cannot "speak without emotion and admiration. They put their heart into everything they do. . . . It was our people," he emphasized, "and not the soldiers who built the fortifications of Leningrad." Popkov went on to say that "during the three black months of 1941, 400,000 people were working in three shifts, morning, noon and night, digging and digging." He remembered "going down to Luga during the worst days, when the Germans were rapidly advancing on Luga." While there he witnessed " a young girl who was carrying away earth inside her apron. It made no sense," he said. When he "asked her [why] she was doing that . . ., she burst into tears, and said she was trying to do at least that—it wasn't much, but her hands simply couldn't hold the shovel any longer." When Popkov looked at her hands, he "saw that they were a mass of black and bloody bruises. Somebody else had shoveled the earth onto her apron while she knelt down, holding the corners of the apron with the fingers of her bruised and blood-stained hands." Popkov reported that "For three months our civilians worked on these fortifications. They were allowed one day off in six weeks. They never took their days off. There was an eight-hour working day, but nobody took any notice of it. They were determined to stop the Germans. And they went on working under shell fire, under machine-gun fire and the bombs of the Stukas." [22]

Anna Ivanova, a resident of Leningrad, believed that her work on the lines of fortification would help secure the safety of the people living within the city. In a letter she wrote: "I want every woman working on the defenses to understand what I feel. We are building for ourselves, for our children. The more we sweat here at our toil, the less the blood of our sons, brothers and husbands will be spilled. And every step the enemy takes here will be lethal. The enemy will not pass here."[23]

Often the women would leave letters in the defense works which they had built for the soldiers who would be assigned to defend them. One of these letters read as follows: "Our dear son! Our dear defender and friend! We have dug this trench for you, so don't let the enemy break through to Leningrad. This is my behest. I know that you don't know me but take my letter. Your own mother would tell you to do the same as I am telling you: smash the Nazis, son."[24]

In the end, the results of the operation were truly significant. In terms of actual work performed there is no precise agreement among the various sources. One source gives the total length of earth walls that were built as over 998 kilometers (620 miles). Another source records the completion of 626 kilometers (388 miles) of anti-tank ditches and 935 kilometers (580 miles) of open trenches and communication passageways. Almost 635 kilometers (394 miles) of barbed wire defenses were erected along with 306 kilometers (190 miles) of forest obstacles. Constructed within and behind the defenses were thousands of gun and machine gun pillboxes made of earth, timber and reinforced concrete.[25]

The majority of the draftees did not question the value of the fortifications and most of the workers did exactly what the authorities demanded. Leon Goure who did extensive research on the siege of Leningrad and wrote an excellent study on the subject believed that there were several reasons for this. One reason was that all policies were determined by the State, and the people were taught to accept and carry out the decisions made by the leadership. Furthermore, the belief that the State was all-knowing and all-powerful left most citizens convinced that they were unable to manage without their leaders. There was also the fear of the NKVD which seemed to see everything and be everywhere (see Glossary- NKVD). No one dared to oppose the State for to do so would result in arrest and severe consequences. Therefore, most draftees obeyed orders and outwardly behaved like loyal, patriotic citizens. Some of the people who did grumble, felt that the digging was nonsensical and for little purpose. There were others who were indignant that adolescents and elderly citizens were forced to do hard, manual labor. To bolster the morale of the workers, the authorities sent to the construction sites hundreds of Party propagandists.

The people in Leningrad were constantly exposed to propaganda produced by the Communist Party. Up to June 22 the Party's propaganda machine had treated Hitler as a partner of the Soviet Union, but after the outbreak of the war one of the principle objectives of the Party was to persuade the people that the friend of yesterday was in reality a monster. Hitler's aim, it was reported, was to become the master of the world. It was pointed out that he had already deprived many nations of their independence.

A description of Hitler's war aims became quite specific. Stalin in his radio speech on July 3 said:

> *The enemy is cruel and implacable. He is out to seize our lands, which have been watered with our sweat, to seize our grain and oil secured by our labor. He is out to restore the rule of the landlords, to restore Tsarism, to destroy national culture and the national state existence of the Russians, Ukrainians, Byelo-Russians, Lithuanians . . . and the other free peoples of the Soviet Union, to Germanize them, to convert them into the slaves of German princes and barons. Thus, the issue is one of life or death for the Soviet State, for the peoples of the USSR; the issue is whether the peoples of the Soviet Union shall remain free or fall into slavery.*[26]

Stalin's analysis left the Soviet citizens with the belief that a German victory would have serious consequences. The analysis was repeated in the Party's propaganda, and it was incorporated in all of the declarations, resolutions and editorials published in the press.

The image of a cruel, bloody and inhumane enemy was strengthened by the Soviet Information Bureau. In July the bureau began to report and describe in its daily war communiqués acts of atrocity committed by German soldiers. The bulletins emphasized that in the territories that were occupied by the Germans the native populations were stripped of all their food and left to starve. At the same time defenseless people were being tortured, maimed and shot and the young women were being raped. Letters that were found on the bodies of dead German soldiers were printed if it was believed that their content would instill within the readers a deep hatred for the enemy. In an unfinished letter printed in a Leningrad newspaper, a German soldier described Russian women as being dangerous. He and his buddies stripped them naked before they assaulted them sexually:

> It was easier in Paris. Do you remember that Honeymoon? These Russian women are like devils. You simply have to bind them. At the beginning I liked bustle. But now I am bitten and scratched, so I act differently. I hold a gun near their temples and that calms them down a bit. Recently a Russian girl with a hand grenade blew up herself and our First Lieutenant Gross. So now we undress them fully, search them and then . . . afterwards they disappear without leaving a trace.[27]

The Party's propaganda also appealed to patriotism and to the local and individual pride of a citizen. Bulletin boards were set up along the streets and in offices, factories and shops, and posted on these bulletin boards were newspapers, pamphlets, posters and leaflets that the Party used to expose the people to its propaganda. It referred to Leningrad's glorious history and the city's cultural and artistic heritage. It reminded the people that their city was the cradle of the October Socialist Revolution (see Glossary—October Socialist Revolution) and that it had never been conquered by an enemy. Most Leningraders felt tremendous pride in their city and regarded their city as unique and superior. Individual pride was appealed to by placing upon the citizens the responsibility for the fate of Leningrad. The city's future depended on the conduct and work of each citizen and on a person's willingness to make every sacrifice. Part of the daily news communiqués was devoted to the heroic deeds of individual soldiers or small groups of soldiers at a military front or to the accomplishments of civilians on the production line.

The population was also exposed to German propaganda. Since the citizens of Leningrad had been ordered by the authorities to turn in their radio receiving sets, Germany's propaganda efforts consisted mainly in dropping leaflets over Leningrad and the surrounding countryside. The leaflets were aimed at undermining the morale of the people and making them believe in the invincibility of the German military. They urged that Leningrad be declared an open city in order to avoid unnecessary destruction and so that its people would not suffer. They denounced the Jewish-Bolshevik leaders of the Soviet Union and ridiculed the city's defense efforts. In an attempt to prevent the leaflets from having an effect, the authorities dispatched special squads to the drop areas to collect and destroy them. The great majority of the population never saw the leaflets. The people who did read the leaflets, although it was forbidden to do so, told others about them and eventually by word of mouth their contents would become widely known.

The German advance on Leningrad was resumed on July 10. Fierce Soviet resistance, mine fields and poorly constructed roads slowed the advance of German Army Group North. On the flanks, the Eighteenth Army made some gains in the direction of Tallin and the Sixteenth Army advanced toward Lake Il'men (see Map 1). Fearing that their slow advance would give the Red Army time to build more fortifications and raise new divisions, the German commanders decided to bypass the most fortified defenses of the Luga Line and ordered the Fourth Panzer Group to cross the Luga River at Sabsk (see Map1). The Germans succeeded in crossing the river and establishing a bridgehead on the east shore of the river. At the same time the Germans directed offensives toward Kingisepp and Shimsk, but in spite of their superiority in numbers the Germans were stopped by the Soviet soldiers and the men of the People's Volunteer Army. From July 14 through July 18 the Soviet forces and the volunteers carried out a counter offensive near the town of Soltsy (see Map1). They succeeded in driving the Germans back some forty kilometers (25 miles). After stopping the Soviet counteroffensive, the German commanders decided to wait for reinforcements before continuing the advance on Leningrad. It was a wait that would last three weeks.

Most of the people in Leningrad knew little about the military situation along the Northwestern Front. Only the Soviet Information Bureau was authorized to issue daily news communiqués, and they were usually vague about the extent of the German advance. Most often the fighting was described as taking place in the direction of a certain city. The loss of a city was either reported after a great delay or it was not announced at all. For example, fighting in the direction of Pskov was not reported until July 12, 1941, yet the city had actually been taken by the Germans on July 8. Pskov continued to be reported as a battleground until July 24; thereafter, the communiqués ceased to refer to it. Fighting around Porkhov continued to be reported until August 2, 1941; however, the city was actually captured on July 12. The advance of the Germans in the Estonian sector was merely described as taking place, and by August 20, 1941, the communiqués had still reported nothing specific concerning the fighting in Estonia. Nor was anything reported about the battles around Luga.[28]

Rumors concerning the military situation became inevitable. To explain why Germany had not yet bombed Leningrad, some people claimed that the city was being defended by no less than 20,000 Soviet airplanes. Others asserted that Hitler had decided not to do any physical damage to Leningrad but to capture the city intact. Leningrad was full of rumors. One of the more absurd rumors was that the district which included Vasilievsky Island would not be bombed because "a lot of Germans lived there, old St. Petersburgers whose families had lived there since Peter the Great's time." There was also the rumor that Vasilievsky Island was the birthplace of Alfred Rosenberg, one of Hitler's early supporters and the philosopher of the National Socialist German Workers Party (Nazi Party). Rosenberg was born in Tallin but a number of Leningraders, believing the rumor, took up residence with relatives and acquaintances that lived on Vasilievsky Island.[29]

NOTES

1. Neil Mishalov, Radio Address of 22 June 1941 by Vyacheslav Molotov, Assistant Chairman of the Council of the People's Commissars of the U.S.S.R., and the People's Commissar for Foreign Affairs (Transcribed and translated by Novosti Press Agency, June, 1941), <http://www. mishalov.com/Molotov-22 June 41. html> (29 May 2007).

2. Mishalov, Radio Address of 22 June 1941 by Vyacheslav Molotov.

3. Nikolai Kislitsyn and Vassily Zubakov, Leningrad Does Not Surrender, trans. Barry Jones (Moscow: Progress Publishers, 1989), 30–31.

4. A.V. Karasev, Leningradtsy V gody blokady (Moscow: Izdatelstvo Adademii Nauk SSSR, 1959), 34.

5. David M. Glantz, The Siege of Leningrad 1941–1944 (Osceola, Wisconsin: MBI Publishing Company, 2001), 18–19.

6. Glantz, The Siege of Leningrad 1941–1944, 17.

7. Leon Goure, The Siege of Leningrad (Stanford, California: Stanford University Press, 1962). 59.

8. James H. Meisel and Edward S. Kozera, Materials for the Study of the Soviet System (Ann Arbor, Michigan: George Wahr Publishing Co., 1950), 365.

9. Goure, The Siege of Leningrad, 23.

10. Goure, The Siege of Leningrad, 52–53.

11. Goure, The Siege of Leningrad, 30.

12. Neil Mishalov, Radio Address of 3 July 1941 by Joseph Stalin, Chairman of the Council of People's Commissars of the U.S.S.R. (transcribed and translated by Soviet Russia Today, August 1941), <http://www.mishalov.com/Stalin-3 July 41.html> (30 May 2007).

13. Mishalov, Radio Address of 3 July 1941 by Joseph Stalin.

14. Goure, The Siege of Leningrad, 31–32.

15. Alexander Werth, Leningrad (London: Hamish Hamilton, 1944), 110.

16. Goure, The Siege of Leningrad, 33.

17. Goure, The Siege of Leningrad, 33–34.

18. Goure, The Siege of Leningrad, 24–25.

19. Louis Fischer, ed., Thirteen Who Fled (New York: Harper and Brothers, 1949), 184– 85.

20. Goure, The Siege of Leningrad, 26.

21. Goure, The Siege of Leningrad, 27.

22. Werth, Leningrad, 165–66.

23. Kislitsyn and Zubakov, Leningrad Does Not Surrender, 39.

24. Kislitsyn and Zubakov, Leningrad Does Not Surrender, 39.

25. Kislitsyn and Zubakov, Leningrad Does Not Surrender, 40.

26. Mishalov, Radio Address of 3 July 1941 by Joseph Stalin.

27. Boris Skomorovsky and E.G. Morris, The Siege of Leningrad (New York: E.P. Dutton and Company, Inc., 1944), 70.

28. Goure, The Siege of Leningrad, 68–69.

29. Ales Adamovich and Daniil Granin, A Book of the Blockade, trans. Hilda Perham (Moscow: Raduga Publishers, 1983), 262.

Chapter Three

Increasing the Interior Defense

During the three-week military stalemate along the Northwestern Front, the Leningraders improved the city's existing civil defense. On July 27 the Executive Committee of the Leningrad City Soviet decided that much of the city's civil defense was to be the responsibility of housing administrators and "commanders" of public buildings. They were ordered to organize, train and equip part-time civil defense teams. They were to show them how to extinguish incendiary bombs, put out fires and provide first aid to the injured. The administrators and "commanders" were authorized to draft all persons residing in the buildings under their care who were not employed in industry and to assign them tasks during their free time. The tasks included guard duty on roofs, in attics, on stairways and in entrance halls of buildings. A daily twenty-four hour watch was to be maintained at each building. The resident who was found guilty of refusing to comply with a civil defense order was liable to punishment. Supervision over the implementation of the city's new civil defense measures was assigned to the chief of the militia, the chief of the fire department and the chief of Leningrad's housing administration.[1]

The great majority of Leningrad's part-time civil defense workers were women and young people. In one city district, there were said to be 16,000 women doing civil defense work. There were also older men who served in their free time. In the city's schools the civil defense teams were composed of teachers and the older students. The Philharmonic Orchestra organized a group of musicians to stand watch for fires. There were some people who worked for civil defense at their place of employment as well as at their place of residence. The physical burden on the people who were employed was great since they had to stand watch on roofs or to do some other type of guard duty after having worked at regular labor for eight to eleven hours.[2]

The equipment used by the civil defense groups was standard. Most of the groups were equipped with helmets, axes, crowbars, shovels, buckets, fire extinguishers or hand operated water-sprayers, hoses and sand. Some groups were supplied with one or two suits made to be worn in gas contaminated areas. The amount of equipment was determined in part on the size and importance of the building for which the group was responsible and in part on the initiative, persistence and connections of the house administrator or building "commander." The fire department and the district civil defense organization could be called to assist but only when a local civil defense team needed assistance.

Large-scale damage caused by heavy air raids was the responsibility of the city's two repair and rescue regiments and three civil defense battalions. The regiments and battalions were formed on July 17 by the Executive Committee of the Leningrad City Soviet. One regiment was drawn from the personnel of the Administration for Housing Construction and the other regiment from the Administration for Construction of Cultural and Public Buildings. One of the battalions was created to repair roads and bridges that had been damaged, another was assigned to repair damage that was done to the city's water system and the third was responsible for housing repairs. Each regiment had 2,051 men, and each battalion had 600 men.[3]

The Komsomol organization also contributed to Leningrad's civil defense. Large fires in the more vulnerable areas of the city, such as the harbor and the warehouse and storage areas, were a major concern. Thus, during the first half of August a Komsomol fire fighting regiment was formed. It consisted of some 1,600 male students. At the same time the Komsomol organized a militarized regiment for the purpose of assisting the militia in maintaining public order. The regiment would eventually consist of more than 2,000 members, and many were young women. The work of both regiments was not restricted to civil defense tasks. At various times, the Komsomols were assigned to construct fortifications, to lay mine fields and to deliver messages.[4]

The existing air-raid shelters and medical first aid posts were improved, and more of these kinds of facilities were built. Work on reinforcing the ceilings of basement shelters began in July. Slit trenches were dug in parks and gardens and around factories. In some places large dugouts were built. By August 20 Leningrad had enough air-raid shelters for 918,000 people and enough slit trenches to accommodate 672,000 people.[5] A large number of schools, hotels and public buildings were requisitioned to serve as hospitals. The Red Cross and the public health authorities established nearly 5,000 medical first aid posts, and a total of 18,000 people were registered as blood donors.[6]

In time, Leningrad's chemical industry provided gas masks for the majority of the population. It was feared that the enemy would use poison gasses, a fear that originated with the capture of enemy gas shells in July. There were also reports which indicated that the Germans were considering the use of poison gasses against the city.[7]

Measures were carried out to reduce the vulnerability of the city and its people to air attacks. Air defense was provided by Soviet fighter planes that patrolled the skies during the day and at night. Hundreds of hydrogen-filled barrage balloons were launched and hovered above the city. The balloons were anchored to the ground with steel cables which prevented enemy dive bombers from striking their targets within the city. Anti-aircraft weapons were placed in the city parks and squares, on wide streets and on the more than one hundred islands in the Neva River. Light guns were mounted on the roofs of some of the city's larger buildings.

Camouflage was used to protect factories and public buildings and to cover structures that might provide reference points for enemy aviation. The first structure to be camouflaged was the golden spire of the Admiralty building in the center of the city. Many unsuccessful attempts were made before a cable loop was dropped over the building's spire from a balloon. Cliff climbers were then able to climb to the top and hang a camouflage cover over the spire. The dome of St. Isaac's Cathedral was coated with gray paint. The Smol'ny Institute and a number of neighboring buildings were covered with netting that from the air had the appearance of trees and gardens. Trams and trolley buses and the entrances to housing complexes were lit with blue lamps. Street lighting and advertisements were switched off.[8]

Numerous alerts were sounded in Leningrad. Except for a bomb that was dropped by a German airplane on July 18, there were no attacks from the air. Yet, there were sometimes as many as four alerts in a day. The alerts were announced by the sounding of sirens and factory whistles and over the radio loud-speakers, which by order of the Executive Committee of the Leningrad City Soviet were to remain turned on twenty-four hours a day. When an alert was sounded, everyone who was not on duty was supposed to enter an air-raid shelter or get into a slit trench. At nighttime people were reluctant to use a shelter especially if the shelter was not located in the building in which they lived. Many people preferred to take shelter in a multi-storied building because they believed that such a building provided more cover overhead. Failure to maintain discipline during an alert or black out was punishable by a fine. Failure to obey any civil defense regulation could lead to an accusation of sabotage.[9]

The city's leadership considered it important to set up safeguards against saboteurs and enemy agents. The militia was assigned to patrol the streets and enforce the curfew regulations. With the assistance of Komsomol guard units, the militia spot-checked the identity cards of people walking the streets. It also maintained check points at the entrances to Leningrad in order to verify the documents of the people entering or leaving the city. Persons coming from or going to a military front or leaving for or returning from a fortification construction site were checked at the railway stations. Militia guards were posted at all factories and important buildings. Furthermore, the militia was responsible for issuing residence permits and making sure that no unauthorized person remained in the city.

On July 20 the city authorities decided to tighten the registration requirements. House managers and private owners of houses were ordered to make sure that new residents registered with the militia within twenty-four hours. The delinquent managers were threatened with fines and imprisonment. Even during peacetime conditions, no person was permitted to reside within a Soviet city without registering with the militia and obtaining a residence permit. Illegal residence was punishable by up to two years of imprisonment. Factory and office managers were warned against employing persons who were not in possession of residence permits. The new registration requirements were designed to prevent the infiltration of German agents.

The press warned the people daily about German agents and urged them to report anyone who they suspected of being an enemy spy. The population became suspicious of everyone. Clothes that were Western in style, a foreign accent or any suspicious behavior such as taking notes or asking questions would cause people to become suspect. Streetcar conductors stopped calling out street names so that it would be more difficult for enemy agents to orient themselves. Suspects who were arrested by citizens were often beaten before they were turned over to the militia or the NKVD (see Glossary—NKVD).

The teenage son of Elena Skrjabina almost became a victim of the spy-mania that had become so prevalent in Leningrad. Elena described the near arrest of her son Dima as follows: "Spy-mania has hit the city. Every day they catch one here, find one there. As a rule, these spies turn out to be law-abiding citizens who somehow accidentally have aroused the suspicions of some very zealous arm of the law. Even my poor Dima has been a victim. His height, his fair, curly hair, and particularly his glasses, must have provoked the suspicion of a militiaman [policeman]. We were walking to the train station, and on the way I stopped at a store for a moment. Dima was waiting for me on the street. When I came out after ten minutes, I saw the militiaman demanding something from Dima, who was obviously very frightened. I hurried to them. The militiaman was ready to take the boy to headquarters to clear up his identity since Dima did not have any documents with him. I had to argue with him and point out that Dima could not possibly have a passport because he is under sixteen. To prove what I was saying, I dragged out all my papers and my husband's military certificate which, luckily, I had with me. I finally convinced him that Dima really is my son and not a German spy. He let him go. We will have to be more careful. It is dangerous for Dima to go out on the streets alone." [10]

The NKVD considered collaborators equally as dangerous as enemy agents. Potential enemies of the State were people with anti-Soviet or deviationist records and those who had relatives that were incarcerated in concentration camps. People who had served in the imperial Russian government before the October Socialist Revolution or who were related to persons who had, were not to be trusted (see Glossary—October Socialist Revolution). Citizens who were of foreign origin or who had foreign names were identified as untrustworthy. About 12 percent of Leningrad's population was of German, Baltic or Finnish origin and most were either arrested or ordered to leave the city. The latter action that was taken by the authorities was a process of forced evacuation.

The arrests of people most often occurred at night. It happened to one of Elena Skrjabina's friends and she would write about it in her diary: "I am shaken by the terrible news. My friend and co-worker Byelskaya was arrested. Why? Another one of many puzzles. Of course, no one will explain anything. They came at night, searched, found nothing, confiscated nothing, but took her away anyway. All I know is that the head of the institute where we both work is very hostile toward her. It could be that the charge is 'foreign ties.' I am greatly concerned for her. Moreover, I know her family situation: her brother, drafted, a tubercular sister, an aging mother, and a three-year-old daughter. I went to see them and spent nearly a half of an hour. At my house, they had all decided that I, too, had been arrested."[11]

NOTES

1. Leon Goure, The Siege of Leningrad (Stanford, California: Stanford University Press, 1962), 39.

2. Goure, The Siege of Leningrad, 40.

3. A.V. Karasev, Leningradtsy v gody blokady (Moscow: Izdatelstve Akademii Nauk SSSR, 1959), 87.

4. Karasev, Leningradtsy v gody blokady, 87–88.

5. Karasev, Leningradtsy v gody blokady, 86, 87.

6. Karasev, Leningradtsy v gody blokady, 83, 89.

7. Goure, The Siege of Leningrad, 42.

8. Nikolai Kislitsyn and Vassily Zubakov, Leningrad Does Not Surrender, trans. Barry Jones (Moscow: Progress Publishers, 1989), 37.

9. Goure, The Siege of Leningrad, 43.

10. Elena Skrjabina, Siege and Survival, trans. Norman Luxenburg (New York: Pinnacle Books, Inc., 1973), 32–33.

11. Skrjabina, Siege and Survival, 21–22.

Chapter Four

Industry and Evacuation

After Germany launched its attack against the Soviet Union, Moscow ordered that Leningrad's industries supply the Soviet military with weapons, ammunition and other supplies. Reorganizing and converting the city's industries to war production would be a complex and difficult endeavor. Leningradskaya Pravda, the important city newspaper, described the task as follows:

> What does it mean to convert a factory to wartime conditions? It means to learn quickly, without losing an hour, to change over to producing those goods that are most needed today and to make the output two, three or even ten times greater than before. It means to plan, to build and to acquire still with new machines and apparatus much faster than before. It means the administrators, directors, shop chiefs and foremen must learn to fulfill the plan with fewer workers, engineers and office workers and must make the entire factory organization more maneuverable and flexible.[1]

The administrative arrangements for these measures were cumbersome. Since the city's heavy industries were under the direct control of the ministries located in Moscow, the local managers were not permitted to act without instructions from their superiors in the capital city. For example, when in August Leningrad's authorities wanted to expand the production of bottles for Molotov cocktails, it required the approval from the State Defense Committee to allow one of the city's bottling plants to convert to this type of production (see Glossary—Molotov cocktail).[2] Often Leningrad's industrial managers, fearing criticism, executed orders coming from Moscow even if the orders were unrealistic. Local control over industry would increase as the Germans gradually cut off the city from the rest of the country; however, orders coming from Moscow never ceased.

Converting Leningrad's industries to war production was hampered by the shortage of raw materials. From the start of the war there was a severe shortage in several critical materials. In June Leningrad's entire stock of TNT was only 284 metric tons, but ammunition production required thousands of metric tons. There was also a shortage of steel, non-ferrous metals and other essential materials. Yet, Leningrad's industries were required to produce military equipment, ranging from tanks and artillery to mess kits.[3] Some of the shortages were partly overcome by the use of substitutes. Leningrad's scientists developed a new explosive and devised methods by which cast iron and a mixture of iron and fiber were substituted for steel in the manufacture of shell casings.

Another chief difficulty was that the trained labor force in Leningrad's industries had been reduced considerably as a result of the various mobilizations. The Kirov Works, which produced ammunition, guns, tanks and heavy equipment, released nearly one-third of its employees so that they could join the People's Volunteer Army. The Stalin Metallurgical Factory lost 1,300 workers to the People's Volunteer Army and still more of its employees were drafted into the army. The Elektrosila Works, the largest electric motor plant in the Soviet Union, suffered a similar loss in workers. The shipyards were required to make repairs on naval vessels; however, some 25,000 yard workers had been mobilized for military service.[4]

Replacements for a portion of the departed workers were found. Retired workers and the wives of soldiers and workers were recruited as replacements. Additional help was drafted under the Compulsory Labor Decree of June 27. Some of the clerical and administrative personnel in factories were transferred to the production lines. Students from factory schools were sent to work in the factories. All the replacements were important, but they were not able to fill the gap caused by the loss in skilled labor. In the Stalin Metallurgical Factory the welders could fulfill only 50 percent of the program. In some factories, engineers were forced to work at machines to keep up the production norms and skilled employees sometimes worked on rush orders for lengths of time from twenty-four to thirty-six hours.[5]

Pressure was exerted continually on workers to increase productivity. On July 12 the city's Komosol began organizing production competitions among young factory workers for the purpose of encouraging them to fulfill production norms by 150–200 percent.[6] Party propagandists held up the better workers as examples to others. The press praised Stakhanovites and urged all factory managers to require each worker to operate several machines instead of just one (see Glossary—Stakhanovite). Posters that showed a soldier pointing a finger at the reader and asking, "You! How have you helped the Front?" were effective.[7] They implied that unless the workers produced more, soldiers would be killed and the city might fall to the enemy. In some factories, signs were posted at each machine bearing the slogan "What have you done for the defense of Leningrad?" and showing the output per shift of each worker stationed at the machine. In other factories daily report sheets and wall graphs showed the performance of each worker, to the shame of the less productive.[8]

In August an order was issued requiring some workers to live in the factory. There were several reasons for this measure. The authorities wanted a trained worker defense unit in each factory at all times. If the enemy should enter the city, the resident workers would defend the factory. Another reason was to keep a labor force at the factory for emergency work assignments. Finally, returning home each evening would take time and expend energy, and this new arrangement prevented that. The factory resident workers were permitted to return home once a week to visit their families. Many of the workers welcomed the new arrangement because they benefited from the additional rest, and they were fed at the factory canteen.[9]

Efforts to increase the productivity of Leningrad's factories were further disrupted by the industrial evacuation that began in July. As the Germans advanced closer to Leningrad, an increasing number of factories were ordered by Moscow to be dismantled and transported to locations in Siberia. After the capture of Pskov and particularly after the Germans breached the Luga Line the removal of industrial equipment from Leningrad was carried out with great haste. Among the first industries that were ordered to leave was an optical instrument plant and some aircraft factories. These were followed by factories producing tanks and other war goods. Usually a factory shop was evacuated as a unit, and according to one source, eighty-six factories were completely or partly removed.[10]

Much of the equipment evacuated from Leningrad suffered considerable damage. According to eyewitnesses, the "dismantling and crating was carried out with such carelessness that part of the equipment was broken." Many of the machines that had been packed and loaded on freight cars did not leave the city immediately. Soviet sources report that over two thousand freight carloads of machinery remained trapped in the railway freight yards after the Germans blockaded the city. The equipment that was left on the open cars would soon rust and deteriorate. A part of this machinery was later moved to the East in the winter and in the summer of 1942. The chief engineers of the Elektrosila Works reported that the trains carrying their factory's heavy equipment would remain in the railway yards of Leningrad until March 1943.[11]

Along with industrial equipment, a large number of managers, technicians, engineers and skilled workers were evacuated. It was decided that at least a part of a factory's original work force needed to be present if the evacuated plant was to be reconstructed and operating satisfactorily in the East. Management of each factory was ordered to draw up a list of workers to be evacuated. The evacuees were permitted to take their families with them unless the latter were not free to leave because of their work. They were also permitted to take a certain amount of luggage. After obtaining the required authorization for departure and their travel papers, they were then transported to Siberia in fourth-class passenger cars or in freight cars. Some of the leading factory administrators and technical personnel were evacuated by air. In all, more than 164,300 workers and employees were reported to have been evacuated by August 27, 1941.[12]

Industrial evacuation forced some factories to begin manufacturing products for which the plants had not been designed. It was a transition that was carried out in a factory that for many years had made the optical instruments used in the Soviet navy, in cinema projectors and in cameras. After the bulk of this factory's optical equipment was transported out of the city and most of its skilled workers were evacuated, the workers that remained began making shells, hand grenades and detonators for anti-tank mines. The workers had no experience in this kind of production; nevertheless, they learned quickly and in time hundreds of thousands of these items were made. One soldier who had been a worker in the factory visited his former place of employment to congratulate the workers. He told them that he had been using their grenades and said "they were grand." He thanked them for "keeping up the standard of the old firm." The factory also began making a flat, dagger-shaped bayonet; it was called the Leningrad bayonet.[13]

Some factories were not evacuated. Shops that were needed to repair Leningrad's naval or military equipment remained. Plants that had machinery which was old and not worth moving but would be useful to Leningrad's defense were not evacuated. The city's foundries were too bulky to be moved, and much of their equipment remained. There were also factory buildings that were empty due to the evacuations, and these were used to house the equipment of other plants whose locations were endangered by the enemy's advance on the city.

In addition to industries, nearly one hundred institutions of various kinds were evacuated. They included institutions of higher education, research institutes, theatrical companies and museums. At the Hermitage, the largest museum in the Soviet Union, staff members and volunteers worked day and night to pack the museum's treasures into crates to be transported to Sverdlovsk. The first train of crates left on July 1 and contained nearly 500,000 articles. When the articles reached their destination they were stored in three locations: an art gallery, a church and the basement of the Ipiatyev Mansion. The latter was the mansion where Tsar Nicholas II and his family were housed before they were executed in 1918. The second train carried 1,422 crates that contained nearly 700,000 articles. They were evacuated on July 20, and fourteen members of the museum staff accompanied the treasures. The articles for the third train were still being packed when the Germans cut the railroad connections between Leningrad and the rest of the country. These treasures were moved to the cellars of the Hermitage where they would be watched daily by the museum's staff members who remained in Leningrad.

The staff at the Leningrad State Library succeeded in evacuating an estimated 360,000 items out of a total of over 9,000,000 that the library had within its collection. Evacuated were the most important incunabula, some Russian and foreign eighteen and nineteen century books and a unique collection of newspapers published during the Russian Civil War. The valuable items that could not be evacuated were stored in the basement of the building. Thereafter, the library staff began the enormous task to protect the library. The attics of the building were filled with a layer of sand. The windows were bricked up and sand bagged. Water tanks, pumps, barrels of sand and fire extinguishers were secured and a fire fighting system was organized.[14]

Throughout Leningrad the statues and monuments that could not be evacuated were either hidden or camouflaged. Trenches were dug under the linden trees in the Summer Garden and the eighteenth-century marble statues of Greek goddesses and gods that adorned the garden were buried in them. Sculptor Peter Klodt's four bronze horses were taken off their pedestals on Anichkov Bridge and buried in the gardens of the Young Pioneers' palace. The Bronze Horseman, the equestrian statue of Peter the Great on the embankment of the Neva River, and the statue of Vladimir Lenin in front of the Finland Station were surrounded with bags filled with sand and then covered with boards and logs. The statue of Generalissimo Alexander Suvorov in front of the Troitzky Bridge and the statues of General Field Marshals Michael Kutuzov and Michael Barklai de Tolli in front of the Kazansky Cathedral on Nevsky Prospect were not removed or covered; they were left in their places as an inspiration for all Leningraders to defend their city. The trees in the city's parks and gardens were declared protected and would remain untouched even during the upcoming winter when there was a shortage of firewood.

On July 8 a special evacuation commission was organized to deal with the refugees who had come into Leningrad since the beginning of the war. Refugees had arrived in the city from several directions.[15] From the north came people who had settled in the areas that had been taken from the Finns in 1939. Evacuees came by sea from Riga and Tallin; they were mostly the families of Soviet soldiers and Soviet officials. From the south and west came people who had fled from the Germans advancing on Leningrad. In each of the city's districts an evacuation committee was formed, and the committees requisitioned schools or empty barracks near railway stations to house the refugees. In all, some forty-two command centers were established where the refugees lived until they could be evacuated and sent east. Some of the refugees stayed with friends and relatives in the city, but they continued to remain under the care of the city authorities. Most of the refugees were used as laborers and were paid a minimal wage; however, the authorities did their best to evacuate the refugees as quickly as possible. They were concerned over the problem of taking care of large numbers of destitute persons. They were also afraid that some of the refugees might be enemy agents. Furthermore, they felt that the refugees undermined the morale of the Leningraders by spreading defeatist stories. Only those refugees who had the right connections in Leningrad or who were needed in the city were permitted to stay.[16]

A certain portion of the population was encouraged to leave the city. They included children, women, elderly citizens and those who were unemployed. People who had obtained a release from their jobs or who had received a transfer to jobs elsewhere in the country were also evacuated. A number of wives of officials left the city. By August 10, 1941, a total of 467,648 persons had left the city. On that date it was decided to evacuate from the city an additional 400,000 people, primarily women and children under the age of fourteen. Less than a week later it was decided that the number of people to be evacuated should be 700,000 at a rate of 30,000 per day. The German advance on the city prevented the planned evacuation from being completed. By August 29, 1941, a total of 636,203 citizens had been evacuated including 147,500 refugees.[17]

Authorization for evacuation had to be obtained from special commissions. The commissions checked whether the applicant had been properly released from all labor obligations or employment. If the applicant had been released, he or she was given a travel order showing the person's destination. In many cases the destination was determined by the authorities regardless of a person's wishes. Travel orders sometimes showed the date of departure, the car number of the train and the compartment number. Most people were permitted to take with them only that which they were able to carry.[18]

The execution of an evacuation often involved difficulties. In many cases the father of a family was evacuated separately from his wife and child. Sometimes children were separated from their parents. There were times when evacuees were forced to wait for days at the Leningrad railway stations or in the marshaling yards before the trains left. At other times evacuees were left stranded en route, either because their train was requisitioned for some other use or because the railway line was blocked by military traffic. A shortage of food or water became a serious problem for the evacuees during the long delays.

The attitudes that people had toward evacuation varied. Sources report that many people, from academicians to artists and writers, did everything they could to avoid compulsory evacuation. Sometimes they even pretended to be ill. There are reports of skilled workers who argued and pleaded with factory managers not to be included in compulsory evacuation. They did not want to leave their native city, their factory and their friends. Some people felt that to leave the city in time of danger was cowardly, and they referred contemptuously to evacuees as vermin. There were people who did not want to leave because they feared the hardships that they would have to face if they became refugees. Moreover, people hated the thought of leaving behind their possessions which they had acquired with great difficulty and which were so hard to replace under Soviet living conditions. Then there were those who were anxious to leave because they feared the Germans, and they wanted to be out of harm's way. A number of people also wondered if it was necessary to leave the city. Maybe the Soviet forces would stop the advance of the enemy.

Few people if any left the city without authorization. The control that was exercised by the authorities over railway and highway travel made unauthorized departures very difficult. A person leaving his job without permission was liable to severe penalties. Some people did leave the city in a quasi-legal manner by registering as relatives of members of evacuation groups from factories, hospitals, institutes and theaters. Some arranged to be sent on assignments to safer areas outside of the city. The latter course was possible only for persons in important positions. Most of the people who held positions of influence were trapped by the existing circumstances like everyone else. There was no escape from Leningrad except through authorization.

Some of the men whose wives were evacuated to safety would find friends among the young women who remained in the city. These liaisons would continue after the end of the blockade. Thus, Peter Popkov, head of the Executive Committee of Leningrad City Soviet, was reported to have told foreign correspondents in 1944 the following joke: "The evacuated wives, for instance, learning of what was going on in Leningrad, took as their slogan: 'Death to the foreign invaders!' But when the wives returned, the girls who had taken their places adopted as their slogan: 'Now we go underground to become partisans and continue the struggle secretly.'"[19]

NOTES

1. Leon Goure, The Siege of Leningrad (Stanford, California: Stanford University Press, 1962), 45.

2. A.V. Karasev, Leningradtsy v gody blokady (Moscow: Izdatelstve Adademii Nauk SSSR, 1959), 55.

3. Karasev, Leningradtsy v gody blokady, 50–51.

4. Goure, The Siege of Leningrad, 46.

5. Goure, The Siege of Leningrad, 46–47.

6. Karasev, Leningradtsy v gody blokady, 57.

7. Goure, The Siege of Leningrad, 182.

8. Goure, The Siege of Leningrad, 49.

9. Goure, The Siege of Leningrad, 48–49.

10. Karasev, Leningradtsy v gody blokady, 94.

11. Goure, The Siege of Leningrad, 51.

12. Goure, The Siege of Leningrad, 52.

13. Alexander Werth, Leningrad (London: Hamish Hamilton, 1944), 71.

14. Werth, Leningrad, 144.

15. Goure, The Siege of Leningrad, 58.

16. Goure, The Siege of Leningrad, 59.

17. Karasev, Leningradtsy v gody blokady, 91, 94.

18. Goure, The Siege of Leningrad, 53–54.

19. William L. White, Report on the Russians (New York: Harcourt, Brace and Co., 1945), 108.

Chapter Five

Advance on Leningrad

In mid-August, after a three-week delay, German Army Group North resumed its advance on Leningrad. On August 16 the forces of the Fourth Panzer Group captured Kingisepp, and three days later the Panzers reached the area of Krasnogvardeisk, some twenty-seven kilometers (17 miles) south of Leningrad. They then stopped and turned back to attack from the rear the Soviet forces that had been by-passed earlier and who were still defending the Luga Line. The Germans succeeded in taking prisoner thousands of Soviet forces and capturing a large number of tanks and guns. On August 24 the Germans occupied the town of Luga (see Map 1).

On the left flank, the Eighteenth Army advanced toward the Estonian port city of Tallin, the main base of the Soviet Baltic Fleet. By August 27 the Germans had reached the outskirts of Tallin, and on the following day, after heavy fighting, the Russians abandoned the city. The soldiers of the defending Red Army were evacuated, but getting the troop transports and the ships of the Baltic Fleet out of the port and reaching Kronstadt proved to be very difficult. The Germans had mined in many places the Gulf of Finland, and they attacked the Soviet ships from the air. Of the twenty-nine large troop transports that escaped from Tallin, twenty-five were sunk; three had to be beached on Gogland Island and only one reached Kronstadt (see Map 1). In addition, ten Soviet warships were sunk. More that twelve thousand Russians were rescued from sinking ships or pulled out of the water while some ten thousand perished.

On the right flank, the Sixteenth Army advanced northeast on a broad front toward Lake Il'men. Their destination was the Neva River. South of Lake Il'men the Germans became engaged in heavy fighting at Toropets and Kholm. On August 19 they captured Novgorod, and then they raced northwards to occupy Chudovo on August 20. At the same time the Germans severed the Moscow-Leningrad railroad line. Nine days later, after passing through extensive Soviet mine fields, the Germans took Tosno. They continued on to Iam-Izhora but encountered the second ring of fortifications which had been built by the people of Leningrad (see Maps 1 and 2). The Germans were unable to expand their bridgehead. Further to the northeast German forces cut the Leningrad-Ovinichi railroad line and advanced to the area of Mga as well as the Neva River at Ivanovskoe. Thus, the innermost ring of fortifications which extended from the Gulf of Finland to the Neva River was reached along a considerable part of its length (see Map 2). On August 29 the Germans entered the town of Mga, and on August 31 they had full control of the town's railway station (see Map 2). It was the last railroad connection that Leningrad had with the rest of the country.

In the North, Finland had negotiated a military alliance with Germany. The negotiations dated back to a Finnish-German agreement signed in December 1940. The agreement permitted Germany to station troops in Finland, and in the months that followed German troops arrived in Finland in large numbers. Hitler wanted to use Finland as a staging base for Germany's invasion of the Soviet Union in the North. Finland's people knew little about their government's agreement with Germany; however, the great majority approved of their country's pro-German policy. They wanted to recover the territories that Finland had been forced to cede to the Soviet Union in March 1940, and they believed that this could be accomplished with Germany's assistance. By the spring of 1941, the Finnish military had joined Germany's military in planning for the invasion of the Soviet Union. On June 9 the northern Finnish air defense troops, consisting of 30,000 men, were put under German command. On June 17 the general mobilization of Finnish troops was ordered and four days later Finland's chief of the general staff was informed by his German counterpart that the invasion of the Soviet Union was to begin.

The Finns would join the Germans in a military offensive directed toward Leningrad in June. Finland did not take part in the initial German invasion of the Soviet Union conducted on June 22 because the Finnish government did not think it wise to appear as an aggressor. On June 25, however, Finland was given the pretext it needed to begin hostilities against the Soviet Union. On the previous day the Soviet High Command was informed that the German air force had been given permission to use several Finnish airports for the purpose of bombing Leningrad, Kronstadt, Murmansk and other places that were vital to the Soviet Union. In response to the information, Soviet airplanes bombed on the twenty-fifth of June Finish airports near Helsinki and other cities. On the following day the government of Finland declared war on the Soviet Union.

On July 10 the Finnish army began a major offensive in two directions. Their Southeastern Army was to strike south, smash the Soviet forces on the Karelian Isthmus and enter into Leningrad from the north. Finland's Karelian Army was to reach the Svir River, advancing between Lake Ladoga and Lake Onega. The two armies represented a total force of fourteen divisions and one German divison. They were to be supported from the air by the Fifth German Air Fleet and by the Finnish Air Force.[1] By July 21 the Finns had reached Salmi on the northeastern shore of Lake Ladoga, and they continued their push toward the Svir River (see Map 1). In the Karelian Isthmus the Finns, on August 22, attempted to encircle the city of Vyborg (see Map 1). The Soviet forces counter-attacked, but on August 25 the Finns cut the Vyborg-Leningrad railroad line. Four days later the Finnish forces entered Vyborg and by the end of the month they had reached the 1939 Russo-Finnish frontier. They were within thirty-two kilometers (20 miles) north of Leningrad (see Map 2).

The stage was set for the final assault on Leningrad. Earlier, on August 21, 1941, Hitler had issued an order which stated that the encirclement of Leningrad by combined German-Finish forces was a top priority. German Army Group North was instructed not to attempt a direct assault on Leningrad but to carry out a speedy encirclement of the city. There were reasons why Hitler wanted to avoid a direct attack on Leningrad. One reason was his dislike of street fighting; he believed the propaganda statements of the Soviet Union that promised a house-to-house defense of Leningrad should the Germans enter the city. A second reason was that Hitler did not know what to do with the millions of Leningraders following the capture of their city. They could not be eliminated, yet he did not want to feed them.[2]

If the German forces were to encircle successfully Leningrad they would need the military cooperation of their allies, the Finns. While the Finns were still fighting on the Karelian Isthmus, the Commander-in-Chief of Finland's army, General Field Marshal Gustaf Mannerheim, received a letter from Germany's General Field Marshal Wilhelm Keitel requesting the cooperation of the Finnish army in an attack on Leningrad.[3] Keitel also requested that Finland's military offensive east of Lake Ladoga be pushed across the Svir River and that the Finnish forces link up with the Germans advancing on Tikhvin (see Map 1). Mannerheim rejected the request on August 28, 1941. The Germans once more urged the Finns to join them in an attack on Leningrad, but on August 31, 1941, the request was once again rejected. Mannerheim intended to bring his forces to the narrowest part of the Karelian Isthmus where he planned to build a line of defense. The Finns further decided that advancing beyond the Svir River was not in Finland's interest.[4]

NOTES

1. Nikolai Kislitsyn and Vassily Zubakov, Leningrad Does Not Surrender, trans. Barry Jones (Moscow: Progress Publishers, 1989), 18.

2. Leon Goure, The siege of Leningrad (Stanford, California: Stanford University Press, 1962), 84.

3. Marshal Mannerheim, The Memoirs of Marshal Mannerheim, trans. Count Eric Levenhaupt (London: Cassell and Co., Ltd., 1953), 426–427.

4. Goure, The Siege of Leningrad, 84.

Chapter Six

Encirclement

The military developments in August forced the Soviet authorities to reorganize Leningrad's defense. After mid-August it was no longer possible to maintain a Northwestern Front and a Northern Front command. On August 23 the Northern Front was divided into the Karelian Front and the Leningrad Front. The Karelian Front was responsible for military operations north of Leningrad and was placed under the command of Lieutenant-General V. Frolov. Because the Germans in their advance on Leningrad had cut in half the forces of the Northwestern Front, the command of the Northwestern Front was merged with that of the Leningrad Front.

On August 24 a military council of the newly restructured Leningrad Front was organized. Marshal Kliment Voroshilov was the military council's first chairman since he was also the commander of the Leningrad Front. The military council included administrative leaders such as Andrei Zhdanov and Aleksei Kuznetsov. Marshal Voroshilov's chief of staff and the commander of the Soviet Baltic Fleet, Vice-Admiral Vladimir Tributs, were also members of the military council. The composition of the Military Council of the Leningrad Front indicated that its zone of operation was the city of Leningrad and the surrounding region. The military council had the authority to command the obedience of all Soviet, Party and economic organizations in its zone of operations as well as the area's inhabitants. However, the military council remained under the direct control of the State Defense Committee in Moscow.[1]

The Military Council of the Leningrad Front ordered the local authorities to prepare Leningrad for a street-by-street defense in case the enemy should succeed in entering the city. The Internal Defense Staff was organized for this purpose. The staff had at its command 36,000 members of the People's Volunteer Army.[2] Newly created People's Volunteer Army units had been hurriedly formed; they were recruited as before, but little attention was given to the physical condition of the volunteers. The authorities appealed particularly to the youth of the city, young men and women who were sixteen to eighteen years old. The Internal Defense Staff also presided over thousands of men who had joined the workers' battalions. Most of the men in the workers' battalions were supplied with shot guns, small caliber rifles, Molotov cocktails and hand grenades and some were armed with rifles and machine guns.

Leningrad and its suburbs were turned into an enormous fortress by the thousands of people who were recruited for this purpose. All entrances to the city were covered with iron hedgehogs and other anti-tank obstructions. The streets and avenues were blocked by barricades in front of which deep ditches were dug. The barricades were made of paving blocks, timbers, railroad iron and steel tubing. The barricades were at least 2.5 meters (7.2 feet) high and 3.5 meters (11.5 feet) deep, massive enough to stop an enemy tank. Anti-tank devices such as pyramid-shaped concrete blocks were placed throughout each of the city's districts. Machine gun pillboxes were built in the ground floors of corner buildings. Underground communication lines and supply routes were created in the city's sewers. Using the network of sewers, reinforcements and ammunition could be moved quickly to wherever they were needed in the city. Special points for directing fire at German tanks and soldiers were built into the sewer inspection manholes and sewer openings. In each district, members of the People's Volunteer Army were organized to fight the enemy invaders at the barricades, in the streets and from the buildings. Each factory had its own defenses, and from these defenses the members of the workers' battalions were to fight the enemy at a moment's notice.

If it became evident that the defense of Leningrad was crumbling, the city was to be destroyed to deny the enemy the use of its industries and facilities. The order came from Moscow and the Military Council of the Leningrad Front issued tons of explosives that, if it should become necessary, were to be used to blow up the bridges across the city's canals, as well as the Neva River and its tributaries. Demolition charges were laid under port and railroad installations. Important buildings including factories were mined in such a way that upon detonation they would collapse across the streets so as to form barriers to the enemy's advance within the city.

On September 1, 1941, the German forces were poised south, southwest and southeast of Leningrad at a distance of nineteen to thirty-five kilometers (12 to 22 miles) from the city's outskirts. Despite this proximity to their final objective, the Germans were faced with obstacles that hindered further advance. The Red Army had been regrouped and reinforced by units of the People's Volunteer Army and by sailors of the Soviet Baltic Fleet that were organized into marine brigades. The stubborn resistance of the Soviet forces had slowed significantly the German advance. Up until July 10 the Germans had advanced an average of twenty-six kilometers (16 miles) per day but subsequently that was reduced to five kilometers (3 miles) per day and in August to less than three kilometers (1.9 miles).[3] The Soviet soldiers were also supported by the heavy naval guns of the warships positioned in Leningrad and Kronstadt. Furthermore, the Germans had to break through a triple line of extensive fortifications to which the civilian population of Leningrad was constantly adding.

Hitler believed the encirclement of Leningrad would be achieved quickly. In Directive No. 35, issued on September 6, 1941, the German forces were ordered to breach the Soviet fortification lines, cross the Neva River and advance north to join the Finnish forces on the Karelian Isthmus. The directive stated in part:

> On the northeast front it is essential . . . to encircle the enemy forces fighting in the Leningrad region so that by September 15 at the latest a substantial part of the mechanical troops . . . be freed for employment with [German] Army Group Center. Before this, the close encirclement of Leningrad in the east is to be achieved, and, if the weather permits, a major air attack by the Luftwaffe is to be carried out.[4]

The directive went on to say that the primary target of the air attack was to be Leningrad's waterworks. The plan of attack did not include an actual ground assault on the city.

During the first week of September the forces of German Army Group North made slow but steady progress against strong Soviet resistance. On September 8 the Germans took Schlusselburg, a town located where the Neva River flowed out of Lake Ladoga, thus eliminating Leningrad's last communication by land with the rest of the country (see Map 2). Two days later, on September 10, the Finns succeeded in reaching the Svir River east of Lake Ladoga and stopped to turn their attention to the capture of Petrozavodsk on the shore of Lake Onega (see Map 1). (The Finns succeeded in taking Petrozavodsk on October 2.) At the same time the Germans, hoping to link up with the Finns who had reached the Svir River, were advancing slowly in the direction of Volkhov (see Map 1).

Germany's advance on Volkhov was spearheaded by the Fourth Panzer Group. It was launched on September 9 from the area of Krasnogvardeisk. The Panzer divisions made slow progress due to strong Soviet resistance and also because of the numerous fortifications that had been constructed by Leningrad's populace. By the end of the first day, the German tanks had succeeded in breaching the first or innermost ring of fortifications. By nightfall on September 11 the Germans, after suffering heavy losses despite extensive air support, took the Dudergof Heights, and the following day they entered Krasnoe Selo (see Map 2).

By this time Leningrad was under long-range artillery fire and aerial bombardment. The Germans began shelling the city on September 4, 1941, and four days later they started conducting daylight air raids. On September 8, German airplanes dropped on the city more than 6,000 incendiary bombs containing napalm, a highly combustible substance. More than 170 fires broke out at industrial plants and in residential places in various districts. Heavy black clouds of smoke rose slowly into the sky contaminating the air with a putrid odor of burning buildings and the things within them. On the same day more than 40 high explosive bombs ranging in weight from 250 to 500 kilograms (551 to 1,102 pounds) were also dropped on the city. Twelve dwelling places were destroyed, the pumping plant of the city waterworks was severely damaged, as many as twenty-four people were killed and more than one hundred people were wounded.[5]

Lydia Okhapkina's recollection of the air raid on September 8 was very detailed: "When I heard the alarm I rushed to the shelter, but didn't get that far and took refuge in the entrance of a stone building. I stood there quaking with fear. A woman invited me [and my children] into her flat. . . . We had just gotten upstairs and in the door when we heard a deafening explosion with an incredible crash and crackling of fire. We were all deafened by the roar of engines. We heard bombs exploding somewhere nearby. The air, everything around, was cracking, booming. The house was shaking through and through. The earth, too, seemed to be seized with convulsions, as in an earthquake. My teeth were chattering from fear, my knees were shaking. I squashed myself into a corner and pressed the children to me. They were crying with fear. I had the feeling there were moments when I was about to lose consciousness. I thought that this was the end, that now a bomb would fall on us and we would all be killed. We stood there like people condemned to die. The woman who invited us in stood open-mouthed, her eyes dilated, whispering something. Her mother, an old woman, fell to her knees and crossed herself." [6]

One German target on September 8 was the Badayevsky warehouses in the southern area of Leningrad. The warehouses were the largest food storehouses in the city. The wooden buildings were separated from one another by no more than ten meters (33 feet). When one of the buildings was struck by an incendiary bomb the flames ignited the wooden structure, and the fire then spread from building to building until the entire depot covering 16,188 square meters (4 acres) was engulfed in flames. After the fire was extinguished, it was determined that 3,000 tons of flour had been destroyed. The sugar supply, 2,500 tons, had melted and turned into a thick syrup with a black crust on top.[7] Later it was made into a hard candy-like substance and sold to the people in that form. The destruction of the Badayevsky warehouses would reduce substantially the city's food supply which was already dangerously low.

Following the initial air raids, the enemy began dropping on Leningrad delayed-action bombs. A special bomb-disposal squad would rush to the site where a bomb had landed and try to dismantle it. Since a delayed-action bomb might go off while it was being dismantled, the work of disarming it was done by a single individual. The most used method was to take a hammer and knock off the metal clamp of the detonator. It had to be done quickly, and the work required enormous self-control. There were incidents when such bombs did go off, and the people working on them were blown to pieces. The civil defense detachment in each city district had a bomb-disposal squad and most of these squads included young girls who were Komsomol members.

One day Anna Nikolaevna Kovaleva, a platoon commander of a civil defense detachment, was called upon to dismantle a delayed-action bomb. The weapon had fallen on the streetcar depot on Serdobolsky Street. It had smashed through the ceilings and floors and had finally landed in the cellar. Everyone was immediately evacuated from the area and the site was cordoned off. Soon after the civil defense headquarters was informed about the bomb, the young Kovaleva arrived to disarm it. She began by surveying the hole in the floor to determine the approximate size of the bomb. She then lit a candle and crawled into the cellar to disarm the bomb knowing that it could explode at any moment. It was to be her first attempt at disarming a bomb:

> The flickering light of the candle in the dark cellar revealed rows of posts, 0.6 of a meter in height, over which ran water pipes and electric cables stretching away into the distance. Somewhere in the dark, damp cellar, filled with the monotonous hum of the cables, the monster was lurking, ready to blow up the depot and the houses around it. Lighting her path with the candle, Kovaleva picked her way among the posts on hands and knees, trying not to touch an uninsulated cable somewhere, and looked for the bomb. And there at the end of the cellar, between posts, she saw a high-explosive bomb lying on its side.
>
> When she got to the bomb, Kovaleva began to knock the clamp ring off with a hammer. Having removed it with difficulty, she took out the detonator and unscrewed the priming cap. The monster was now harmless. When Kovaleva came out of the cellar, she was asked how she had felt. "I was a little upset," said Anna, "because I was afraid the candle would burn down before I got the detonator unscrewed, but everything turned out all right."[8]

During the last three weeks of September some 2,700 German aircraft were sent to fly over Leningrad, but no more than 480 penetrated the city's air defenses. Soviet aircraft and the anti-aircraft artillery regiments stationed along the western and southwestern outskirts of the city and in the city parks and squares shot down some 270 German airplanes.[9] The anti-aircraft batteries mounted on the Soviet Baltic Fleet ships in the Gulf of Finland also protected Leningrad. The city's air defenses forced the Germans to fly higher and conduct more of their raids at night. To combat the night raids, searchlights were used to penetrate the skies and silhouette the German bombers for the higher-flying Soviet aircraft.

It was the city's searchlights that helped Junior Lieutenant Alexie Sevastyanov, while on patrol one night, notice a German bomber. The Soviet pilot immediately turned his airplane in the direction of the Heinkell-III. When he got within firing range he shot several bursts from his machine gun, but the German pilot maneuvered his aircraft out of the way. Fearing that the enemy bomber would escape the searchlights, Sevastyanov flew up close and again pulled the trigger. Nothing happened; he had run out of ammunition. Sevastyanov knew that if the enemy was permitted to escape, he would be back the next day to drop a load of bombs on Leningrad. Thus, Sevastyanov decided to ram the German airplane. He succeeded in bringing down the bomber, but in doing so his own aircraft crashed. Before it hit the ground, Sevastyanov parachuted out and landed on the roof of the Nevsky Engineering Plant. Here he was taken by the workers, and after they checked his papers he was warmly embraced. The German pilot had also bailed out; he landed on Mayakovsky Street and was apprehended by people in the street.[10]

The aerial bombardment of Leningrad strengthened the widely held belief that there were enemy agents in the city who were signaling the location of targets to German bombers. It was believed that this was done with lights and rockets and hence the enemy agents were given the name "rocket men." It was further believed that the agents had either entered the city before the war or had been parachuted in later. The authorities responded to these beliefs by organizing in each city district a special destruction detachment made up of members of the Komsomol and the NKVD. Each detachment was 150 to 200 persons strong. It was their duty to find the enemy agents and arrest them. The so-called "rocket men" caused a great deal of excitement, but there is no evidence that they existed.[11]

The Germans used their long range guns to strike Leningrad's industrial centers. The enemy's artillery bombardment caused heavy casualties among the workers, and it lowered their morale. One factory director explained: "In our experience a direct hit has a very bad effect. . . . In a workshop that's had a direct hit, production slumps heavily for twenty-four or forty-eight hours, or stops almost completely, especially if many people have been killed or injured. It's a horrible sight, all the blood, and makes even some of our hardened workers quite ill for a day or two. . . . When we see," he continued, "that a man or a girl is going to pieces we send him or her to a rest-home for a fortnight or a month." The director commented that except for one or two very sick people, he had not come across anyone in his plant who wanted to quit and get a quieter job elsewhere.[12] Most workers felt that through their efforts they were supporting the soldiers among whom they had relatives and friends.

Since the southern districts of the city were nearest to the military front and most exposed to enemy artillery fire, the authorities decided to relocate a part of this area's industry and population to safer districts. The relocation began in September. Usually the factory shops that were moved were those that produced items for the war effort. Factories that were engaged in less vital production or those in which the equipment was too difficult to move were not relocated and continued to operate under enemy fire. Shops that were relocated were generally given space left by factories that had been evacuated from the city. About 54,000 inhabitants in the exposed districts were relocated as well. Some were moved by streetcar and some on foot. Many of the people were quartered in empty schools and offices or in apartments and rooms whose occupants had been evacuated from the city or who were away in the army. Some were moved in with residents who had excess living space. The city's refugees had to leave behind most of their furniture and other belongings, to be retrieved later.[13]

Fuel shortages would hamper the operations of Leningrad's industry. In September the factories exhausted their supply of liquid fuel and many depleted their supply of coal. Electric power was also in short supply. Before the war, Leningrad obtained its electric power from six hydroelectric power plants located at various distances from the city and from a number of thermoelectric power plants located within the city. The latter produced less than half of the total amount of electricity needed by Leningrad, and most of them operated on coal imported from other parts of the country. By September almost all the hydroelectric power stations had either been captured or cut off by the Germans. It put almost the entire burden of producing electricity on the thermoelectric power plants within the city, and each had a limited supply of coal. Furthermore, some had been damaged by enemy bombardment. Consequently, it became necessary to ration electric power for industrial use and this in turn led to a decline in industrial output.[14]

The methods of defending Leningrad along the city's military fronts changed after the tenth of September. On this day Stalin ordered General Georgy Zhukov to go to Leningrad and replace Marshal Voroshilov as the chief commander of the Leningrad Front. General Zhukov had been the head of the Red Army General Staff since the beginning of the war. Upon his arrival in Leningrad, he joined Andrei Zhdanov at the Smol'ny Institute, the seat of the Leningrad Communist Party and the local government and the headquarters to which the top military commanders of the Leningrad Front were summoned. General Zhukov made it clear that he was willing to sacrifice anybody and anything to defend the city. He informed the commanders that a withdrawal would be considered a crime against the homeland. If they should withdraw they would be brought before a military tribunal and shot. General Zhukov's deputy, Lieutenant-General Ivan Fedyuninsky, liked to repeat the words: "Our principle is this: if you retreat, I will kill you. If I retreat without orders, you will kill me. And Leningrad will not be surrendered."[15] General Zhukov also ordered the commanders to attack, attack and attack again. It made no difference to him if their military units were weak and had few weapons and no ammunition. The commanders who failed to carry out his orders were removed and faced execution.

On September 14 Germany's Panzer divisions reached the Pulkovo Heights beating back all Soviet counterattacks (see Map 2). The German tanks were now poised to dash into Leningrad, which was only about eleven kilometers (7 miles) away. At that moment they were ordered to halt and establish defensive positions in preparation for their withdrawal three days later. The Fourth Panzer Group had received orders to leave Germany's northern front and join German Army Group Center. The orders were in compliance with Hitler's Directive No. 35 issued earlier on the sixth of September.

Elsewhere on September 16 the Eighteenth Army captured Uritsk, Petergof and Strel'na and reached the Gulf of Finland (see Map 2). By doing this the Germans cut off the Soviet forces along the Gulf of Finland between Kopore and Oranienbaum. Two days later the Germans completed the encirclement of the Soviet forces around Oranienbaum (see Map 2). It was a bridgehead that the Soviet forces would not surrender. Toward the east of Oranienbaum, the city of Pushkin was taken by the Germans late on September 17 and the following day they occupied Slutsk (see Map 2). Alexandrovka, the terminal of a Leningrad trolley car line, was taken by the Germans as well. On September 18 the armored and motorized divisions of the Eighteenth Army, in compliance with Directive No. 35, began their transfer to German Army Group Center.

Thereafter, the fighting south of Leningrad was marked by minor German advances and Soviet counterattacks. Due to exhaustion, the Germans were unable to cross the Neva River, and a junction with the Finns was not achieved. Nor had the Germans succeeded in approaching Leningrad to within range where they could strike the city with their light artillery. The drive on Leningrad had been halted. The Germans had no choice but to dig a network of trenches, build dug-outs, lay mines and put up barbed-wire entanglements. The network of trenches became their military front. On the evening of October 6, General Zhukov received a telephone call from Stalin at Smol'ny Institute; he was ordered to return to Moscow. General Zhukov handed over his command at Leningrad to Lieutenant-General Fedyuninsky.

The close encirclement of Leningrad that Hitler had ordered was in reality a wide arc that would remain a siege line until January 1943. It began on the shore of the Gulf of Finland at Novoikerson and then curved eastward in a semicircle to Petergof. Within this arc, which faced the island fortress and naval base of Kronstadt, was the so-called Oranienbaum bridgehead defended by Soviet military forces (see Map 2). No assault on Kronstadt or against the western side of Leningrad would be possible unless the Oranienbaum forces were destroyed. These forces were supplied by sea and during the winter months over the ice, and they were defended by coastal and naval artillery. The bridgehead tied down a number of German divisions that were needed elsewhere and constantly threatened the German forces that held Petergof and Uritsk. From the Gulf of Finland east of Petergof the military front swung in a semicircle through Pulkovo, Pushkin and Slutsk and on to Schlusselburg on the southern shore of Lake Ladoga (see Map 2). The Germans along the western portion of this arc were within artillery range of a major part of Leningrad. From Schlusselburg the military front followed the southern shore of Lake Ladoga for several kilometers, then swung sharply southeastward to the vicinity of Kirishi and from there followed the Volkhov River south, via Novgorod, to Lake Il'men (see Maps 1 and 2). Below Lake Il'men the German Sixteenth Army had pushed forward during September into the Valdai Hills beyond Demiansk and was in touch with the Ninth Army of German Army Group Center.

To the north of Leningrad the encirclement included the military postions that were held by the Finns, Germany's allies. On the Karelian Isthmus the Finnish advance had come to a halt some thirty kilometers (18 miles) from Leningrad. Here the Finns built four lines of fortification that extended from the Gulf of Finland to Lake Ladoga (see Map 2). The first line, the one closest to Leningrad, was three to five kilometers (2 to 3 miles) deep. The second line was built fifteen to twenty-five kilometers (9 to 15 miles) behind the first and it too was three to five kilometers (2 to 3 miles) deep. The third line was similar to the first two and was built sixty to sixty-five kilometers (37 to 40 miles) from the first. The fourth line, constructed in the Vyborg area, consisted of minefields, barbed-wire entanglements, granite anti-tank obstructions and anti-tank ditches. It also included concrete, earth and wooden weapon emplacements and gun turrets. The Finnish forces stationed at these defense lines were ordered to hold their postions whatever the cost.

On the eastern shore of Lake Ladoga the Finns had stopped at the Svir River (see Maps 1 and 6). North of the river the Finns constructed lines of defense that were similar to the ones they built across the Karelian Isthmus. Together they were 180 kilometers (111 miles) deep and ran from Lake Ladoga to Lake Onega.[16] The eastern shore of Lake Ladoga between the Svir River and the German military front to the south was in Soviet hands. Thus, a considerable gap existed between the Finns and the Germans. The survival of Leningrad depended in large measure on the ability of the Soviet defenders to prevent the junction of their enemy forces. During the months of encirclement, which Leningraders called the blockade, the fighting along the military fronts consisted primarily of Soviet attempts to push their enemies back and of the efforts of the Finns and the Germans to retain their grip on Leningrad. At the same time, the Germans were confident that starvation would force the Leningraders to surrender.

NOTES

1. Leon Goure, The Siege of Leningrad (Stanford, California: Stanford University Press, 1962), 111–13.

2. Goure, The Siege of Leningrad, 114.

3. Nikolai Kislitsyn and Vassily Zubakov, Leningrad Does Not Surrender, trans. Barry Jones (Moscow: Progress Publishers, 1989), 76.

4. Goure, The Siege of Leningrad, 85.

5. Dimitri V. Pavlov, Leningrad 1941, trans. John Clinton Adams (Chicago, Illinois: The University of Chicago Press, 1965), 25.

6. Ales Adamovich and Daniil Granin, A Book of the Blockade, trans. Hilda Perham (Moscow: Raduga Publishers, 1983), 284.

7. Pavlov, Leningrad 1941, 56.

8. Pavlov, Leningrad 1941, 27–28.

9. Kislitsyn and Zubakov, Leningrad Does Not Surrender, 83.

10. Kislitsyn and Zubakov, Leningrad Does Not Surrender, 84.

11. Goure, The Siege of Leningrad, 116–17.

12. Alexander Werth, Leningrad (London: Hamish Hamilton, 1944), 116–18.

13. Goure, The Siege of Leningrad, 105.

14. Goure, The Siege of Leningrad, 108.

15. Harrison E. Salisbury, The 900 Days: The Siege of Leningrad (New York: Avon Books, 1970), 400–01.

16. Kislitsyn and Zubakov, Leningrad Does Not Surrender, 264.

Chapter Seven

Hunger and Starvation

By the end of September the encircled city of Leningrad was faced with a siege that was designed to destroy its inhabitants. There were more than 2,500,000 Leningraders living in the city and more than 340,000 Soviet citizens residing in the areas bordering the outer limits of the city.[1] Trapped in Leningrad with its citizens were more than 100,000 refugees from the Baltic Republics and from areas within the Leningrad region. They had abandoned everything when they fled from the enemy, either the Germans or the Finns. Added to Leningrad's population were Soviet soldiers who had been brought into the city to receive medical treatment for the wounds that they had acquired while fighting for the city's defense. All would suffer starvation unless the blockade was broken and food was brought into Leningrad.

The city's food supply was such a major concern that a rationing program was already in place. The rationing of food was introduced on July 18, 1941. Ration cards were issued to the population by the city administration through district executive committees, through heads of enterprises, offices and schools and through managers of housing buildings. All of these people were responsible for keeping exact records in their own areas and places of jurisdiction. All working persons received their ration cards at their place of employment. People who were not employed received them at their place of residence. Each card was good for one month.[2]

The ration system divided the population into four categories based on each person's importance and contribution to the war effort. The first and highest category included managers of defense enterprises, technical and engineering personnel, defense workers, key personnel in utilities and services, the armed forces, troops of the NKVD and other persons in similar jobs. The second category included office workers in nonessential jobs, including education. The third category comprised all unemployed persons. In addition, there was a category for children under twelve years of age. No special mention was made of Party officials and full-time Party workers, but they were presumably included in the first category.[3]

The ration of bread, the basic food of the population, was set at a fairly high level. According to official Soviet sources, the people in the first category received 800 grams (28.2 ounces) of bread per day. People in the second category were allotted 600 grams (21.2 ounces) daily. Unemployed persons were given 400 grams (14.1 ounces) and children under twelve years of age received 400 grams (14.1 ounces). According to Leningrad Communist Party records, industrial workers received in addition to bread 800 grams (28.2 ounces) of butter, 2,000 grams (70.6 ounces) of cereal and 2,200 grams (77.6 ounces) of meat per month. Office workers received 1,500 grams (52.9 ounces) of cereal and 1,200 grams (42.3 ounces) of meat per month. Unemployed people received 1,000 grams (35.3 ounces) of cereal and 600 grams (21.2 ounces) of meat and children under twelve years old received 1,200 grams (42.3 ounces) of cereal and 600 grams (21.2 ounces) of meat per month.[4]

The food rations were reduced as the city's food reserves decreased. The first reduction was made on the second day of September. It was decided that workers and white collar employees would receive 600 (21.2 ounces) and 400 grams (14.1 ounces) of bread a day respectively or 200 grams (7.1 ounces) less a day than before. Dependents, non-workers and children would receive 300 grams (10.5 ounces) of bread or 100 grams (3.5 ounces) less a day than before. In order to make the supply of bread go farther it was decided, on September 6, to add to the bread such admixtures as malt, corn flour, barley flour, oat flour, soya flour and other ingredients. On September 10 the bread ration of workers and office workers was reduced to 500 grams (17.6 ounces) and 300 grams (10.5 ounces) a day respectively and that of adult dependents to 250 grams (8.8 ounces). It was a decision made by the Military Council of the Leningrad Front after the civilian and military food reserves were pooled. Workers were to receive monthly 1,500 grams (52.9 ounces) of meat, 1,500 grams (52.9 ounces) of cereal, 2,000 grams (70.6 ounces) of sugar and 950 grams (33.5 ounces) of fats. Office workers were to receive 800 grams (28.2 ounces) of meat, 1,000 grams (35.3 ounces) of cereal, 1,700 grams (60.0 ounces) of sugar and 500 grams (17.6 ounces) of fats. Adult dependents were to receive 400 grams (14.1 ounces) of meat, 600 grams (21.2 ounces) of cereal, 1,500 grams (52.9 ounces) of sugar and 300 grams (10.5 ounces) of fats. Children under twelve years of age were to receive 400 grams (14.1 ounces) of meat, 1,200 grams (42.3 ounces) of cereal, 1,700 grams (60.0 ounces) of sugar and 500 grams (17.6 ounces) of fats. Substitutes were to be made. Instead of meat, the population was to be issued sausages of poor quality. Cereal was to be replaced with potato starch, flour by vegetables and sugar often by hard candy.[5]

Reducing the people's rations was not a solution to Leningrad's food crisis; food needed to be brought into the city. On September 9 the Military Council of the Leningrad Front ordered the construction of a harbor at the bay of Osinovets (see Map 2). The bay was on the west bank of Lake Ladoga within a thirty-kilometer (19 mile) stretch of land that was occupied by the Soviet Union and was covered by a thick forest of high pine trees, which would conceal warehouses and access roads. The bay was just nineteen kilometers (12 miles) north of the Germans at Schlusselburg and eleven kilometers (7 miles) south of the Finns who controlled the northern part of Lake Ladoga. Osinovets was located near the end of a railway line, the Irinovsky Railroad, which connected Leningrad to the bay, a distance of fifty-five kilometers (34 miles).[6] It was believed that food and other supplies could be brought from the Russian mainland to the eastern shoreline of Lake Ladoga south of the Svir River, an area that was still in Soviet hands. The supplies could then be ferried across the lake on barges to the newly constructed harbor at Osinovets. There the cargo could be taken off the barges and placed on trucks and freight-handling carts and be brought from the harbor to the small station at the end of the Irinovsky Railroad line located within the proximity of the bay (see Map 2). After the cargo was loaded on railroad cars it could then be transported into Leningrad.

A harbor at the bay of Osinovets was built. The shore at the bay, which was sandy, low and sloping, was dug out to deepen the draft so that water vessels would not run aground. Army units and workers built four large piers for mooring boats. Warehouses were constructed for the storage of fuel and ammunition and for the temporary storage of food and other supplies as they arrived from the eastern shore of Lake Ladoga. They were also to be used for the temporary storage of industrial equipment that was to be evacuated from Leningrad and transported across the lake to the eastern shore and the Russian mainland. From Leningrad were brought commercial docks, freight-handling carts and other machinery. Bunkers were dug for various defense purposes.

Toward the middle of September a supply line across Lake Ladoga was in operation. Food and other supplies were transported from the mainland by freight train to Gostinopolye through Vologda, Cherepovets, Tikhvin and Volkhov (see Maps 3 and 4). At Gostinopolye, a river port on the Volkhov River nine kilometers (6 miles) south of Volkhov, the cargo was unloaded onto docks and then placed on river barges. The barges were pulled down the river to Novaya Ladoga on the eastern part of the south shore of Lake Ladoga where the Volkhov River emptied into the lake. Here the cargo was reloaded into lake barges and pulled to Osinovets (see Map 3). On the twelfth of September a steamer pulling two barges carrying 800 tons of cereal and flour arrived at Osinovets from Novaya Ladoga.[7] News of the initial success of the lake's supply line was encouraging to the Party leadership of Leningrad, but the boost in morale was brief. Three days later five more barges arrived from Novaya Ladoga with three thousand tons of wheat. Shortly after their arrival, they were spotted by a German reconnaissance airplane. Within thirty minutes German dive bombers arrived and sank three of the barges.

From then onward the Germans patrolled the lake route with bombers and shelled the harbors at Osinovets and Novaya Ladoga. In response to Germany's actions, the Soviets mounted anti-aircraft guns at both harbors and ordered the gunboats of the Ladoga Naval Flotilla, headquartered at Novaya Ladoga, to accompany the tugboats pulling the supply barges across the lake. All the barges left the two harbors in darkness. The crossing took from twelve to sixteen hours, and when the barges were halfway across the lake German aircraft arrived to bomb them in daylight. During the last two weeks of September only 10 percent of the food that was loaded at Novaya Lodaga arrived at Osinovets. The remainder of the food along with the barges and their crews lay at the bottom of the lake. By the end of the month only 9,800 tons of food had been brought into Leningrad from the east shore of Lake Ladoga. It represented an eight-day food supply for the civilians and soldiers in Leningrad.[8] The city's leaders knew that unless greater supplies of food were brought into the city, the people would die from starvation.

On October 12 the city authorities decided to take drastic measures. They ordered 3,000 Party workers to check every ration card. The citizens of Leningrad were required to appear personally with their identity papers and prove that they were the rightful holders. The cards that survived this process were stamped "Reregistered." Those that were not reregistered were confiscated on presentation. As was suspected, some people were using cards belonging to friends or relatives who had either left Leningrad or who had died. There were orders to look for ration cards that had been forged or that were printed without authority. One woman who worked in a ration card printing shop was found in possession of one hundred cards; she was immediately shot. The measures used by the Party workers revealed that more than 300,000 unauthorized ration cards had been in use. Their elimination created a significantly fairer distribution of food, and after October 18 ration cards that did not bear the stamp of the Party checkers were invalid.[9]

In an effort to further resolve Leningrad's food crisis, the authorities evacuated by water transportation a large number of the city's inhabitants. More than 33,000 persons, primarily children and unemployed adults, were evacuated by boat across Lake Ladoga before the freezing temperatures turned the lake's surface to ice. These people were not contributing to the city's defense, and by evacuating them the authorities were in turn reducing the number of mouths that needed to be fed. The evacuations, however, were dangerous because enemy aircraft patrolling the waters would attack the passenger transports.

On November 4 a large boat carrying more than 350 evacuees, mainly women and children, left the western shore of Lake Ladoga for the harbor at Novaya Ladoga. A German bomber spotted the large boat just a few kilometers from the port. The captain of the vessel took evasive action and succeeded in avoiding the bombs, but then another enemy bomber appeared and one of its bombs hit the large boat. The force of the blast swept many of the passengers into the water, and the boat barely stayed afloat. Meanwhile, the German airplane was circling above and strafing the people as they struggled in the water. More than two hundred people died on this transport.[10]

A further reduction in the city's population was achieved through evacuations by air transportation. In mid-October the State Defense Committee in Moscow decided to establish a tank factory in Cheliabinsk located in the Ural region of Siberia. The skilled workers, technicians and administrators from the tank shop at the Kirov Works and their families were placed on airplanes and transported to Cheliabinsk to organize and operate a new tank plant. In addition to these industrial people, families of high army and navy officials were evacuated. By the end of the year more than 35,000 people had been brought out of the city by air transportation. The evacuations did not, however, resolve Leningrad's food problem.[11]

At this same time Hitler wanted to tighten Germany's stranglehold on Leningrad. General Field Marshal von Leeb, the commander of German Army Group North, was instructed to concentrate his efforts on pushing forward north in the direction of Tikhvin, a Soviet held railway station located eighty kilometers (49 miles) east of Volkhov (see Map 4). The railway station was a supply center for both Leningrad and the Soviet forces that were attempting to break through the German encirclement from the east. Hitler also wanted the Finnish and German forces poised along the northern shore of the Svir River to advance south toward Tikhvin thereby closing the ring around Leningrad along the eastern shore of Lake Ladoga. If that should be accomplished then Leningrad would no longer be able to use the lake as a route to bring food and other supplies into the city.

The Germans launched an attack in the direction of Tikhvin on October 16. They advanced slowly over difficult terrain and in the face of strong Soviet resistance. On November 8, during a snow storm, they captured Tikhvin but were unable to continue an advance northward. Contact with the Finnish and

German forces stationed north of the Svir River was never made. These forces were held back by Soviet attacks and by the need to wait until the river froze over. A military encirclement of Lake Ladoga by the Germans had been prevented, but Leningrad's leadership knew that as long as Tikhvin remained in enemy hands it was impossible to supply the city with the food and materials that were necessary to prevent its fall.

German forces also advanced to the vicinity of Volkhov and Voibokalo in the direction of Lake Ladoga's southern shore (see Map 4). As a precautionary measure, the Soviet leadership ordered that the Volkhov hydroelectric power station be dismantled and removed to a safer area; they did not want the power station to fall into the hands of the enemy. It was the last hydroelectric station that supplied Leningrad. The power station was dismantled and moved. The Soviet forces were also able to stop the Germans from reaching the southeast shore of the lake.

In the early days of November Lake Ladoga began to freeze and after it ceased to be navigable Leningrad was supplied only by air. Moscow upon the request of the Military Council of the Leningrad Front granted that cargo airplanes be used to transport food into the city, and on November 16 the airlift began. The cargo airplanes were loaded at the airfield at Novaya Ladoga with smoked foods, canned goods, powdered eggs, condensed milk, lard, butter, meat compressed into blocks and other compacted foods. Because of the short flight distance, about one hundred sixty-one kilometers (100 miles), it was possible for an airplane to complete five round trips in one day. However, the frequency of the flights alerted the Germans, and they began bombing the airfield at Novaya Ladoga. The Soviets responded by transferring at least two thirds of the cargo airplanes to more distant airfields, and from there they continued to bring supplies into Leningrad. These airplanes were able to complete only two flights a day. They were armed with machine guns and would leave the airfields in groups of six or nine. For added protection they would often be escorted by a fighter aircraft. Because there was limited cargo space in the airplanes, the food airlift into Leningrad did not solve the city's food supply problem.[12]

On November 20, 1941, the Leningraders began receiving the lowest bread ration during the entire length of the siege. Workers in priority shops, engineers and technical workers received 250 grams (8.8 ounces) of bread per day and office workers, dependents and children received 125 grams (4.4 ounces) of bread per day. Front line soldiers, naval crews and flyers and other air force personnel received 500 grams (17.6 ounces) of bread per day. Military men stationed in the city received 300 grams (10.5 ounces) of bread per day.[13] The dark brown bread that was rationed out was 73 percent rye flour, and its other ingredients were 10 percent cellulose, 10 percent cottonseed-oil cake, 3 percent corn flour, 2 percent chaff and 2 percent flour sweepings and dust shaken out of flour sacks. There were other food products to be issued on the ration cards, but during the days in the winter of 1941–1942, the distribution of these foods was irregular.

Bread was the people's main source of sustenance, and in an attempt to satisfy their hunger they developed their own routines in eating it. Some people would eat their daily ration all at once soon after they received it. Others divided the ration into three parts, the first for breakfast, the second for lunch and the third for supper. It was this routine that required great self-discipline. Some people would eat their bread by biting off a piece and other people would break off or pinch off tiny pieces and put them in their mouths trying to make the ration last throughout the day. There were people who would cut the sticky bread into tiny pieces, dry the pieces on the stove and then chew them as little biscuits. Some people would dry the entire portion, pour hot water over it and catch the water as it filtered through the bread. They then added salt and pepper to the water and drank it. They would repeat the process, and after that they would eat the water-soaked bread.

The organization of the sale of food added to the difficulties of the population. Earlier, on August 24, the authorities had reduced the number of food stores in Leningrad; only fifty-nine food stores and fifty-four bread stores were to remain open to the people.[14] In October the number of bread stores was reduced from fifty-four to thirty-four. Under the rationing system, bread had to be purchased daily. Since the people were free to buy their food in any store, the number of purchasers in each store fluctuated from day to day so that sometimes the supply of bread in a store was depleted before everyone who came to the store was able to buy their ration. Consequently, people would rise at 5 o'clock in the morning to line up in front of a bread store and would stand in a long line several hours in the intense cold weather waiting for the store to open. If the supply of food in a store should run out then those who had not gotten their daily ration would be forced to walk to another store in the hope that it would have food for sale. Later, the authorities remedied this situation. On the first of December everyone was ordered to register with a store of choice and was to purchase rations only from that store.[15]

Finding food to feed the people was a chief concern for the authorities. They sent out search parties to find food and urged experts to come up with food substitutes. Warehouses, grain elevators and freight cars were swept, and several tons of flour were reclaimed. Sacks that had been used to hold flour were turned inside out and beaten, and the flour dust was gathered in containers. The sweepings of the floors in a tannery building produced leather dust that was mixed with sawdust to make a paste that was added to so-called food patties. In the port of Leningrad 2,000 tons of sheep guts were discovered. The guts were processed into jelly, and the jelly was flavored with aromatic herbs to disguise the revolting smell. The jelly was then mixed with flax seed and machine oil and supplied to ration card holders as a meat substitute. Any food substitute was considered provided that it could be made digestible and that it contained calories. Botanists pointed out that some common plants were edible. The countryside was scoured for stinging wattles which made a nourishing soup. Branches of young trees were ground up and stewed and then mixed with peat and salt to make a nourishing paste. In time, the workers at the defense enterprises were issued acorn "coffee," kelp casein glue, protein yeast, fermented soybean milk and other substitutes that would dull the feeling of hunger.

Survival on the official ration was impossible, and people were forced to seek other means to acquire additional food. Many turned to barter market sources. In the barter market firewood or vodka could be exchanged for a day's bread ration. Valuable objects such as watches, gold jewelry and even wedding rings were exchanged for food. One woman bartered a bottle of perfume (which people drank for alcohol) for 200 grams (7.1 ounces) of bread, and later she would exchange some silver spoons for a piece of meat.[16] Lydia Okhapkina posted a notice at the bread store saying that she had a gramophone and would exchange it for bread. The next day a soldier arrived at her place with an entire loaf of bread. Lydia then posted the sale of her sewing machine. "Not long after a woman came. She did not offer me an entire loaf but only just over half. I hated to part with the sewing machine, but there was no option—I gave it to her. That woman did not look particularly undernourished. I asked her where she worked. But she told me it was none of my business. By then the price of bread was extremely high."[17]

People searched throughout their homes for anything that would give them nourishment. Rats were caught, skinned and roasted or put in stews. Pets such as dogs, cats and birds were eaten as well. The bones of dead animals were stewed for hours in order to extract a little marrow from them. Books were stripped of their covers, and the glue in the bindings was melted down as an ingredient for soup. Wallpaper was stripped from the walls; the dried paste on the back was used as an admixture with flour. Caster oil and hair oil were used instead of fat.

For sixty rubles Nil Belyaev could make himself a meal that would sustain him for at least a little while. Thirty of the rubles were used to purchase a piece of animal hide that was ten centimeters (4 inches) by ten centimeters large. The other thirty rubles were spent on a small slab of carpenter's glue. He boiled the hide until it became a thin jelly-like substance and then added the carpenter's glue. The boiled mixture of the two ingredients produced a "nice and thick" jelly. "Of course it was quite disgusting to eat, but if you flavored it with mustard, pepper and vinegar, which we received regularly on our ration cards, and got it down somehow, you could just about manage to exist."[18]

For some Leningraders the new concoctions that were considered edible were too disgusting, and they refused to eat them. Faina Prusova wrote in her diary: "On the advice of one elderly woman I boiled the wallpaper. But it made me feel so nauseous that I threw it out at once—what a waste of water! Boiled a leather belt too (the yard keeper suggested it)—got the same muddy, dirty water. Poured it away immediately. . . . And at this point we all promised one another not to get hysterical and not to eat any muck, come what may!"[19]

Already in November most people suffered from starvation, which was described as "alimentary dystrophy." Their bodies bore the marks of hunger and carried the destructive qualities of deprivation. Many adults suffered from heart and lung diseases, nausea, physical weakness, dropsy and scurvy. Their hands and legs were swollen, and the pain in their joints made it difficult to move. Every movement was slowed down. Hands were raised slowly, and fingers moved slowly. No one ran; they walked slowly, raising their feet with great difficulty. Their eyes protruded from fleshless sockets, their lips were drawn back from teeth that were embedded in dry gums and their paper-thin skin was pulled tightly over their skull and bones. There was not a drop of fat under the skin. The stomachs of children were swollen; their heads appeared huge and their arms and legs looked like match sticks. Pubescent girls did not begin menstruating, and adult women stopped. Their breasts shriveled. Their desire to have sexual intercourse disappeared, and they made no effort to beautify themselves. The eyes of people who were about to die conveyed an attitude of resignation and indifference. They were aware that death was nearby ready to snatch their lives at any moment, and then suddenly their wasted bodies would become lifeless.

Death in the streets was common, and those who saw others collapse could give them no assistance for fear that they might themselves collapse and die. Snow would drift over those who died, and their bodies would not be seen again until the spring thaw. On November 15 Elena Skrjabina entered the following words in her diary: "Death reigns in the city. People die and die. Today, as I made my way along the street, a man was walking ahead of me. He could barely put one foot in front of the other. Passing him, I reluctantly turned my attention to his blue, cadaverous face. I thought to myself that he would surely die soon. Here, certainly, one could say that death had placed its stamp on the face of this man. After several steps, I turned around and stopped to watch him. He sat down on a hydrant, his eyes rolled back and then he slowly slipped to the ground. When I finally reached him, he was already dead." [20] The enemy was no longer the German army outside of Leningrad; it was within the city as well, slowly and painfully gnawing the inhabitants to death.

Under these extreme circumstances an increasing number of people began to participate in theft and looting. Their object was food, and they either stole it or they took goods that they could use to exchange for food. There were people whose only occupation was looting damaged houses and taking from corpses whatever was considered valuable. The theft of ration cards, especially from older women and from people who had collapsed in the streets, became frequent. Sometimes a starving child would go up to a person who was leaving a bread store and try to tear the ration of bread from the person's hands. One "young boy tore the bread from the hands of a woman and ate it before her eyes. She beat him with her fists, but she was too weak to take it back and had to watch as her bread disappeared. She cried like a child." [21] When it became too dangerous to carry food rations openly, people hid them on their persons.

"True, sometimes people would snatch your bread in the shop," wrote Yekaterina Vovchar, "but after all they were crazy with hunger. Neither then nor now can I find it in my heart to condemn them." Yekaterina admitted that there came a time when the urge to steal someone's bread rose within her as well. "I too," she confessed, "wanted to take someone's bread once when my family was dying and there was no way I could get bread for the next two days. I saw a very small woman in the baker's with a whole loaf of bread, and I started to follow her to seek a convenient moment, but then I came to my senses and was horrified at what I had been contemplating. Evidently, I was not yet absolutely crazy. . . ." [22]

Acts of theft committed by people who worked with the production and distribution of food were not uncommon. In her diary, Elena Skrjabina writes about Marusa who she had not seen for quite some time and who was employed at a food warehouse: "My former maid, Marusa, appeared unexpectedly, unexplainably. She brought a loaf of bread and a voluminous sack of cereal. Marusa is unrecognizable. She is not the same barefoot, unkempt girl I knew. She wore a squirrel jacket, an attractive silk dress and an expensive scarf. Added to all this, a blooming appearance just as if she had come from a vacation. She is not at all a citizen of a hungry, embattled city. I asked why. It turns out that the reason is very simple. She works in a food warehouse. The director of the warehouse is in love with her. Whenever the workers are searched before they leave, Marusa is searched just for the sake of appearance. She carries out several kilos of butter, sacks of cereal, rice and canned goods — all hidden under her fur jacket. Sometimes, she says, she has even managed to take out several chickens. She takes everything home, and in the evenings the director comes to eat and relax." [23]

The theft of food became a concern of the authorities. In order to prevent acts of theft, Party and Komsomol members were mobilized to watch over the personnel that prepared, transported and sold food. Control teams were sent to food processing plants, warehouses and transportation centers. Similar control teams were sent to food stores to check on the sales force and to ensure that the customers were not being cheated. Persons caught in acts of theft were liable to trial by a military tribunal, which under wartime laws could impose the death penalty. In a speech that was made in April of 1942, Aleksie Kuznetsov, a member of the Military Council of the Leningrad Front, declared: "I must say straight off that we shot people for a half pound of bread stolen or withheld from the population." [24]

People became so desperate in their need to eat that they would turn to items which they would not have eaten before the blockade. Yelena Nikitina wrote that she was so hungry she would consume whatever she believed would give her nourishment: "I remember coming home and so wanting to eat! At the time I lived in Voitik Street. There I had some firewood lying by the stove—one or two logs. So I took a log, it was pine, I recall, and began to gnaw. I was desperate to eat. I chewed and chewed away at that log, and resin oozed out. The fragrance of [the] resin gave me a sense of enjoyment that I was at least chewing something. I had to eat something otherwise death was inevitable from starvation, and this is even worse than being killed under bombardment. One dies a very terrible death from starvation." [25]

Hunger would drive some Leningraders to turn to cannibalism. Reports indicated that cannibalism was first practiced on those who had died. In the streets, corpses were found that were missing pieces of flesh that had been cut from arms and legs. There were rumors that people were exchanging personal items such as clothing, watches and jewelry for meat patties that contained human flesh. It was rumored that this was being done at Hay Market, the center of Leningrad's black market activities. There were cases of murder for food by starvation-crazed people. Soldiers, the best-fed people in the city, reportedly were killed on their way home from the front. As a measure of protection, the soldiers carried their weapons with them at all times and moved about the city in groups. It was also said that children were beginning to disappear. Boys and girls were easy to seize, and their flesh was tender. Rumors spread that husbands ate their wives, wives ate their husbands and parents ate their children.[26] Stories spread that gangs of well-fed cannibals roamed the city. Anyone who appeared well-fed and looked healthy was under suspicion.

Suicide is considered the final alternative to hunger, yet few if any people in Leningrad committed suicide. Yura Ryabinkin, a sixteen-year-old young man, contemplated suicide, but in the end he decided that he wanted to live. In his diary he wrote: "Each day brings me closer and closer to suicide. There is truly no way out. It's a dead end. I can't go on living like this. Hunger. Terrible hunger. Once again, no more news about evacuation. Life is becoming a burden. To live to no purpose, dragging out this life of hunger and cold. . . . I'm not alone, there is Mum and Ira, and I just can't take their last piece of bread away from them. I can't because I know the value of even a crumb of bread now. But I can see them sharing their food with me. . . . That dreadful hunger! I know that if anyone offered me a lethal poison now, which [will bring] painless death in . . . sleep, I would swallow it without a moment's hesitation. I want to live, but I cannot live like this! And yet I want to live! So what is the solution?" [27]

In addition to starvation, the people were suffering from severe shortages in all types of fuel. Earlier, in September, the population was issued a last kerosene ration of 2.5 liters (.65 gallons) per person. The situation with regard to electric power was worse. On September 11, 1941, electricity by order of the city's leadership was to be rationed. Citizens were forbidden to use electrical appliances in their homes, whether for heating, cooking or any other purpose. Anyone who was caught using electrical appliances was to be deprived of electricity and jailed for six months or fined 3,000 rubles. The use of electricity in offices and homes was sharply curtailed, and the amount of electricity allotted to each household was determined by its location and record of normal use. Control over the proper observance of the limits set for electric lighting was given to house managers. Violators were to be fined five times the cost of the electricity they used above the authorized limit. In general, electricity was available for only a few hours each day.[28] It was during those hours that the people could listen to broadcasts over their wired radio loud-speakers. When there was no electricity and daylight turned to darkness, the people would take out a homemade lamp fueled with machine oil and light the twisted piece of cloth that served as a wick. At the end of September both oil and coal supplies in Leningrad were virtually exhausted.

By mid-October most of the supply of firewood available to the population was exhausted. The cutting of some timber that was available in the blockaded territory slightly eased the fuel problem, but it did not solve it. On October 20 the city leadership authorized the house administrators to take the firewood from vacant apartments and redistribute it among the remaining residents of their buildings. On November 17 the heat level in buildings with central heating was set at 53 degrees Fahrenheit in apartment houses, 50 degrees Fahrenheit in offices and 46 degrees Fahrenheit in factories. In practice, the central heating in most buildings ceased to function altogether, and most factory workshops remained unheated. Because of the lack of fuel and the consequent freezing of water pipes, all laundries, barber shops and public bathhouses were closed.[29]

Most of the people in Leningrad heated their homes with a small temporary stove called burzuikha. If it was homemade it was constructed with a variety of materials such as tin cans, bricks and metal barrels. Many homemade stoves were badly built and caused numerous fires. A burzuikha was usually placed on the floor or on a stool. It had a small chimney that went out through the smoke duct of a larger stationary stove or through the small ventilating window of the room in which it was placed. The stove was used for both heating and cooking. Generally only one room in an apartment would be heated and then only for short periods of time. Everyone lived and slept in this room, but even here the temperature could be kept barely above freezing. The winter of 1941–42 was particularly cold.

People who had no reserve firewood might acquire some from damaged houses. On their way home from work they would visit the city's bombed neighborhoods and take from the vacated buildings pieces of broken doors and other scraps of wood to burn in their small stoves. Many people burned their books and furniture or they tore up their wooden floors and huddled around their stoves in an attempt to stay warm. The leg of a chair or table would give a blaze that would last for thirty minutes or longer. Most people wore their warmest clothes and kept their overcoats on permanently at the work place and at home and when they went to bed.

It was in bed where Nadazhda Kupriyanova found her three neighbors. They had become indifferent toward everything. It was day time and Nadazhda realized that if she did not intervene in their lives, Lyudmilla Bokshitskaya and her mother and sister would die. She left their apartment and soon thereafter returned with some firewood. "She lit their stove and fetched some water. Then, saying that she had been given a rabbit at the military hospital where she worked, she put it in a pot and on the stove." While the soup was cooking, she washed the three women shielding them from the cold with a blanket. The floor of the room was so cold that the warmth of the fire extended only a meter (39 inches) from the stove. After bathing the women, Nadazhda fed them. It was not until after they had finished the soup that Nadazhda told her neighbors that they had eaten a cat and not a rabbit. It was this meal and the care that Nadazhda gave to her neighbors that saved Lyudmilla's life.[30]

Shortages of fuel and water would affect the care that patients received from the city's medical establishment. By the end of the year most hospitals were without electricity, water and heat, and most were short of medicines. Alexander Pokrovsky who was a medical student in Leningrad gave the following description of a hospital to which he was assigned in December: "The absence of electricity, heat and water made work extremely difficult. The temperatures in the wards usually stood between 30 and 35 degrees Fahrenheit. The patients lay fully clothed, with coats and blankets and sometimes even mattresses piled on top of them. The walls were covered with frost. During the night the water froze in pitchers. The hunger had the effect of causing diarrhea among the patients, many of whom from weakness were unable to use the bedpans. Sheets on the beds were filthy—no water for laundering. The only medicine available was sodium bromide, and the doctors prescribed it to patients under various names."[31]

Breakfast at the hospital where Pokrovsky worked consisted of "a cup of ersatz coffee, a few grains of sugar and two slices of bread." Following breakfast, the doctor in attendance would make his rounds wearing an overcoat, a fur cap and gloves. "Coming into the ward he could see no patients—their heads were under the covers. He proceeded to lift the covers at the foot of each man's bed and pull his leg. If the patient showed no reaction, he nodded his head—meaning 'take him to the morgue.' After the doctor had gone, the corpses were loaded on a truck and carted away."[32]

Most hospitals had been requisitioned for the use of the armed forces. Getting a bed for a civilian in a hospital often involved several days of effort, and many people who needed medical attention did not receive it. Civilians who did receive medical care were usually brought to other facilities such as school buildings. The Leningrad State University buildings, the Technological Institute, the Palace of Labor and Hertzen University had all become temporary hospitals. The number of doctors available in the city was inadequate since about 60 percent of Leningrad's medical personnel was either with the armed forces or had been evacuated. To make up for this loss, general practitioners were given two weeks training and were then assigned to work as surgeons.[33]

Cold and starvation would bring to an end the lives of thousands of people every day. The victims were struck down by death at all times and in various places. They died at midday, while they were asleep at night, by the workbench in the factory, when walking to the bread store or while waiting in line within the store. It was in a bread store where Ivan Korotkov almost stumbled over someone who had died: "I was queuing at the baker's for bread. A dim lamp was burning there, and they were allowing a soggy piece of bread on each card. I felt myself come up against something, and I stepped over it. I had no realization that it was a human being. I wondered who had thrown a sack down there. I could not understand at all what was happening. I stepped over it, and others did the same. It was only as I was going out of the shop that it hit me that we had been walking over a person who had fallen there!

We had been stepping over him, and no one had acknowledged that fact. What a fearful state we were in!"[34]

There were people who could sense that they were about to die. One senior factory worker asked his director to do him a favor: "Comrade Chief, I have a request to make. I am one of your old workers and you have always been a good friend to me, and I know you will not refuse. I am not going to bother you again. I know that today or tomorrow I shall die. My family is in a very poor way — very weak. They won't have the strength to manage the funeral. Will you be a friend and have a coffin made for me, and have it sent to my family, so they don't have the extra worry of trying to get a coffin? You know how difficult it is to get one."[35]

The concern expressed by the factory worker was one that was voiced by many people who believed that they were about to die. They did not want their death to be a burden to their family. Yaketerina Yanishavskay wrote that while walking down Engels Prospekt she overheard an old woman express such a concern to "an old man pulling sledges full of dead bodies [that were] barely covered with bast matting. Behind him was the old woman who could scarcely totter along. 'Wait deary, let me on.' He stopped and said, 'what do you mean old woman, can't you see what kind of a load I've got?' 'I can see, I can see, I'm going the same way. I lost the ration card yesterday, I'm going to die anyway, and so [that] my family won't have to bother about me when I'm dead, take me to the cemetery. I'll sit on a tree stump there and freeze, and right there they will bury me. . .'"[36]

The worry of the old woman was one that plagued the minds of people who had no means of getting a dead family member to a morgue or cemetery. It was a worry that was witnessed by a man named Savchenko who saw a woman leading a man across a road. It was obvious that the man could barely move and when he "collapsed by the tram line — the woman got him back on his feet, and he took a few more steps, but he did not make it to the pavement. He fell by a mound in the snow." When Savchenko reached the couple, the man was already dead. "The woman, the man's wife, was fussing over the body. Passers-by, on learning what had happened, advised the woman not to let it be known that she was the man's wife, but to give the impression she was merely a stranger." They assured her that it was then the responsibility of "the militia to take the corpse and dispose of it in the proper way. And that is just what she did. A militiaman stopped a passing sledge and the corpse was hoisted onto it to be taken to the morgue."[37]

If a person died at home the members of the family were faced with two choices. If they chose to bring the dead body to a cemetery they would tie the body to a child's sled or lay it on a piece of plywood and pull it through the snow-covered streets to the nearest cemetery. They could also choose to bring the body to a morgue from which it was later removed by truck to a cemetery. Generally, the dead were left in the corner of a cemetery to await burial, and most of the bodies were buried in mass graves which were long trenches that had been opened with explosives. Upon burial the dead were simply tipped or thrown into the trenches. People who were anxious to obtain an individual grave would not only have to pay for it at the regular price but would also have to bribe the grave digger with food or with ration cards. Coffins were not provided by the authorities and were usually not available. Most of the corpses were wrapped in a blanket, a bed sheet, a curtain or a rug.

When Yelena Averianova-Fyodorova brought her grandmother to the cemetery she witnessed scenes that horrified her. She would describe the scenes in her diary: "We took my grandmother to the cemetery on a sled, pulling it in turn—I , mother, Tanya and Shura. We could barely drag our own feet along. With such food, I don't know how we are still alive. . . . And now we are behind someone else—in an endless chain of dead people, mostly without coffins. But that's not the only thing . . . lines of trucks are going past filled with bodies, undressed, unshod bodies, all lying every which way and in different bits of clothes. . . . They were collecting people in the streets. A person would be walking along, he would drop, die and be put onto a truck. And there in the cemetery, there were such enormous common graves. . . . While we were there six trucks and three horse-drawn carts full of bodies arrived. It was horrible to see! And how many more there were that had been brought there earlier but had not yet been buried!. . . . Now everyone's buried in common graves, one on top of another."[38]

As the death rate rose, certain rules and regulations were either ignored or could not be enforced. It was a requirement that all deaths be registered with the Bureau of Vital Statistics. Many deaths were not reported because the families of the deceased were unable to do so. There were also families who deliberately kept secret the deaths of relatives in order to make use of the ration cards of the deceased. There were corpses that could not be identified. These human beings had died in the street and had been stripped of their ration cards and papers of identification. The authorities did not have the personnel or the transportation necessary to determine the identity of these people.

Regulation dictated that after a person died, the manager of the building where the person resided was to make an inventory of the contents in the person's apartment and then seal it. The empty apartment was then to be registered by the manger with the housing department within the district. No one was allowed to obtain or use that apartment without permission from the authorities. These regulations were ignored by managers who permitted unauthorized persons to use empty apartments on a temporary basis. In some cases house managers allowed residents of upper floors to move into the vacant apartments on lower floors where they would be safer from bombardments.

NOTES

1. Nikolai Kislitsyn and Vassily Zubakov, Leningrad Does Not Surrender, trans. Barry Jones (Moscow: Progress Publishers, 1989), 89.

2. Leon Goure, The Siege of Leningrad (Stanford, California: Stanford University Press, 1962), 76.

3. Goure, The Siege of Leningrad, 76.

4. Goure, The Siege of Leningrad, 76–77.

5. Goure, The Siege of Leningrad, 128–130.

6. Dmitri V. Pavlov, Leningrad 1941, trans. John Clinton Adams (Chicago, Illinois: The University of Chicago Press, 1965), 97.

7. Kislitsyn and Zubakov, Leningrad Does Not Surrender, 91.

8. Pavlov, Leningrad 1941, 102.

9. Pavlov, Leningrad 1941, 71–72.

10. Kislitsyn and Zubakov, Leningrad Does Not Surrender, 93.

11. Goure, The Siege of Leningrad, 183–84.

12. Pavlov, Leningrad 1941, 104–05.

13. Pavlov, Leningrad 1941, 118.

14. Goure, The Siege of Leningrad, 132.

15. Goure, The Siege of Leningrad, 156.

16. Goure, The Siege of Leningrad, 215.

17. Ales Adamovich and Daniil Granin, A Book of the Blockade, trans. Hilda Perham (Moscow: Raduga Publishers, 1983), 370.

18. Adamovich and Granin, A Book of the Blockade, 45.

19. Adamovich and Granin, A Book of the Blockade, 314.

20. Elena Skrjabina, Siege and Survival, trans. Norman Luxenburg (New York: Pinnacle Books, Inc., 1973), 53.

21. Goure, The Siege of Leningrad, 216.

22. Adamovich and Granin, A Book of the Blockade, 422.

23. Skrjabina, Siege and Survival, 56–57.

24. A.V. Karasev, Leningradtsy v gody blokady (Moscow: Izdatelstve Adademii Nauk SSSR, 1959), 193.

25. Adamovich and Granin, A Book of the Blockade, 31.

26. Harrison E. Salisbury, The 900 Days: The Siege of Leningrad (New York: Avon Books, 1970), 550.

27. Adamovich and Granin, A Book of the Blockade, 410.

28. Goure, The Siege of Leningrad, 133.

29. Goure, The Siege of Leningrad, 165–66.

30. Adamovich and Granin, A Book of the Blockade, 419–20.

31. Louis Fischer, ed., Thirteen Who Fled (New York: Harper and Brothers, 1949), 188.

32. Fischer, ed., Thirteen Who Fled, 188–89.

33. Goure, The Siege of Leningrad, 162.

34. Adamovich and Granin, A Book of the Blockade, 57.

35. Alexander Werth, Leningrad (London: Hamish Hamilton, 1944), 73.

36. Adamovich and Granin, A Book of the Blockade, 85.

37. Adamovich and Granin, A Book of the Blockade, 327–28.

38. Adamovich and Granin, A Book of the Blockade, 146–47.

Chapter Eight

Blockade Artist

The starvation and cold from which the Leningraders suffered and died were recorded in several ways. People kept diaries in which they described what they witnessed and how they felt about their circumstances. Their entries were uninhibited expressions and in many cases were not to be read by anyone except by the diarists. There were letters sent to family members, to friends and to military personnel outside of Leningrad which described the horrific conditions that existed in the city. The letters were honest expressions, but many were also tempered by the writer's knowledge that they might be reviewed and censored. Essays were assigned and the school children who wrote them were encouraged to convey what it felt like to live in a city that was being besieged. The essays contained astonishing details that were expressed with unbridled emotions. Soviet writers and foreign correspondents were sent to Leningrad to interview the city's inhabitants. The interviews were recorded and published, and they too were informative. Finally, there were artists in the city who drew on paper and painted on canvasses the sights to which they were exposed during the blockade. One of these artists was Elena Martilla. In the conversations that the author and a friend had with Elena, the artist shared with them her memories and her drawings.

Elena learned about the invasion of the Soviet Union on the day after she attended the graduation ball that was given by the secondary school from which she had just graduated. She and her friends, who had graduated with her, responded to the news by walking to the regional Komsomol office to volunteer their services whenever and wherever they were needed. The people at the office told the girls to go home. They were promised that they would be contacted if they were needed. Eventually, Elena was assigned to a Red Cross squad that provided first aid and treatment to the wounded soldiers who were brought into the city from the front lines.

Later, Elena was sent to a children's hospital to work as an aid. Here she prepared bandages and assisted the resident physician whenever he performed surgery. Many of the children that were brought to the hospital had severe burns; they were victims of fires that had been started by the incendiary bombs dropped on the city. Elena's other duty was to bring the bodies of those who died in the hospital to the morgue within the building. She was always shocked to see the piles of dead children in the morgue and dreaded each trip that she had to make to this place of death.

When Elena was told that a school for aspiring young artists was still in operation in the city, she was surprised. Most schools in Leningrad were closed. Art was Elena's passion. Prior to the war she had studied drawing and painting and was one of thirty students who had been chosen throughout the Soviet Union to attend a special art school created by the Russian Academy of Arts in Leningrad. The experience had been wonderful for her. While working at the children's hospital, Elena often thought back to the days when she was a student of art. She missed drawing and painting very much and wondered if she would ever become an accomplished artist. Becoming a professional artist had been her dream for as long as she could remember, and it continued to be her desire.

Elena decided to find the school for artists and apply for admission. The school, she discovered, was housed in a magnificent mansion that dated back to Tsarist times. She knocked on the front door of the building and after a brief wait saw a handsome man appear in the doorway. He was Yan Shablovsky, the director of the school. He invited Elena to come in and after a few words of introduction gave her an appointment to take an entrance examination. Elena had no difficulty with the examination and was admitted as a second year student.

The art school was located a long distance from Elena's apartment, and she walked the distance every morning. It was a dangerous journey that included a lengthy trek across the frozen ice that covered the Neva River. Elena knew that if the enemy should bomb or shell the river while she was crossing it, she would become a casualty. There was no place to hide on the river. When she reached the place where the river passed the Summer Garden she would climb up the staircase along the steep embankment of the river. The climb was difficult because the staircase was always covered with ice.

Elena then continued to cross the old city district. Many of the buildings in the district had been damaged; they had either been bombed or shelled. The fire fighters were unable to attend to all of the fires in the city, and some buildings in the old district would burn for many days. One large old building had been burning slowly for more than a month. It was at this building where Elena would stop to rest and warm her hands with the heat of the smoldering fire. After she passed the Suvorov Museum, Elena knew that she was almost at her destination, the art school. She had walked eight kilometers (5 miles).

The warmest room in the art school was the director's office. Upon the students' arrival in the morning, they gathered around the wood stove in Mr. Shablovsky's office. He would ask them about their lives and instruct them repeatedly that during their walks to school they should be observant of everything around them. They should store away in their memory all that which they witnessed in order to visually record later the scenes on paper or on canvass. He said it was their duty to record the effects of war so that the misery and suffering to which Leningraders were being subjected would not be forgotten. "Future generations must know what is now happening in Leningrad," he would say. Elena listened intently to Mr. Shablovsky, a man she had come to admire, and made a conscious commitment to carry out the director's instruction.

Early one day Elena met two of her friends near the Suvorov Museum. As the friends approached, Elena noticed that they were distraught. The face of one of the friends, Zoya, was drawn and had lost its color. The girls informed Elena that upon Zoya's return home, the previous day, she had found her mother dead. The woman had died alone. As Zoya was expressing her grief, Elena noticed a truck filled with the corpses of human beings coming toward them. Elena grabbed her friend immediately, embraced her tightly and turned her so that she would not see the dead bodies. Later in the evening, in the privacy of her apartment, Elena drew with a pencil the horrible morning scene from which she had protected her friend. It would be one of many scenes of human suffering and death that Elena would draw or paint in Leningrad during the blockade.[1]

NOTE

1. A.V. Vinogradov and A. Pleysier, *Bitva za Leningrad v sud' bakh zhitelel goroda I oblasti: vospominahiiy a zashchitnikov I zhitelei blokadnogo goroda I okkupirovannykh territorii* (Saint Petersburg, Russia: Saint Petersburg State University Press, 2005), 224–25.

Chapter Nine

Enemy Bombardment

On September 22, 1941, Hitler decided "to wipe the city of Petersburg [Hitler would not call the city Leningrad] from the face of the earth" and turn down all requests for capitulation. The Finns had informed the German leadership that they too had no interest in the future existence of the city. A letter to the Naval Chief of Staff on September 29 elaborated on Hitler's decision as follows:

> The Fuhrer has decided to erase from the face of the earth St. Petersburg. The existence of this large city will have no further interest after Soviet Russia is destroyed. Finland has also said that the existence of this city on her new border is not desirable from her point of view. . . .
>
> It is proposed to approach near the city and to destroy it with the aid of an artillery barrage from all weapons of different caliber and with large air attacks. . . . The problem of the life of the population and the provisioning of them is a problem which cannot and must not be decided by us.
>
> In this war . . . we are not interested in preserving even a part of the population of this large city.[1]

German Army Group North was not capable of wiping Leningrad "from the face of the earth." To do this the German forces along the military front south of Leningrad needed to be closer to the city; they were too far away to hit the city with their medium and small caliber artillery. They also needed at their disposal a large bomber force. When the German Eighth Corps was withdrawn from the Leningrad region and sent elsewhere, on September 29, German Army Group North lost most of its dive bombers and was left with fewer than 300 airplanes of all types.

The Germans did strike Leningrad with their long-range guns that were emplaced at Strelna, Uritsk, Pushkin and Dudergof. During the month of October Leningrad was struck by 7,590 shells and in November by 11,230 shells. The enemy's artillery fire was particularly dangerous because no warning to the civilian populace could be given in time for them to take shelter. The shelling would begin suddenly at any time of the day or night, and the Germans would constantly change the direction and range of their fire. All of this was done with the purpose of spreading panic and fear among the citizens. The bombardments resulted in many casualties and did considerable damage to buildings.

Many of the shells that struck roofs and entered the attics of buildings were made harmless immediately by people who were standing watch. Yura Ryabinkin was one of several students who did watch duty at night on the roof of his school. On October 13 he entered in his diary: "Last night was more or less calm and David and I went out onto the roof. . . . The search lights were sweeping the sky, when quite suddenly we heard the furious hiss of a bomb, a sound rapidly gaining in volume. In an instant David and I were in the attic. . . . Having decided that it would be dangerous to stay in the attic, we went out onto the staircase, and just then we heard a brief whistling sound, followed by an explosion right over our heads. It became lighter than day. David was the first to grasp what had happened and, grabbing a spade, rushed to put the bomb out. I ran too. We plunged into furious activity. We were working in thick, acrid smoke, which got into the throat, irritated it, and penetrated right into our lungs. Sweat ran down our faces all the time we were busy with [the] incendiaries. I rushed to the first post. A woman was standing shouting in fright: 'A bomb! Put it out!' She grabbed handfuls of sand and threw it at the burning pieces of thermite. I grabbed a spade and in half a minute had covered with sand anything still burning. Brilliant light was replaced with pitch darkness. I somehow managed to get down from the attic and . . . ran to the second post. There all the bombs had already been extinguished. I looked at the roof. About ten people were scurrying about there. I felt I needed to breathe in some fresh air, clear my mind [and] come to. Soon the all-clear was sounded." [2]

Bombardments were responsible for the destruction of Leningrad's elaborate water system. For months the Germans had damaged the system, but brigades of specialists checked daily the water mains and made repairs where they were necessary. When the temperature dropped, the exposed pipes of the city's water system burst. Damage to water pipes led to a sharp drop in water pressure, and with the shortage of fuel and electricity many of the pipes in buildings began to freeze often bursting as a result. Consequently, there were fire hydrants that failed to work, and the Leningraders were often forced to use snow to extinguish fires that were started by the careless use of small homemade stoves or by the enemy's incendiary bombs. People were also forced to get their water for consumption from the Neva River or from one of its tributaries that flowed through the city or from one of the city's canals. If a citizen managed to bring home a pail filled with water and succeeded in carrying it up the ice-covered steps of the steep staircase in the apartment building, he or she would have enough water for a few days. The water was used primarily for drinking and cooking. Few people shaved or washed themselves or their clothing.

Golina Petrova and her father acquired water from a hole that had been made in the ice that covered the Neva River. To get to the ice hole they had to make their way down the river's snow covered embankment. The embankment was also covered with a layer of ice that was formed by the water that had spilled out of filled containers that had been pulled up the embankment by their owners. "I remember it very clearly," Golina would say. "It [the ice hole] was opposite the Bronze Horseman. We went to it through the Alexandovsky Garden. There was a large ice hole there; we kneeled at the edge of it and drew up the water in a bucket. I always went with my father, and we had a bucket and a big milk can. By the time we would get home with the water it would be frozen, of course, and . . . we had to thaw it out. The water was, naturally, dirty. Well, we boiled it. There was a little [water] for food, and then we had to have some for washing. We had to go for water frequently. It was terribly slippery and to get down to the ice hole was very awkward. You see people were very weak. It often happened that they would get their pail full of water and then could not get it to the top of the bank. Everyone helped one another. They dragged the buckets to the top, but the water would spill out again." [3]

When bomb damage and freezing temperatures made inoperable the city sewage system, the people solved this problem in the simplest manner. Garbage and human excrement were either thrown into the courtyards and streets of the city or else dumped into abandoned rooms. Fortunately, these practices due to the freezing temperatures did not create a serious health problem. There were some people who would use the human waste. They would gather it, dry it and burn it in their small iron stoves.

The enemy's bombardments were not discriminatory; many housing complexes were hit. Shells would tear open roofs which then permitted the snow and freezing temperatures to enter the buildings resulting in extensive damage. The breakage of windows also imposed great hardships. Leningrad's authorities were unable to provide glass for private dwellings, and they had very little of it for public buildings. Yet the intense cold, the snow and the blackout regulations made it necessary to cover up the broken windows in some fashion. The population resorted to putting blankets and carpets over the

openings or boarding them up with lumber or plywood if they had these materials. It meant that many places of residence were deprived of daylight.

The residential buildings that were not hit directly suffered damage as well.
The exploding shells and the concussions of the bombs caused the plaster of
the walls and ceilings to crack and eventually fall to the floor. In a letter, fif-
teen-year-old Susanna Ivanova described the damage that was done to her
family's apartment by the daily shelling and bombing. She witnessed the pro-
gressive damage because she visited the vacant apartment everyday to practice on her piano. Susanna wrote:

> My baby grand piano, my Becker, remained in the cold apartment house. The
> apartment was empty and the ceiling came down. The falling plaster covered the
> soft chairs, rugs and books, but the grand piano stood there like a saint.
>
> I went there to play. I tried to come before the beginning of the [daily] bomb-
> ing. At the corner of the Fontanka [River] stood a trolley bus hit by a bomb; it
> looked like a vessel between icebergs. I always tried to walk a distance around
> it for fear that I might stumble over the long frozen wires.
>
> The apartment house was even colder than the street. I heated the tea kettle
> and the iron to warm me a little, and I would sit down immediately at the baby
> grand in my fur coat and ear muffed hat, only lowering my earmuffs to hear my-
> self playing. I started to play my scales—the plain ones and the elaborate ones.
>
> I did not leave Leningrad with my conservatory mates because my papa took
> sick that very day. When they departed, at first I thought that [their departure]
> was the end of my life; there in Tashkent they will be able to practice everyday
> and I will forget everything. But then I got used to the bombings and shelling,
> and I played as before every day. I played Chopin's *Concerto*. In the first part
> there is a passage; the right hand takes the tercets, a note after a note, and the
> left hand the octaves. Every time at that point an air-raid alarm would sound. As
> soon as I reached that passage I would hear the siren. I would sit and wait until
> it stopped howling.
>
> Now, when they begin to bomb, I begin to play from that same passage. Mu-
> sic makes me fearless; shell fragments hit upon the roof, but I play. The plaster
> begins to fall down but I go into the melody. I can't stop; I do not want to be be-
> hind my conservatory mates.[4]

The enemy's bombardments were so frequent that many Leningraders began to disregard the civil defense regulations that made it mandatory for them
to seek shelter during an alert. Many people preferred to conserve their energy by remaining where they were, at least when no bombs or shells were
dropping nearby. At night, particularly, people chose to stay in bed during
alerts. Elena Skrjabina wrote: "I don't especially believe in the protective
quality of our cellar. To make him [her husband] happy, I usually take the

boys and crowd down into the basement with the rest of the household. Lately we have had to stay there from seven in the evening to twelve at night. The Germans do not give us any respite and drag out the bombardment through several hours. . . . That is why I try to avoid those trips to the basement and go to bed early. Often, in dreams, you picture a table full of all sorts of snacks, lots of delicious things. You don't want to wake up. And when you do, it is gloomy reality and the gnawing feeling of hunger again." [5]

People who refused to seek shelter during an air raid were challenging death, and those who witnessed a victim struck by a shell would not soon forget the scene. One military officer recalled how he saw a shell decapitate a man who was walking a distance from him: "I was in the Nevsky [Prospect] once when a shell landed close by. And ten yards away from me was a man whose head was cut clean off by a shell splinter. It was horrible. I saw him make his last two steps already with his head off—and a bloody mess all around before he collapsed. I vomited right there and then, and I was quite ill for the rest of the day—though I had already seen many terrible things before. . . . It's bad for one's nerves to see such things happen; our ambulance services have instructions to wash away blood on the pavement as quickly as possible after a shell has landed." [6]

Leningrad's industrial workers suffered terribly from the enemy's bombardments, and working conditions in the factories became appalling. The holes in the roofs and walls made by artillery shells or bombs and the shortages of fuel and electricity left the factories unheated. Many workers kept their overcoats on and wore gloves. One factory director told Alexander Werth, a British correspondent: "When they started bombing us in a big way in October 1941, our workers fought for the factory more than they fought for their own houses. There was one night when we had to deal with three hundred incendiaries in the factory grounds alone. Our people were putting the fires out with a sort of concentrated rage. . . . They realized by then that they were in the front line. . . . And then one day in December in twenty degrees of frost, we had all of our windows blown out by a bomb, and I thought to myself: 'No, we really can't go on. Not till the spring. We can't go on in this temperature, and without light, without water and almost without food.' And yet, somehow—we didn't stop. A kind of instinct told us that we mustn't— that it would be worse than suicide. That it would be a little like treason. And sure enough within thirty-six hours we were working again—working in altogether hellish conditions, with eight degrees frost in the workshops. . . . Oh, we had stoves of sorts, little iron stoves or little brick stoves that warmed the air a couple of feet round them. The conditions were really incredible, but still our people worked, worked with a kind of frantic determination, with furious defiance. And mind you, they were hungry, terribly hungry." [7]

Another factory shop that was still in operation at the end of the year was described by Soviet writer Nikolai Tikhonov:

> From outside, the workshop walls looked dark and gaunt, like the ice-covered cliffs of an Arctic bay. It seemed as though all life were extinct in this dreary space, with its litter of frozen metal, barrels and slag heaps. Piles of snowdrift rose like frozen waves on all sides. Not a single light gleamed through the darkness. . . .
>
> If a stranger were brought here and put down in this silent yard, he would say he was in a wilderness of ice kilometers away from any human dwelling. Yet it was the yard of a giant factory.
>
> And if you found a little door and opened it you would be looking into a place that might have been a cave with stalactites. This was the workshop. The sky showed darkly through the shell holes in the roof, a gleaming layer of ice covered the rafters and walls, carefully-shaded, dim electric lamps cast patches of light at intervals, if you stared intently you would see a good number of people in the various sections of the vast hall. They were at work.
>
> They were wrapped in all sorts of coverings and threw strange shadows in the feeble light. The sharp lines of their sunken faces would have frightened an outsider. . . .[8]

The workers suffered from hunger and exhaustion. Some were so swollen from hunger that they could not sit down or get up without assistance, and others were so weak that they fainted at the machines. It was said that in one factory the workers tied themselves to the tanks they were repairing because they feared that they would fall off when they became dizzy from hunger. To conserve the energy of the workers it became necessary to reduce the daily work hours from eleven or twelve to eight. In order to avoid the long walks to and from work, which sapped a worker's strength, many factories organized dormitories for all their employees and also arranged for them to receive their rations at the factory. Many administrators of enterprises, like their workers, became residents of their factories and lived in their offices. Some of these men were too exhausted and weak to go anywhere.

The workers who returned home on the weekends would force their legs to take them back to the factory when it was time to return. These people not only wanted the larger food rations that they were given as workers, they also sought the companionship of their fellow workers. For many workers, the factory or office was a sort of home where a person was surrounded by friends and familiar activities and where one would find assistance when in need. Many people worked being motivated by the will to live; they believed that if they did not stay busy they would die. Some who knew they were going to die preferred to do so in the factory among friends rather than in their cold, dark apartments alone. In the words of one factory director: "Many a man would drag himself to the factory, stagger in and die." [9]

By the end of the year most factories had stopped producing. According to the director of the Kirov Works: "On December 15 everything came to a standstill. There was no fuel, no electric current, no food, no street cars, no water—nothing. Production in Leningrad practically ceased. We were to remain in this condition until the first of April."[10] Some factory shops continued to operate after a fashion, either by switching to hand-manufacturing methods or by managing to obtain a very small amount of electric or steam power. They were able to produce small amounts of munitions, mines and hand grenades and they repaired guns, electric motors and tanks. For the most part the workers used this period of idleness to clean and repair machines, to keep the water and fuel pipes in working order, to clean the shops and to cut lumber for fuel. The factory administrators kept their workers employed so that they would not be relegated to the lowest ration category, that of the unemployed. To be left without employment was a great calamity. Such workers were required to turn in their ration cards and obtain new ones from the authorities. The issuing of new cards took time which would mean that these people would be left without food for days and that would mean death not only for the workers but for their families.

When the Kirov Works stopped its operations Konstantin Mikhailovich, the foreman of one of the shops, stayed living in his empty shop. He had built the shop twelve years before and he considered it his child, a child to whom he had given birth. His family had earlier been evacuated from Leningrad so throughout the remainder of the winter he kept busy during the day working on various projects. In the evenings he would place himself in front of the small office stove to stay warm. It was quiet in the large empty shop, and he would hear only the howling of the wind that entered through the blown out windows. Many evenings Konstantin would take up a book and read with the light from the stove. He would read and think.

Later, while reflecting on those evenings, Konstantin would say: "There was much to think about. Human beings showed what they were like in those days. I don't suppose people had ever before witnessed such a revelation of greatness of soul on the one hand and of moral degradation on the other. . . . I remember when the shop was working in December; in spite of the fearful cold and hunger . . . we had a wonderful old man with us here. He mixed the sand for the moulds—he was a skilled man at the job; he was . . . one of those elderly craftsmen who work like an artist and cannot himself explain how he does things. If you asked him what proportions he used in his mixtures he would reply: 'There are no definite proportions, I can sense things, I can tell by the feel what to add and how much.' People think a man like that must have a secret which he keeps all to himself, but the whole secret is in his hands. For instance, instead of the sand for our moulds that had been specially brought to us, we were obliged to use sand from pits in the suburbs here. Everybody said it would not do. And indeed none of the moulders could do anything with it. But the old man had a try and everything turned out all right. . . . And then his strength began to fail. Every day . . . he became weaker. But he didn't give up work, and he began to teach his old woman how to mix the sand. He kept on explaining things to her, demonstrating, making her try for herself. . . . Then one day a boy came running to me and said: 'He's calling.' I understood at once who he meant. I went along and found the old man lying on the sand he knew so well how to mix. His old woman, her eyes dry, was standing beside him. There were other old workers standing around too. He was very feeble now. 'Well Konstantin Mikhailovich, I am dying. . . . My old woman will take my place.' And he turned away from us and kept his eyes on the old woman and begged her not to forget what he had taught her about mixing the sand. . . . She repeated everything he said and kept on saying: 'Don't be afraid, I won't forget.' She was still dry-eyed. It was a scene which might have brought tears to anybody's eyes, though in truth they said that the tears of the people of Leningrad were frozen by now. But there he was instructing her and suddenly he broke off, leaving a phrase unfinished, and died. . . . These were the sort of things one witnessed. And yet in another case somebody had sunk so low that he would steal a comrade's last piece of bread. . . . "[11]

NOTES

1. Leon Goure, The Siege of Leningrad (Stanford, California: Stanford University Press, 1962), 141–42.

2. Ales Adamovich and Daniil Granin, A Book of the Blockade, trans. Hilda Perham (Moscow: Raduga Publishers, 1983), 308–09.

3. Adamovich and Granin, A Book of the Blockade, 75–76.

4. Boris Skomorovsky and E.G. Morris, The Siege of Leningrad (New York: E.P. Dutton and Company, Inc., 1944), 54.

5. Elena Skrjabina, Siege and Survival, trans. Norman Luxenburg (New York: Pinnacle Books, Inc., 1973), 46.

6. Alexander Werth, Leningrad (London: Hamish Hamilton, 1944), 81.

7. Werth, Leningrad, 72–73.

8. Nikolai Tikhonov, The Defense of Leningrad (London: Hutchinson and Co., Ltd., no date), 18.

9. Werth, Leningrad, 73.

10. Werth, Leningrad, 114.

11. Alexander Fadeyev, Leningrad in the Days of the Blockade, trans. R.D. Charques (Wesport, Connecticut: Greenwood Press, Publishers, 1971), 59–60.

Chapter Ten

The Road of Life

An organization of ice roads across Lake Ladoga had been discussed by the Military Council of the Leningrad Front ever since the blockade of the city had begun. It was decided that the ice roads should be built in the southern part of Schlusselburg Bay, where the distance between the shores was only about thirty kilometers (18 miles) and where the ice would form quicker and be stronger than in the other parts of the lake. A military engineer by the name of B. Yakubovsky was placed in charge of the operation, and on November 14, 1941, Yakubovsky traveled to Osinovets to organize the preparations necessary for the construction of an ice road. On November 15 through November 19 several reconnaissance groups were sent out to mark a route across Lake Ladoga.

One reconnaissance expedition was conducted by Lieutenant E. Churov, a hydrographer who was in the service of the Ladoga Naval Flotilla. Assigned to the expedition were several other men along with ten armed sailors who were to watch for and protect the group from an approaching enemy. Each person was given a ration of 800 grams (28.2 ounces) of salted fish, 250 grams (8.8 ounces) of bread and three pieces of sugar. In preparation for the expedition, Lieutenant Churov was taken on a reconnaissance flight over Lake Ladoga to determine how much of Schlusselburg Bay was covered by ice. Lake Ladoga did not freeze uniformly; strong winds made the ice pile up, and there were always some crevices that never froze over.

Before setting out from Osinovets, the men on the expedition tied themselves together with a rope so that they could walk a distance of twenty meters (22 yards) apart from each other (see Map 3). If someone should fall through a crevice or through a thin patch of ice the others would be able to pull him out of the icy water. Lieutenant Churov was at the front guiding the group with his compass. Every five hundred to six hundred meters (547 to 656 yards) the men would drill a hole in the ice to measure its thickness and then insert a thin black rod into the hole. The markers were to map the way for a future road across Schlusselburg Bay.

After the men had walked about five hours they stopped to rest and eat some food. When Churov looked up from his meal he noticed that the heavy, dark clouds that had filled the sky when they left Osinovets earlier that evening had disappeared. The sky was now spotted with stars, and he could see the North Star blinking an alert telling him that the expedition was off course; they were going southeast instead of due east. If they continued in this direction they would fall prey to the Germans who controlled the southern shoreline of Lake Ladoga. How could he have been so wrong? Was his compass faulty? The location of the group was a major concern, and it was decided that they should wait till morning to continue the journey.

The following morning the expedition would suffer another complication. After they had continued their journey walking east using the beacon of the light tower at Osinovets as a point of reference, Lieutenant V. Dmitriyev, one of Churov's assistants, suffered a serious injury to his leg. Churov decided it was necessary to bring Dmitriyev back to Osinovets as soon as possible. There, at one of the huts, he could be given medical attention. After unloading the sledge that was being used to transport the supplies for the expedition, Dmitriyev was lifted onto the empty sledge. Churov and three sailors then began the trip back to Osinovets pulling the sledge behind them. When the sledge became too cumbersome, Churov lifted Dmitriyev on his back and carried him the remainder of the way.

Upon Churov's return to the others the expedition continued. By the morning of November 17 they had arrived safely at Kabona along the eastern shoreline of the lake (see Map 3). The path for a future ice road had been marked. The next day the expedition team left Kabona pulling two sledges loaded with flour and made their way to the western shoreline of the lake following the path that they had marked. Upon their arrival at Osinovets, Churov and his assistants submitted their findings to the authorities.[1]

On November 19 the Military Council of the Leningrad Front ordered that a vehicle road be constructed across the ice of Lake Ladoga's Schlusselburg Bay. Since it was to be a military road it was to be operated and protected by the army. The civilians who were to be mobilized under a compulsory labor decree for work on the road or for loading and unloading supplies were to be placed under military control.[2]

In order to build a proper motor road across the lake, it was essential that the ice covering the lake be at least 200 millimeters (7.9 inches) deep. By the twentieth of November most of the ice covering Schlusselburg Bay had

reached a thickness of 130 millimeters (5.1 inches) and in certain places the
ice had reached a thickness of 180 millimeters (7.1 inches). On November 20
a string of almost 350 sledges pulled by horses left Vaganovo village located
along the western shore of Lake Ladoga and was brought to the eastern shore
(see Map 3). At the same time two automobiles left Vaganovo and crossed the
lake to Kabona (see Map 3). One of the vehicles transported military engineer
Yakubovsky, the man who had been placed in charge of the construction of
an ice road.

On November 22 the first convoy of trucks left Vaganovo for Kabona. The
ten trucks, each a GAZ-AA, were the first of sixty trucks that had been assigned to make the trip across the lake. Eight of the ten trucks succeeded in
arriving at Kabona; two had fallen through the ice. Thereafter, the remaining
fifty trucks began their successful trek across the lake. On November 23 the
entire convoy left Kabona and returned to the western shore of the lake. Each
truck carried five to six sacks of flour and each pulled a sledge which was
loaded down with five to six sacks of flour. Upon the completion of their journey, on November 24, the trucks had delivered to the western shore thirty-
three tons of flour.[3] The normal consumption of food in Leningrad was about
three thousand tons a day; therefore, the supplies that arrived on November
24 would do little to feed the entire population. The success of the truck convoy, however, was proof that the ice covering Lake Ladoga in its southern
area could be crossed, and the authorities were encouraged by that.

The drive across Lake Ladoga was dangerous. The ice was so thin that only
small loads could be carried by the one-and-a-half ton trucks that were being
used. The system of tying sledges to the rear end of the trucks and placing half
of the cargo on the sledges was used to distribute the cargo's weight and de-
crease pressure on the ice. The trucks were also spread wide apart and were
driven at a slow speed. Yet there were many casualties. Trucks fell through
the ice and their drivers and loads disappeared into the icy water. Some were
shelled by German artillery fire or destroyed by bombs dropped from German
dive bombers. Soldiers were stationed along the ice road from Osinovets to
Kabona, and one of their duties was to lay prefabricated wooden bridges over
any hole or crack in the ice caused by German shelling or bombs. At this time
the supply route across the lake was called "The Road of Death" by those who
drove it.

On November 24 the Military Council of the Leningrad Front decided to
organize a road that was to link Osinovets with the railway station at Zaborye. The road was to begin at Osinovets, cross the ice of Lake Ladoga, arrive
at Lednevo and from there go north and pass around the German held community of Tikhvin and end up at the railway station at Zaborye. The section
of road from Lednevo to Zaborye would be more than two hundred kilome-

ters (124 miles) long and it would need to be built through forests and across swamplands and small rivers. It was to go through a series of villages: Syas'stroy, Karpino, Novinka, Yeryomina Gora, Shugozero, Lakhta, Velikiy Dvor and Serebryanskaya (see Map 4). Thousands of villagers, men, women and children, were recruited to assist the Soviet soldiers in the construction of the Wilderness Road. The workers were given picks and shovels to mark the road and handsaws to cut down trees. Army trucks and tractors and occasionally a tank were used to pull down thousands of trees which were laid across the swampy areas of the forests; however, the bulk of the work was done by the physical labor of the people. They were fed but very little, and those who died from accidents were buried along the Wilderness Road. Work went on every hour of each day. Makeshift shelters made of branches and tarpaulins were built to house the workers whose turn it was to sleep for several hours. On December 6 the road reached the end of the forest and was brought across a few farms to its final destination, Zaborye (see Map 4).

Within an hour after the road's completion, the first convoy of trucks loaded with supplies left Zaborye for Lednevo. The convoy had been prepared for the journey three days before the road was completed. For the first few kilometers the convoy progressed rapidly across the open farmland, but when it entered the forest it experienced difficulties. The leading truck became stuck in snow. The road was so narrow that the other trucks could not be driven around it, and there was a delay while the leading truck was dug out. The delay was the first of many caused by snow, inadequate construction and enemy fire. The maximum distance that was traveled by the convoy in any day was thirty-two kilometers (20 miles). After six days had passed, the convoy arrived in Lednevo. From there the convoy crossed Lake Ladoga to Osinovets. It had brought less than a day's supplies needed to feed the people of Leningrad.

The Soviet leadership became convinced that the recapture of the railway station at Tikhvin was necessary for Leningrad's survival. Orders were given to send additional troops to Army General Kirill Meretskov who commanded the Soviet forces of the Volkhov Front. Meretskov was assigned the objective of liberating Tikhvin, and on December 7 his forces reached the outskirts of Tikhvin. On December 9 the German forces withdrew from Tikhvin and made their way westwards to the Volkhov River over roads that were covered with deep snow. As the Germans withdrew, Meretskov's forces took control of Tikhvin and on December 10 began their pursuit of the enemy. The campaign to retake Tikhvin was a huge military success for the Soviet forces and an important development for Leningrad. After Tikhvin was recaptured, goods supplied by various areas in the Soviet Union were brought by freight trains to its railway station. Hundreds of workers and soldiers unloaded the

trains and placed the supplies on trucks that were then driven to either Lednevo or to Kabona along the eastern shore of Lake Ladoga (see Map 5). The
major proportion of the supplies was food, but there was also medicine, fuel
and military equipment.

Many people kept the ice roads operational. When the ice weakened in one
spot, a new section of road had to be built. Snow had to be cleared repeatedly,
and eventually the roads were flanked with walls of snow which helped guide
the drivers of the trucks. At each kilometer on a road stood a traffic guide
wearing a white camouflage outfit and holding white and red traffic flags. Repair shops were organized where the vehicles were serviced. Maintenance
was difficult, especially since all sorts of vehicles, even city buses, were being used as trucks. Because of frequent accidents, enemy shelling and strafing and cold temperatures causing frostbite, medical aid stations were established along the entire length of each road. At these stations doctors and
medical assistants worked in tents that were protected by walls of ice and
snow. Communication stations, rescue stations, feeding stations and combat
security stations were also placed strategically along the roads. There were
days when as many as 19,000 people were working on the ice roads, and col-
lectively the roads became known as "The Road of Life." [4]

Adjustments were made to further increase the transport of supplies to
Leningrad. It was decided that the trucks should be driven at night and with
their headlights on and not just during the day. The convoy system, which had
been used, was abandoned, and each driver was encouraged to make as many
round trips as he could without stopping. Two round trips, which was the average, would take from sixteen to eighteen hours. Along the roads there were
signs with slogans of encouragement such as "The Fatherland and Leningrad
will never forget your labor" or "Every two trips provide bread for 10,500
Leningraders." [5] Party workers were sent to the ice roads to urge the drivers
to complete more than two round trips a day. It was possible, but not easy, for
a driver to complete three and sometimes four round trips in a day. When a
driver completed more than two round trips, a sign was erected at his base
reading "Salutations to the leader of the ice road driver _____, who made
_____ trips today." [6] Many drivers fell asleep and some fainted from exhaustion. To assist them in their difficult work, the drivers and traffic controllers
were given a larger daily ration of food.

Measures were enforced to improve the individual performance of the drivers. Signs were pasted in the cabs of trucks whose drivers were careless or
had poor driving habits, admonishing the drivers to mend their ways. Because
the gasoline that was being used was of low grade quality, the drivers had to
filter it through cloth before putting it in their vehicles. Those who consis-
tently forgot were reminded with signs reading, "Add up how many times you

lost by blowing out your gas line on the road and tell the Leningraders the total. Will they forgive your sloppiness?" [7] Drivers were embarrassed by the signs which they were not permitted to remove until they had demonstrated that they no longer committed the error. There were drivers who were lazy, and there were those who would drop a sack of food on the ice and retrieve it later to sell the food on the black market. The authorities relied on organized social pressure to eliminate laziness and theft. Culprits were made to appear before "courts for cowards" and to face the criticism of their fellow workers. They were also threatened with serious punishment.[8]

The ice roads were subjected to almost constant enemy attacks, and the Soviet military leaders responded by instituting defense measures to secure "The Road of Life." Anti-aircraft units were put in place to defend the ice roads from German air attacks. They also defended the roads and railroads adjacent to Lake Ladoga and the bases and warehouses at the harbors on both sides of the lake. The military fielded some 200 mid-caliber anti-aircraft guns, 50 small-caliber guns, 100 anti-aircraft machine guns and 100 search-lights. Along the lake's shores the military stationed rifle units and naval infantry brigades.

Soviet aircraft fighters from the Leningrad Front and the Soviet Baltic Fleet patrolled the ice roads and engaged in many dogfights with enemy airplanes. On December 3, 1941, Junior Lieutenant Vorontsov ran out of ammunition while in combat with four German Messerschmitts. If he had retired from the battle the trucks that he saw moving across Lake Ladoga would have become easy prey for the German airplanes. Vorontsov instead continued his attack by ramming one of the enemy fighters. In doing this he severly damaged his own airplane and was forced to land it on the ice. The German Messerschmitts then swooped down to strafe him and his airplane. He was saved, however, by the anti-aircraft gunners who put up a barrage of fire that drove off the enemy fighters.[9]

A reported nineteen iceboats were brought to Lake Ladoga to further safeguard "The Road of Life," and they were also to be used as emergency vehicles. Experienced yachtsmen from Leningrad volunteered to operate the iceboats, and each day they would leave their headquarters at the small village of Kokkovero to patrol the length and breadth of the lake. If they came across truck drivers or anyone else that needed assistance, they provided them with the necessary aid. Soldiers who were injured or wounded while on duty guarding the ice roads were brought by the iceboats to medical installations either on the lake or along the shoreline. Military skiers who were assigned to patrol the shorelines of the lake were brought daily by the iceboats to their assigned spots. The iceboats were fast; on windy days the vehicles with their large sails could reach a speed of up to one hundred kilometers (62 miles) per hour. The iceboats were also easy to maneuver.[10]

The increase in the flow of food into Leningrad made it possible for the authorities to increase the people's daily and monthly rations and to open semi-sanitariums. The latter was an effort to help those who suffered the most from the effects of starvation and illness. People who became patients in a semi-sanitarium were admitted upon certification of the medical services and would receive a special diet for one or more weeks. The patients were usually given high proportions of meat and other foods with a high protein content, fats, sugar and cereals. Because it was not possible to provide this assistance to all who needed such help, industrial workers and people who held positions of influence were the first to benefit from this development. For example, the Bolshevik Works sent more than 6,000 employees to the Works' Sanitarium for a three-week rehabilitation period. Party members, scientists and well-known artists, painters and writers were sent to the Hotel Astoria which had been converted into a semi-sanitarium. Despite these efforts, hundreds of the patients died; their bodies were so ravaged by hunger and disease that they could not be saved.[11]

NOTES

1. A.V. Vinogradov and A. Pleysier, Bitva za Leningrad v sud' bakh zhitelel goroda I oblasti: vospominahiiy a zashchitnikov I zhitelei blokadnogo goroda I okkupirovannykh territorii (Saint Petersburg, Russia: Saint Petersburg State University Press, 2005), 65–66.

2. Leon Goure, The Siege of Leningrad (Stanford, California: Stanford University Press, 1962), 151.

3. Nikolai Kislitsyn and Vassily Zubakov, Leningrad Does Not Surrender, trans. Barry Jones (Moscow: Progress Publishers, 1989), 111.

4. A.V. Karasev, Leningradtsy v gody blokady (Moscow: Izdatelstre Adademii Nauk SSSR, 1959), 179.

5. Goure, The Siege of Leningrad, 210.

6. Goure, The Siege of Leningrad, 210.

7. Goure, The Siege of Leningrad, 211.

8. Goure, The Siege of Leningrad, 210.

9. Kislitsyn and Zubakov, Leningrad Does Not Surrender, 113.

10. Vinogradov and Pleysier, Bitva za Leningrad, 66.

11. Goure, The Siege of Leningrad, 213.

Chapter Eleven

Assistance and Encouragement

Leningrad's leaders and the city's Party organizations did what they could to give assistance and encouragement to the civilians and the soldiers. Thousands of volunteers, despite their own hunger and weakness, were recruited to patrol the streets of the city to find and help others get to their homes or receive medical care. Inside apartment buildings special "warming up" rooms were organized where hot water could be obtained. Here people would gather to talk and to drink a cup of hot water or to simply get warm. The city library was kept open for those who wanted to read or do research. Entertainment was important and theatres were opened as often as possible. Correspondence between the city's inhabitants and their loved ones stationed along a military front was encouraged and letters were delivered. To further uplift the morale of the troops, the authorities sent civilian delegations to the front. These delegations would bring with them gifts from the city such as guitars, handkerchiefs, pouches filled with tobacco, razors and hand knitted winter clothes. Lecturers, writers and performers were also brought to the front lines to entertain the soldiers.

The members of the Komsomol won the love and respect of the people with their many acts of assistance. The Party's youth organization divided its membership into everyday life teams. The teams, consisting mostly of teenaged girls, would visit the people in their cold apartments and offer the kind of assistance that was necessary to keep the people alive. They would chop wood and light the small stoves. They would bring pails of water from the Neva River or from a nearby canal. They made tea and cooked meals. They swept the floors of apartments and washed and dressed children. They cheered up and encouraged the tired and weak and entertained them by reading their favorite literature.

News that Komsomol members would visit those who needed assistance quickly spread and letters arrived at the Komsomol organization requesting aid. The following short letter is one of the thousands that arrived:

Comrades of the Komsomol:

I, Balikova Yelena Bogdanovna, am writing to you and beg you to help me. I and my daughter are bedridden. It's cold. Nobody is here to make a fire or boil some water. The windows are bombed out. We are lying here without a doctor, and there is nobody around to call him. Please don't forsake us.

In the corner of the letter was written: "Food is being delivered. A doctor is sent. Windows rapaired."

On a piece of paper torn from a copybook the following message was written:

I beg you to help my mama; she got sick; she cannot go to work. Papa has been wounded, but he went back to the front. Only I with my little brother take care of our mama. Please don't forget us; don't let us become orphans.

Tanya Svetlov

Notations were made in a lead pencil: "Send a Komsomol team immediately." "A doctor was sent. Food is being delivered to the house."[1]

The Komsomol organization was given considerable authority by the city's leadership. On request of the organization, the city opened special food stores to supply the people who were ill. From these stores the members of the life teams would acquire the food rations for the people who were under their care without having to wait in long lines. Komsomols were also permitted to re-settle people in more suitable housing. They placed children whose parents had died from hunger or who were killed during an air raid or a shelling bombardment in children's houses. At a children's house the orphans received food, vitamins and some medical care. Komsomol members also visited the city's hospitals and penned the letters that were dictated to them by patients.

Letters were delivered by Leningrad's postal system which continued to function during the blockade. One postal person who delivered the mail was Natalia Petrushina; she worked in the 129th postal district. Academician Pavlov Street was in Natalia's district and the Experimental Institute of Medicine, Vaccines and Serums was an address on that street. One day, according to Natalia, a man working at the institute told her that if she wanted to live, she must remain active. "I am leaving Leningrad," he said to her, "because they are making me do it. But I tell you—don't ever give up and go to bed. Don't get downhearted. Keep on your feet just as long as you possibly can."

Natalia took seriously the man's advice, and she did not let herself get down-hearted. Whenever there were letters to be delivered, she would gather them in her sack and take them to the correct addresses.

Delivering letters to apartments in a multi-storied building was particularly difficult. Natalia explained that it would usually "take a couple of hours. . . . It was dark on a staircase and slippery." Because "the toilets were not working" the residents of the building threw their human waste out on the stair-case. "Sometimes you would be going up the stairs and you would fall and slide down again, because it was slippery. . . . All the rooms would be open, a flat was not locked at all; it would be dark and you would stumble. Some-times when you came you would find someone lying there. You would think—he's dead! You would shake him a little and say: 'There is a letter for you.' If he was conscious, then of course he would begin to stir. But others couldn't care whether there was a letter or not. Well, you would start pester-ing them. If they asked you to, you would read [the letter] to them. . . . Some-times you would come to a flat and find someone lying dead on the bed."

On one occasion Natalia delivered a letter to a man who was waiting to hear from his son in the military. When she arrived the man was sitting on the stairs. Natalia addressed him by name and told him that she had a letter for him. He asked her politely to read it for him, and she did. The father's "son had written to say that they were engaged in fierce fighting; there had just been an offensive—and that was all." The man took the letter and thanked Natalia and then asked her to help him stand up. He was very thin and "I be-gan to help him up and collapsed onto the stairs myself. We couldn't get up, neither he nor I. What a terrible thing! But another man appeared and he was a bit stronger evidently and so between us we got one another up." [2]

Many letters were written by Leningrad's citizens to the soldiers and sailors defending the city. It was believed that this kind of correspondence would boost the morale of the men at the front, and it did. When a Leningrad paper published a letter written by a soldier who complained that he had never received a letter from anyone, he received within a week more than six hundred letters. [3] Husbands and fathers who were in the service were eager to hear from their wives and children because it meant that they were still alive.

There were also letters that were not uplifting. They informed the recipi-ents about events that were sad and heart-rending. Such a letter was received by a father-soldier from his thirteen-year-old daughter. Her name was Tanya Bogdanov and she wrote:

Dear Daddy! I am writing to you during my illness . . . and write because I am awaiting death and because it comes most unexpectedly and very quietly. I ask you not to blame anyone for my death. I admit that according to my conscience

I myself am to blame since I haven't always obeyed mother. Dear Daddy, I know that it will be hard for you to hear of my death, and I most terribly don't want to die, but there is nothing to be done if that is fate. I know that it will be difficult for you to understand my illness, so I write about it below. Mummy has tried very hard to keep me going and has supported me in every way she could and can. She even took bits off her bread and a little off each of the others for me, but as it was very difficult to keep it up it turns out that I have to die. . . . I am writing this letter to you and crying myself, but I am very much afraid of getting upset as then my arms and legs start [to shake and tremble uncontrollably]. But how can I not cry when I so desperately like to live . . . I am trying so hard not to just pass away; I haven't any desire for that. I lie and every day I wait for you, and when I start dropping off to sleep you begin to appear to me. . . . Well, dear daddy, don't get very upset and take my words about death calmly. I just want to thank Mummy and my sisters and my brother for all their care and attention and especially Mummy to whom I can't find words to express my gratitude. After all, she has helped me in every way she could.[4]

In many of the letters received by soldiers and sailors, the writers expressed great anger and a burning hatred for the enemy. People who had lost their homes or had lost others who were dear to them would request that vengeance be carried out. Such a request was made in a letter written by a young lady to the sailors of the Soviet Baltic Fleet:

Sailors! Two years ago you drank lemonade in the small kiosk near our house; you sat and chatted with girls on the benches. Now there is no kiosk; there are no more benches.

The Germans flew over and dropped a bomb. The house was destroyed and people were killed. . . . It is awful Baltiitsy [sailors of the Soviet Baltic Fleet were called Baltiitsy]. Is it possible that the Germans will be allowed to live on the earth? I am certain they will find their masters. It is impossible that our boys will not overpower the German. I ask you, Baltiitsy, to strike now so that there will be no smell of a German around our city. Do not be chivalrous with this enemy. An eye for an eye, all their teeth for one tooth. That will be right. So I beg you, my sailors, hit the German and defeat him. I shall have a bench for you. I shall put flowers in the yard, and I shall meet you at my house. I am waiting for you to return victorious. Good luck.

> Korolyova,
> Dvornik [Janitress] of House No. 20,
> Ulitsa Kholturina [Kholturin Street]
> Leningrad[5]

One day a woman by the name of Stepanova who was living in Leningrad received a letter from her daughter who had remained in the occupied part of the Leningrad region. Stepanova mailed her daughter's letter to one of the military headquarters of the Leningrad Front so that the soldiers could read the following:

Dear Mama!

I must and I will get revenge for my wounds, for the wounds of my sister, for the death of my friend Anya Fedorova.

You remember her, she used to come to us very often and you would say: "What a sweet, cheerful girl!"

Mother dear, the monsters hanged her on the Station L. Before the hanging they abused and tortured her for a long time. They broke her fingers and her bleeding hands were put into boiling water. They tore her slippers and stockings off and made her walk with bare feet over nails and pieces of glass. After torturing her, they hanged Anya on a pole. With her head held high she went to her death.[6]

The Leningrad State Library kept its door open in order to accommodate the citizens who were lovers of books and those who wanted to research various topics. Before the war there were seven reading rooms in the library, and they daily were visited by 3,000 readers. As many as 9,000 books were issued each day and the library's staff responded to some 400 written queries. During the winter of starvation all of the reading rooms were closed. However, a little brick stove was placed in the staff dining room, and it became the reading room. There were days when as many as five readers were in the staff dining room. The principal readers were engineers, physicians and scientists who were seeking answers to problems. Some studied books that were written about the sieges of other cities. The library staff received queries from soldiers and various organizations concerning problems of nutrition and on how to make matches, and these were addressed. It was important work and when one of the curators at the library, a man who was in his eighties, was urged to leave Leningrad, he refused to be evacuated. "Leningrad won't be taken—," he replied with defiance, "to hell with you!" [7]

There were schools that continued to operate during the winter months but under very difficult conditions. At the school on Tambov Street the headmaster, a Comrade Tikhomirov, and his teachers conducted classes in a large air-raid shelter. Later, Tikhomirov would describe the conditions within the shelter in this way: "We stuck it, and we stuck it well. We had to be worthy of our city. We had no wood, but the Lensoviet gave us a small wooden house not far away for demolition so we could use the timber for heating. The bombing and the shelling [were] very severe in those days. We had about 120 pupils then—boys and girls—and we had to hold our classes in the shelter. Not for a day did the work stop. It was very cold. The stoves heated the air properly only a yard around them, and in the rest of the shelter the temperature was below zero. There was no lighting, apart from a kerosene lamp. But we carried on, and the children were so serious and earnest about it all that we actually got better results out of them than in any other year. It is surprising but true. We had meals for them; the army helped us to feed them . . . all the children in our care survived. Only it was pathetic to watch them during those famine months. Toward the end of the year they hardly looked like children any more. They were strangely silent with a kind of concentrated look in their eyes. They would not walk about . . . they would just sit." [8]

None of the students died who attended Comrade Tikhomirov's school, but several of his teachers did. One had joined the military and was killed in action at Kingisepp. Four others died due to hunger and exhaustion. One of these teachers had taught literature and following his death the headmaster, who recorded the developments at the school in a large scrap book, made the following entry: "He worked conscientiously until he realized that he could no longer walk. He asked me for a few days' leave in the hope that his strength would come back to him. He stayed at home, preparing his lessons for the second term. He went on reading books. So he spent the day of January 8. On January 9 he quietly passed away." [9]

The students appreciated greatly the efforts put forth by the school's headmaster and the teachers. One of the female students expressed her gratitude in an essay: "It became very difficult to work. The central heating was, of course, out of action. It became terribly cold. One's hands and feet were quite numb, and the ink froze in the inkpots. We hid our faces inside our coat collars and wrapped scarves around our hands, but it was still terribly cold. Antonina Ivanovna, our chemistry teacher, came into the classroom and teased us for sitting there all bundled up. Feeling a little ashamed, we put down our collars and took off our gloves. She was always cheerful and always managed to cheer us up. She made jokes which made us laugh. . . . Only thanks to this moral support that we received from all the teachers and the headmaster did we stick it at all. Otherwise we should have stopped coming to school. . . . " [10]

In another essay a sixteen-year-old student named Luba Tereschenkova described the effects that the cold had on her while she attended classes. She wrote: "Frost also joined the blockade and lent Hitler a hand. It was never less than thirty degrees of frost! Our classes continued on the 'Round the Stove' principle. But there were no reserve seats, and if you wanted a seat near the stove or under the stove pipe, you had to come early. The place facing the stove door was reserved for the teacher. You sat down and were suddenly seized by a wonderful feeling of well-being; the warmth penetrated through your skin, right into your bones; it made you all weak and languid and paralyzed your thoughts; you just wanted to think of nothing, only to slumber and drink in the warmth. It was agony to stand up and go to the blackboard. One wanted to put off the evil moment. It was so cold and dark at the blackboard, and your hand, imprisoned in its heavy glove, went all numb and rigid and refused to obey. The chalk kept falling out of your hand, and the lines were crooked and the figures [were] deformed. . . . " [11]

Theaters were opened occasionally to provide the people with entertainment. In the Dramatic Theater on the Fontanka River it was so cold that the actresses who performed in the comic opera Baydere wore their fur coats. The dancers also wore fur coats, but nobody in the audience minded. The people laughed, but it was not a loud laughter, and there was cheering but not frantic cheering.[12] Vladimir Sofronitsky, the great Russian pianist, gave a concert in Pushkin Theater on the evening of December 12. It was "dark, cold, morose" according to Sofronitsky. "There was no heat. The temperature fell to 3 degrees below zero. The public sat in the theater in winter coats and wore felt boots. I myself played in gloves with the finger tips cut out. But frankly I believe I have never played so well. And what a reception from the audience! This evening was one of the happiest days of my life." Four months later Sofronitsky was airlifted out of Leningrad; he would join the many other artists who had been evacuated from the besieged city before him. [13]

The composer Boris Asafyev was one of several artists who refused to be evacuated from Leningrad. In the fall he was asked if he wanted to leave the city. "A place," he was told, "is reserved for you on a plane and you could go deep into the interior, thousands of miles from the front and continue your work in peace." Asafyev smiled and replied, "I am a citizen of Leningrad. Most of my life has been spent here and I have no desire to go anywhere else." Later, however, it did become necessary for him to leave his apartment, the place where he had written the music for The Fountain of Bakhchisarai and had composed The Flames of Paris and had worked on The Prisoner of the Causcasus. Bombs had been dropped on several occasions in the square on which his home was situated. He was moved to Pushkin Theater where he was given a room in which to live and work. The room was not heated and those who entered would see Asafyev seated at the end of his bed with a beret on his head and a white scarf around his neck. Next to the bed there was a big table stacked high with books and perched on top of the books was a lamp with a dull shade that was slanted so that a dim glow fell upon Asafyev's thin face. On his knees was a copy book. When his chilled hand could no longer hold the pen, he would blow on his fingers until some feeling came back and then he would continue. (It was not until March 1943, after the blockade of Leningrad was lifted that Asafyev finally agreed to leave the city.)[14]

In celebration of the New Year the city authorities gave each family in Leningrad a bottle of wine and some candy. On January 1, 1942, Elena Skrjabina described how she and her family had celebrated New Year's Eve:

> It is hard to imagine a more grim celebration . . . they gave each family a bottle of red wine and a small bag of candy. We decided not to wait for the traditional twelve o'clock. We went to bed at ten. We sleep in a room whose windows are boarded with plywood. We don't undress to go to bed, but do quite the opposite. We pull on everything we can. I, for instance, sleep in a fur jacket, a large kerchief and boots, and on top I cover myself with blankets. The little bed of Yura [Elena's son] is next to mine. Only his nose peeks out from beneath the covers. I listen to his breathing to be sure he is still alive.
>
> Around twelve, a noise woke me. I saw my husband. He was sitting at the table in his military coat in front of one little burning candle, hunched, tired, staring into space. The heart bursts with pity for him, for us, for all the others caught in this mousetrap. In front of my husband on the table lay three pieces of black bread. He brought these as a New Year's treat. He wanted to spend this evening with his family. There is a saying—"Those with whom you celebrate New Year's Eve, you will stay with the whole year." This night I didn't sleep. Thoughts turned in my head and wouldn't give me any peace. It seems demeaning and absurd to die of hunger, and there is no hope for a safe escape. Our strength fades with every day.[15]

It had been more than six months since the war began. During this time Leningrad had become a battered fortress, defended by soldiers and sailors and inhabited by weary civilians who were suffering from severe shortages. The city was enclosed in a network of barricades, and within the city fortress military personnel were manning camouflaged anti-aircraft guns that were strategically placed throughout the city. At the cross-roads and bridges there were earthen pillboxes, and the nearby houses concealed fortified machine gun nests. Hovering above the city were hundreds of hydrogen filled barrage balloons that prevented enemy dive bombers from attacking the city. Above the cloud of balloons, Soviet flyers combated the enemy's high-flying bombers; nevertheless, the city continued to suffer from bombardments. The roofs and facades of buildings were torn off. Walls were shattered exhibiting dark gaping holes that exposed the ruined interiors of buildings. The glass in windows was broken, and the openings were boarded up with sheets of plywood or were stuffed up with cushions and mattresses. Residential places that were not padlocked were dimly lit inside by the feeble flame of a homemade wick lamp and were heated by a small iron stove fueled by books, pieces of furniture and other sources of wood. The inhabitants of these places left early each morning dragging their emaciated, weak bodies to assigned bread stores to stand in long lines in freezing temperatures. After they received their daily ration they slowly made their way back passing people pulling sleds that bore the wrapped bodies of their dead loved ones. Upon returning home they would leave again with buckets and pitchers to begin the arduous walk to an ice hole in a nearby canal or river. They could not take a tram or a trolley bus; the cables of these transportation systems hung lifeless above the streets that were empty except for an occasional supply or army truck. After getting their water the people would begin their walk back along snow-trodden paths that took them past walls that had been posted with written announcements. These were offers to exchange a suit or a pair of shoes or pieces of valuable furniture for bread and other foods. If the people decided to shorten their walk by going through a residential yard or a city square they would see piles of human refuse and corpses. Some of the dead had been stripped of their clothes; all were to be picked up later and brought to a local morgue or cemetery. It was the end of the year and Leningrad, shrouded in snow and ice, appeared to be paralyzed and dying.

NOTES

1. Boris Skomorovsky and E.G. Morris, The Siege of Leningrad (New York: E.P. Dutton and Company, Inc., 1944), 134–35.

2. Ales Adamovich and Daniil Granin, A Book of the Blockade, trans. Hilda Perham (Moscow: Raduga Publishers, 1983), 103–04.

3. Alexander Werth, Leningrad (London: Hamish Hamilton, 1944), 132.

4. Adamovich and Granin, A Book of the Blockade, 199–200.

5. Skomorovsky and Morris, The Siege of Leningrad, 120.

6. Skomorovsky and Morris, The Siege of Leningrad, 71.

7. Werth, Leningrad, 131.

8. Werth, Leningrad, 88–89.

9. Werth, Leningrad, 93.

10. Werth, Leningrad, 91.

11. Werth, Leningrad, 91–92.

12. Werth, Leningrad, 54.

13. Skomorovsky and Morris, The Siege of Leningrad, 95.

14. Skomorovsky and Morris, The Siege of Leningrad, 97–98.

15. Elena Skrjabina, Siege and Survival, trans. Norman Luxenburg (New York: Pinnacle Books, Inc., 1973), 65–66.

Chapter Twelve

Letters Never Sent

The effects of the blockade on Leningrad and its people were described by Robert Pershitz in a series of letters that he addressed to his fiancé, Taalah, in January 1942. Taalah and her older sister had left Leningrad in August 1941, before the blockade against the city was established. Robert planned to give the letters to Taalah after the war in the hope that they would be with each other again. In the letters Robert mentioned and described the actions of several people who were related to Taalah or with whom she was familiar. At the same time, he wrote about his own experiences in blockaded Leningrad. In the year 2005, Mr. Pershitz shared his letters with the author and the author's close friend and colleague, Dr. Alexey Vinogradov.

In a letter dated January 12, 1942, Robert wrote:

Dear Taalah,

My last letter to you was dated the first day of December. A month and a half has passed since that time, and I have received nothing from you. I have not written to you since December because I did not think you received my last letter. You will not receive the letter that I am presently writing because I am not going to send it to you. You will have an opportunity to read it when we meet again, unless I should die. The construction of my sentences may seem strange to a person who does not live in Leningrad or to the person who is not experiencing what we in Leningrad are enduring. We, who are witnessing death and see it all around us, do not consider my comments strange. Listen, I have started this letter while I still have the strength and energy to do so.

I would like to describe for you what we are thinking and what we hope for. Later it will be impossible to describe what we are thinking and feeling.

Robert Pershitz as a student before the war

Even now it is very difficult to express my feelings and thoughts. Yet it will be so interesting to read what I am about to describe for you later when we sit around a warm stove after we have eaten a wonderful dinner in the company of friends. These are difficult but heroic times. Look, I am already finishing the first page of the letter, yet I do not know how to begin describing our way of life. It will be a pity if my last four letters do not reach you. In those letters I told you about very important matters. But the misfortunes that I described to you in those letters seem to be minor compared to what we are experiencing now. What we are undergoing now is unimaginable. Let me describe for you our apartment. There are few apartments like ours in the city. It is our good fortune to have such a nice apartment on Nevsky Prospect. Sometimes we actually have electricity. Four days ago we had light. Almost everyday we have running water. In the recent past I had to go to a nearby river for water but only three or four times. Our windows have not yet been broken. We still have enough wood to heat our apartment and that in itself is happiness. In other apartments there is darkness both day and night because the windows are covered with shades. There is neither kerosene nor oil. It is cold in these other apartments because there is no firewood. The people in those apartments must walk two blocks to get water.

Let's return to our apartment. Six people live in our apartment. My parents, me, Lisa, my aunt (her apartment was destroyed by an artillery shell) and Sasha's brother (in his apartment there is neither water nor electricity). We have a seventh sleeping area, and it is often occupied by Moitska because there is no electricity or water in his apartment. Generally speaking we together live in a zoo. I admire my mother because she has saved our lives. It bothers me to look at her because she has become very thin; yet her condition is not unique.

Now our life consists of minor events and activities to which we had never given much attention. Never before did we think about finding a match to light a cigarette or to light our small oil lamp. We never thought about shaving without water, and now that is being done. Now we wonder how we should take a bath at home since there are no bathhouses in the city that are in operation. . . . Forgive me for writing about such detailed matters, but I want you to understand the kinds of problems we are facing in Leningrad.

A half hour ago we suddenly received electricity, but it lasted only a short time. The radio loud-speaker in our apartment began to work. It had not worked for three days so during those days we received no news. The city has not received a newspaper from Moscow for many days. The Leningradskaya Pravda appears in the kiosks the day after it is printed, but sometimes it is not delivered to the apartment for three or four days. The news we do receive is old news. We have not seen trains or freight trains in operation for two weeks because of the cut back in electricity. If you should open a newspaper you would see the dates and times of the theaters and cinemas, but you should not believe everything you read because on the office doors where tickets are sold there are posted signs that read "closed for there is no electricity." While I am writing I am reminded of the other problems that we are facing. Do not be alarmed that I am jumping from one problem to another, and that there seems to be little order or organization in my writing.

Just now everyone in the living room has given a great sigh of relief. The noise in the kitchen means that the water is running again. Everyone has rushed to the kitchen to fill with water all of the containers including our bathtub. Mother is happy because she will be able to clean the apartment with water. What I am describing concerns our lifestyle, and our way of living is not attractive. Beyond this our major difficulty is hunger. We now know what it means to have swollen bodies because of hunger, and we see people lying dead in the streets with a thousand rubles in their pockets. I don't have words to describe the situation because a person must witness what we see daily to truly understand what we are experiencing. Right now my self-made oil lamp is sputtering. Nearby Lisa is trying to persuade mother to lie down and stop bustling about. The radio is whispering, and it is hard to hear what is being said or played. I am writing this letter and looming over each one of us is the shadow of hunger; it never leaves. Subconsciously, I am constantly thinking about food. Involuntarily, I listen for the sound of pans in the kitchen being used to make food. Now almost all of our conversations are about food. We are ready to eat anything that might give us some nourishment. We eat things that before we did not consider to be food. There is no more carpenters' glue in the city. There is no more starch used for starching linens. There is no more bran. There is no more technical gelatin. There is no more castor oil. All of these items were eaten or consumed a long time ago. I have not seen a cat or dog in more than two months. There are no pigeons. I am not sending this letter by mail and that is why I feel free to write so honestly. Former food markets now have a strange look about them. At the markets there are people who exchange their possessions for food. They come to the markets with old items hoping to barter them for something to eat. For those who have money the following are the current prices: one kilogram of bread will cost 300 to 400 rubles, one bar of chocolate will cost 200 rubles and one kilogram of horse meat will cost 200 rubles. These are the prices. But it is almost impossible to find these foods even at these prices. It is possible to acquire these foods but only with a person that one can trust, someone who will not report you to the authorities. There is speculation and speculation is strongly prohibited. The militia are aware of such speculation. They will arrest those who try to victimize the hungry. Barter is not prohibited. The following are examples of the kinds of barter taking place: for a pair of felt boots a person is able to get one and a half or even two kilograms of bread and for an armload of firewood you can get a half kilogram of bread.

It may seem to you that what I am writing is nonsense and unnecessary and if so you will be right but only because you are not experiencing what I am describing. For us the talk of food is all consuming. Our future meeting is dependent on my ability to get food. Without food, I will die. We must be concerned about food and the acquisition of food. I do not want to write about our fellow acquaintances at this time. I first want to talk about the circumstances of our lives so that you can judge more objectively the changes that have taken place in our lives. Let's turn back to the problem of eating. The changes that have taken place in the food markets are changes that are necessary for existence. The main feature in our environment is rations. I don't know if you are suffering from food shortages, but I am certain that our situation is much worse. We receive almost nothing but bread. The norm is the following: workers receive 350 grams of bread per day, and other employees, dependents and children receive 200 grams of bread per day. The above are the new rations that went into effect at the end of December. Before these went into effect, workers received only 250 grams of bread per day and other employees, dependents and children were given 125 grams per day. It is poor quality bread. Half of the bread is made of rye flour and the other half is bran. Nevertheless, it is our main staple because that is all there is. It is almost impossible to get any other food. I would like to describe our situation in detail because I am afraid I will forget the details. I do not want to forget what is happening.

On January 13, 1942, Robert described the effects that hunger had on the human body:

Today was a good day. It was published that during the month of January each person was to receive for the entire month 400 grams of oats. Thus, today we each had a glass of coffee with scones made of oats. We are thankful even for this. Taalah, today my hope for life and our eventual reunion has strengthened. People were talking in the city that it was reported on the radio that Soviet troops had recaptured Mga and that the blockade of the city had been broken. Everybody waits for the arrival of food. I will not believe these rumors; I must hear with my own ears the reports on the radio. In the past it was published that rations of food would increase; yet the stores were empty. Lines of people appear at the bread stores already at 3 or 4 A.M. in spite of the threat of penalty. People are not permitted on the streets after 5 P.M. The mother of one of my friends was fined 30 rubles as a penalty. People stand in long lines even though there is no assurance that they will acquire food. In most cases the stores are open even though they are empty. A ration card may be used only at a designated store, and if that store is empty the owner of the ration card may not use the ration card at another store. People will stand in freezing temperatures for entire days and will not leave the lines.

It is a bit easier for us because Vladimir Orestavitch [Taalah's father] helps us. I have asked him to help us, and he has. I felt uncomfortable asking him. Remember that Vladimir is the director of a bread store, but I will talk more about this later. Let's leave metaphysics for the end. People often use canteens because it is too difficult to acquire food from stores. Only people who work are permitted entrance into a canteen. You can buy soup in a canteen. To call it soup is an exaggeration. It is really just warm water. Before November 10 the canteens in Leningrad would sell soup, but ration cards were not needed to purchase it. After November 10 it became necessary to have ration cards to purchase food at canteens. There are lines of people at the canteens. One day a mother wondered if it was cheaper to buy soup in a canteen or to make it at home. She experimented and discovered that if she bought grain with her ration card at a food store and made soup at home, the soup was better than the soup she ate in the canteen. The cost of the soup she made at home was the same as the soup served at the canteen. I know for a fact that the canteens are not subsidized by the State and that the workers at the canteens steal food for themselves and for their friends. That is why the quality of the soup sold at the canteens is low. People are stealing. The price of soup remains the same, but the quality goes down.

So you see that the shortage of food is our greatest problem. Often the delivery of bread to the bread shop is interrupted. Yesterday afternoon there was no bread in the stores. Today there were long lines at the bread stores, and by the afternoon the delivery of bread to the stores had stopped. The mood in the city is low, and it did not improve when it became evident to the people that the report that Soviet troops had taken Mga was false.

Now I will describe the terrible consequences of starvation. It is difficult for me to do this in the correct sequence. I will try to give you just the facts. Imagine that you are walking on Nevsky Prospect during the daytime. You will not recognize it. Many of the buildings are gone due to the bombing. The windows of buildings that are still standing are broken, and they have been replaced with sheets of wood. You will be greatly astonished at the neglect that is so evident in the most famous blocks of the city. The snow has not been removed from the street, and the rail lines are covered with ice and snow. The sidewalks are also covered with ice. No sand has been thrown over the ice, and in many places the ice is spotted with human blood. Stores are closed because of the absence of electricity. Newspapers have been posted on the street bulletin boards. The loud-speakers on the street corners are not working. The trains are not operating. The trolley buses are not in use. There are only a small number of vehicles that are in use. The horses are gone. They have been butchered and eaten. The type of transportation that you will see is a child's sled. No one is carrying bags or boxes. Items are placed on sleds and then pulled. It is so much easier. If you were to examine the contents on the sleds, you would shudder. A fourth of the contents are house items. Another fourth is firewood. Still another is wooden coffins. The last fourth is corpses wrapped in blankets or bed sheets. Taalah, you cannot imagine what it is like; at least 10,000 people die in the city each day. This is not an official statistic. In fact, the number 10,000 may be lower than the actual count. A month earlier it was reported that 2,000 people died each day. I am certain that when you return to Leningrad you will discover that most of your acquaintances are dead. People have food, but they are given only a small portion of food each day. Therefore, they die a slow death. Their bodies finally give up, and they die. If a person catches a cold the person's body, which is so weakened, is unable to fight the cold, and it dies. The body is so worn out that it cannot fight against a common cold or influenza. The body refuses to walk. The feet and the face of a person swell. The swelling is caused by starvation. There is little to eat so the body consumes water and becomes bloated. After the swelling, the dehydration process begins. A person loses weight. He has no strength to stand up or move. The person lies down and dies. There is also a drop in body temperature. The body loses its fats and because there is no inner warmth, the body feels cold. This is why warm clothes have become so valuable and firewood is as valuable as gold. Now women wear coats made of seal skins and under them blue or purple-colored ski pants. Men wear warm clothes as well. No one is shocked by this. Seeing people dressed this way has become the norm.

The facial features of the people will surprise you. From a distance a woman may look like a granny but then as she walks past it becomes evident that she is only fifteen or sixteen years old. Starvation causes a person to age. One day I saw Nadinkal. Do you remember how she always appeared youthful and fresh? I passed her on the sidewalk. She looked into my eyes and I looked into hers, and it was not until we were just three feet from each other that I recognized her. She did not recognize me. I was in a hurry so I did not stop to talk to her. Her face had aged; it had a greenish hue; it was so unrecognizable.

On January 16, 1942, Robert described death as he witnessed it in the streets of Leningrad:

Dear Taalah,

Today I almost felt happy. I received a telegram from you. Your father was very happy to read the telegram. He had not heard from you for a long time. It was reported that yesterday 11,322 people died in the city. That number represents only the people who were registered as having died; the actual number of people who died yesterday is probably much higher. We see more and more corpses in the streets. Taalah you cannot imagine what it is like to see a person on the sidewalk suddenly stop, sit down and die. A person's legs collapse in a strange manner. The person's eyes shine brightly as he or she is about to die. The eyes are hopelessly begging for something. The face is pallid, and the muscular features are absent. There are only skin and bones, skeletal features. It is wonderful to see two or more people walking together in the streets. It means that these couples will support each other. The person who walks alone has little hope. There is no one to support this person. If the person should sit down due to exhaustion there is no one to help him get up. He may call for help, but the people will pass by without giving him assistance. No one will assist him. Maybe, several hours later, the young girls of some volunteer organization such as the Komsomol will find him and bring him to a hospital. But even then there is no guarantee that he will survive.

There are so many people being brought to the hospitals that they cannot admit them all. Therefore, a person who is brought to a hospital may not be admitted. It is highly probable that the person will not survive. A person who is not admitted may offer people who pass by a lot of money for their assistance, but no one will respond. Money is worthless. It is food that is valuable. No one will expend energy for money. If food should be offered, then people will help. Fortunately, you don't have to choose the shorter route to spare your energy. The only way to get to any destination in the city is by our legs. Distances are our enemies. Today I did not have the energy to walk to Yurka's apartment. [Yurka is Robert's friend.] I did not have the energy to reach the post office to send you a telegram. On the days when I am to go to the university, I divide the long walk into two stages. I first walk from Nevsky Prospect to Sadovia or Syniaya Square to the apartment owned by mother. There I rest for a while. Then I make my way to the university. I return home using the same route and again divide the walk into two stages. The walk back home takes me one hour and thirty minutes. About a month ago I got a job. As a result, I began receiving a worker's ration card and my ration of bread per day jumped from 125 grams to 350 grams. But I have to walk to work, and I get tired. My legs carry me but with great difficulty. I am afraid of distances. Yurka has not visited us for two weeks. He finds that climbing the staircase of our building to reach our apartment is too difficult. . . . He wants to see us but he just does not have the energy and strength to walk the distance to our place. It is another one of our great difficulties. It may be a difficulty that we will have to live with forever. Recently, Volva Ulbensky came over to visit me after his work. He was exhausted, and I urged him to lie down and sleep for thirty minutes before going home. When he left I walked with him down Litany Avenue. He wanted to go to Yurka's apartment on the fifth floor, but he did not have energy to climb the stairs. Volva wanted to discuss with Yurka the possibility of acquiring firewood.

In a letter dated January 17, 1942, Robert described how the dead in Leningrad were being buried:

Taalah, I read what I wrote you yesterday, and I believe that I misinformed you. I told you that I am stronger because of the extra bread that I am receiving with my worker's ration card. This is not true. Today I can hardly walk. Today I had to visit your father twice, and I barely finished the second journey. Right now I am going to bed and will rest awhile. I will feel a little better, but I know it will not last. I know that it will be difficult for me to move around in the apartment this evening. It is weakness. As you can tell, although we have the traditional breakfast, lunch and supper, our hunger is never satisfied. At the same time there are a lot of people who eat only once a day, and all they have to eat is 200 grams of bread. Nobody wants to die in spite of starvation. I am not sure you will believe this, but in spite of all the suffering and difficulties nobody wants to commit suicide. There were mass suicides in other countries that experienced similar situations, but none in Leningrad. I have not heard about a single case of suicide. The desire to live has multiplied for every Leningrader. We will ourselves to survive and to once again experience a better life. It has not been the fate of many people to survive. I will write later about the people who have died.

I would like to write a few words about the contemporary burial ceremony. A dead person has done his duty and that is to die, but the living must do their duty and that is to bury the dead. For many of the living it is too difficult to perform a burial ceremony. One must first purchase a coffin, and a coffin is very expensive. The price of a coffin must be paid for with food. Coffins are made of wood, and wood has become very valuable. After the coffin is ordered, made and finished it then must be brought by sled to the location of the corpse. If the corpse is in the hospital it is unwise to leave the coffin in the hospital overnight. It will be stolen and used by someone who will burn it in his stove. It is also necessary to hire someone to dig a grave for burial at a cemetery. This will cost 3 to 4 kilograms of bread. . . . There is no guarantee that grave diggers will not remove the coffin and use it as firewood. It is very possible that within the next few days another person will be buried in the same grave. It is difficult to dig a grave especially during the winter when the ground is hard. It is much easier for a grave digger to use the same grave. After all he is human and does not want to expend more energy than necessary.

There are very few people who are able to bury a loved one in the traditional way. People die; their bodies are kept in apartments and, in spite of the freezing temperatures, the cadavers rot. Neighbors become angry if a corpse is kept in an apartment too long. So the people bring the corpses to the morgues in the hospitals, and the directors of the hospitals have the dead buried in large collective graves. Dynamite is used to create large holes into which the dead are dumped. This is why there are many people pulling sleds carrying corpses that are wrapped in blankets or bed sheets to local cemeteries. Now you are aware of the kind of nightmares we have. The way we live and even the way we die has changed so much. We could not have imagined this before the war. But it has become the norm. We are no longer astonished by scenes of death. It is a pity that I did not write down my impressions of life behind the blockade before the month of January. It would have been interesting if I had done that. Now it is impossible for me to remember that which has transpired, but I do have the opportunity to describe the events as they take place from now on.

Taalah, I have already written that you will not find alive many of your acquaintances. It is a rare family in the city that has not suffered a death during the last four months. I have already lost two of my uncles, my father's two brothers. Volva Albensky has lost his father and very recently, on January 11, Maria Pavlovina died. I am sure that many more people who I know personally will die, and I will record their deaths as well. I do not think that my expressions are cruel; they are truthful understandings of the situation that exists. It will be very good if death should take only four more people in our three families. I am afraid the number will be higher. I sincerely hope that I am a bad prophet.

On January 27, 1942, Robert described the death of Maria Pavlovina who is the grandmother of Robert's friend, Yurka:

Dear Taalah,

Ten days have passed since I last wrote. It seemed at that time that life and our existence could not be worse. Since that time our situation has become more desperate. A new development has occurred. The water supply system has completely stopped working. Now we have to get our water from the city's rivers. Imagine if you can, people are forced to take pails and churns on children's sleds and go to the Neva River, the Fontanka River and to other rivers in the city. They fill the containers with water from holes made in the ice covering the rivers. Then they try to climb the ice-covered embankments of the rivers. Those who fail to reach the top lose their grip on their water-filled containers. The water spills out and will eventually freeze and become another layer to the already existing layers of ice on the embankments. The people who lose their water will return to the hole in the ice to again fill their containers. Generally there are 33 misfortunes. [This is an old Russian saying.] Because of the absence of indoor plumbing, there is no supply of bread. The bread factories do not receive water, and without water they are unable to make bread. At the same time the temperature has dropped. Today it is 35 degrees below zero Celsius. The water pipes have cracked and burst. This is why yesterday all of Litany Avenue was covered with water that quickly turned to ice. I went to see my uncle who lives on Litany Avenue, number 49, and if I had not worn my high Russian military boots it would have been impossible for me to make my way down the avenue. Generally speaking life is terrible. Right now my mother is standing in line for bread in the freezing cold. She has been standing in line for three hours. What can we do? It is necessary for us to eat. I cannot take her place because I have no felt boots. During the past ten days we have received lots of news. First of all, on January 25, we buried Maria Pavlovina. Her dead body had been lying in her apartment for two weeks. We carried her corpse to the morgue at the Koybescheve Hospital. To be honest, we could not bring the body into the morgue so we placed it on a large mound of other dead bodies that had been brought to the hospital.

It is good Taalah that you left Leningrad before the blockade so that you don't have to see the horrible scenes that I am describing. To see the mound of human corpses outside of the hospital has a lasting effect on a person, much more so than a description in words. The mound of corpses consisted of many people, some of them were clothed, some were naked, some were wrapped in blankets and only a few had been placed in coffins. There were hundreds of corpses. Several had already been attacked by rats. It was apparent that a few were killed by artillery shelling. Most died from starvation. They were thin and had lost much of their body weight. It would have been impossible for them to look thinner than they did. While I was observing the human mound of corpses, a truck arrived and delivered seven more dead bodies from a university dormitory. The men in the truck lifted the dead bodies from the bed of the truck as if they were sacks of coal and threw them onto the mound of corpses. They showed no care or respect for the human bodies. Some were thrown head first. Later, all these corpses will be placed on large trucks and delivered to cemeteries, and there they will be buried in large common graves. Officially, a person is supposed to receive permission from the militia to bring a human corpse to a hospital, but that is only officially.

Taalah, I would like to describe the death of Maria Pavlovina. It will be difficult to do this, but it is necessary so that you will understand the relationship that exists between Yurka and me during this time of starvation. Maria was not a good caretaker of her things and did not provide for the future. When the blockade went into effect she had no food in storage. So she existed only on her ration cards. As a consequence, she suffered from hunger. She ate the food as it was rationed out to her. She did not organize her food intake. Until the end of November both Maria and Yurka had ration cards that were issued to dependents. This was a slow death. At the end of November both were beginning to suffer from dystrophy, and with each passing day their situation grew worse. Yurka behaved foolishly. He would purchase a small bar of chocolate for 200 rubles and would exchange some of his ration of bread for tobacco and matches. He smoked a lot and no one could persuade him to stop smoking. By New Year [1941–1942] Yurka did not have the strength to climb the staircase to his apartment on the fifth floor, and Maria had great difficulty walking and making her way throughout the apartment. [Yurka and Maria lived together.] It was fortunate for them that Anna Ileenichna visited the two and brought them soup. [Anna Ileenichna was the wife of Vladimir Ovestovitch and the stepmother to Taalah.] In spite of Anna's periodic assistance, Yurka and Mariah continued to lose weight. Their apartment was dark inside. The windows in the apartment had been shattered by aerial bombing, and the glass had been replaced with sheets of wood. Because it was dark inside they were unable to wash or clean the floor. All their clothes were placed on one pile. Their small wood-burning stove [burzuikha] was not being used. Thus, it was terribly cold in the apartment. This is how I found the apartment when I visited Yurka on January 8. Yurka was lying in bed wearing all the clothes that he was able to put on. He was also wearing his coat. Maria was sitting in an armchair near the cold burzuikha. She was sitting in the dark. The oil that I had given Maria and Yurka had been used so they had no light. At the market the price of a candle is 50 rubles. The burzuikha was not being used because the firewood that I had gotten with great difficulty for Yurka was stored in Woofka's storage place. Yurka had not had the strength to bring the wood to the apartment. I succeeded in getting Yurka out of bed but with great difficulty and then persuaded him to go with me to Woofka's place to get some firewood. We took with us a sled. On that day Yurka had eaten some bread but nothing more. We were able to get the firewood and brought it back to the apartment. By that time Yurka did not have the energy to cut the wood into smaller pieces. I did it for him. I first sawed a length into two lengths, and then I split the lengths with an axe. With that wood we were able to warm the apartment.

It is very difficult for me to write Taalah because it is so cold and I am so hungry. A new development has taken place. We have the opportunity to purchase 1 ? kilograms of meat. It is a luxury, of course. I can't help but listen to every word that is coming from the kitchen where the development is being discussed. I have difficulty writing as I listen to the talk in the kitchen.

The next day [January 9] I visited Yurka again, and again I sawed and split some wood to be burned in the burzuikha. Maria was unable to walk. She and Yurka had each eaten 200 grams of bread as they had the previous day. They were dying from starvation. Yet Yurka wanted to go to the market to purchase, for any price, a couple of bars of chocolate. At the same time he wanted to visit your father. I accompanied Yurka, but before we were able to get to the end of the block Yurka suddenly stopped and leaned against the wall of a building. He could not continue. With great difficulty I brought Yurka to my parents' apartment.

Please understand Taalah. I brought Yurka to my parents' apartment. He is dying from starvation. It is necessary that he be fed, but we have almost nothing to give him. The little we have we must save for ourselves. I brought Yurka to our apartment because I knew that we had some oats, and I wanted to give that to him. Imagine Taalah, oats, the kind of food we gave to horses. Imagine if you can, Yurka is dying in our apartment from starvation. We used the oats to make Yurka some soup, and I believe that the soup saved him. Nevertheless, I took a risk by bringing Yurka to our apartment and giving him the soup we had planned to eat. After being fed, Yurka lay down and fell asleep. But in time Yurka became ill. He had diarrhea and had severe chest pain. Yurka had been taking heart medicine. I went to visit your father and he gave me 100 grams of flour. Mother used the flour to make gruel for Yurka. Meanwhile, Maria was alone in her apartment sitting in her armchair near the burzuikha. That evening I went to see her. I lifted her out of the armchair and into her bed. I then heated some gruel on the burzuikha and fed her. I also gave her some of the bread that I found in the apartment. Maria looked like a corpse. Her face was made of bones covered with skin. Her eyes shone brightly. I left a portion of the bread on the table next to her bed. I told her not to eat it until morning. She promised me that she would not touch it until the following day. It was rather warm in the apartment because the burzuikha had been burning all day long. When I visited Maria the next day, I found her lying on the bed but her feet were touching the floor. Apparently she had tried to get out of bed. I lifted her legs onto the bed, covered her with a blanket, gave her some gruel and water and brought her some bread. She was so weak that she could not reach for the bread that I had placed on the table. I placed the bread in her mouth, but she had great difficulty chewing it. When I asked if she had difficulty chewing, she said no. She said it was wonderful to have food to eat.

I left her and promised that I would visit her in the evening. I left half of her bread ration on the table next to the bed. Maria, while she was eating, was so preoccupied that she did not even ask about Yurka. It was when I was about to leave that she asked about Yurka. When I returned home I told Yurka that Maria was still alive. She was no better and no worse. I believed that she would survive another day. Early in the evening, Anna Ileenichna arrived at our apartment and brought soup for Yurka. She also brought some chocolate. Anna and I then went to visit Maria. We found her lying on the bed covered with a blanket. I learned later that Volva had visited her before our arrival. He had found her lying on the bed, but her feet were touching the floor. She had apparently tried to reach the bread on the table but had fallen back on the bed. He had lifted her legs back on the bed and covered her. Anna and I filled the burzuikha with wood and started a fire. We then warmed some soup and gave that to Maria. Anna also gave Maria the bar of chocolate that she had purchased for Yurka. Maria appeared stronger than when I visited her earlier that day. Anna was afraid to stay any longer and so at 8 P.M. we left. By this time the fire in the burzuikha was warming the apartment. Before we left the building we asked a neighbor woman to check on Maria in the morning. Anna and I agreed to meet at Maria's apartment at around 11 A.M. the next day.

During all this time Yurka was lying in our apartment. Mother took care of him. But Yurka behaved very childlike. Believe me Taalah. Of course it is necessary to remember that Yurka has already suffered from starvation for a long time. Yurka is no longer able to think quickly or clearly. He has lost his memory. Yet Yurka's behavior made me angry. He was lying in our apartment. He had been eating our food for two days. Yurka also expresses his emotions quite freely whereas the rest of us suffer in silence. Anna had left him a half of a bar of chocolate, but we told Yurka that he should not eat it because of his diarrhea. But Yurka, behaving like a child, ate it anyway. He then expressed a desire to see Maria, but I refused to take him. He was not strong enough. He could barely make it to the toilet. Later on Yurka became hostile toward me. I responded to Yurka's hostility by sitting down and weeping. It was impossible to make him realize that I was not his enemy and that if I had not taken care of him, he would be dead.

The next morning Anna and I went to Maria's apartment. We were met by the neighbor woman and she told us that Maria had died. Anna became frightened, but I persuaded her to go with me into Maria's apartment. I went in first. It was dark. I took out my flashlight and from a distance I directed the light on Maria's face. Maria's head nodded. I cried out in surprise that she was alive. Anna then entered the apartment, and together we walked to Maria's bed. Maria was still alive, but she was unconscious. Anna and I stood by the bed and just watched Maria as she took her last breaths. We did not know exactly when she stopped breathing and only became certain of her death after we placed a mirror against her nose. We then went home locking the door of Maria's apartment as we left. I did not tell Yurka that his grandmother had died. Yurka was a major problem. He could not stay with us because there was no one to take care of him. Mother was ill; her heart was weak, and I was working. It had become necessary to move Yurka from our apartment as soon as possible, but I did not want Yurka to be moved to his grandmother's apartment. Taalah, your father and I carried Yurka to Weo's apartment. [Weo was the name that those who were close to Vladimir Orestavitch used to address Taalah's father.]

In the letter addressed January 28, 1942, Robert announced to Taalah that he was planning his evacuation from Leningrad:

I would like to write down a few facts that characterize our life before I forget them. I wrote several days ago that Litany Avenue was covered with water. Today I walked down Litany Avenue, and I saw several trucks and their tires were frozen in the ice. Nearby I saw a dead woman whose body was frozen in the ice. The people who walked by the spot did not stop and try to move the woman. The spot where the woman was frozen in the ice was near to your home. A shameful discovery was made in your building Taalah. The militia raided the building and uncovered a secret workshop in the basement. In the workshop people had been taking the muscles of human corpses and grinding them into meat patties. Because the muscles of the dead had shrunk, many corpses had been used. The enterprise had been a very profitable business venture. What did they call this meat? That I do not know.

I just returned from Weo's apartment. Today no food was delivered to Weo's store. So our family will have enough grain for just one meal today. Yesterday mother stood in line for some nine hours to purchase bread, but she was unable to get the bread. Today she spent seven hours standing in line and was able to purchase enough bread for three days.

I was very fortunate today. I received permission from the recruiting office to be evacuated out of the city and go to Svertlovsk in the East. All my documents are in order, and now I must find a way to leave Leningrad. I hope to leave within a few days.

Today Weo received a letter from Sophia Gregoryevna. [Sophia was Taalah's aunt and she lived in the Ural region.] She informed your father about the prices of food in the area where you live. I should like to inform you about our prices in Leningrad. One kilogram of sugar is priced at 600 rubles. One kilogram of grain costs 400 rubles. One kilogram of butter costs 1,000 rubles. One kilogram of bread is 400 rubles. One kilogram of fat is 500 rubles. One kilogram of sunflower oil is 400 rubles. A bar of chocolate is priced at 200 rubles. A package of cigarettes is 30 rubles. One box of matches is 10 rubles. Even if a person should have the money to do so, it is almost impossible to purchase these items. Vendors sell only to friends and acquaintances.

During the past ten days another important event took place. My aunt and uncle and my cousin were evacuated from Leningrad. They left by truck and were brought to a railway station. It cost them a huge sum of money. They paid 2,000 rubles for each person. They left the city just in time because they had run out of food. On the day they left, my uncle was unable to walk down the stairs. We had to carry him down. I too desire to leave as soon as possible and will try to use the same means that my uncle, aunt and cousin used to be evacuated. Thus, I believe strongly that I will see you in the spring.

I have not seen Anna since Maria's death because I have not had enough energy or strength to visit her. Tomorrow I will undertake the huge task of visiting her. At the same time I will visit Yurka, and when I return I will describe his condition to you.

Taalah, walking the streets of the city is now a frightening experience. Along each step of the way a person sees the effects of the blockade and the city's isolation. For the past five days we have heard nothing about the situation along Leningrad's military fronts because the radio does not work and newspapers have not been delivered and have not been posted on the bulletin boards in the city. We have not seen a newspaper from Moscow since the middle of December. That is why rumors are spreading that tell of fantastic military victories won by the Soviet troops, but no one is able to confirm them.

Just now my notebook is full so I will finish this letter. Now I will reread all that I have written.[1]

NOTE

1. A.V. Vinogradov and A. Pleysier, Bitva za Leningrad v sud bakh zhitelei goroda I oblasti: vospominauiiya zashchitnikov I zhitelei blockadnogo goroda I okkupirovan-nykh territorii (Saint Petersburg, Russia: Saint Petersburg State University Press, 2005), 170–80.

Chapter Thirteen

Evacuating People

The need to evacuate people who were not essential to Leningrad's defense was considered one of the top priorities, and the authorities decided that the ice roads should be used for that purpose. On December 6 the Military Council of the Leningrad Front authorized the evacuation of civilians over Lake Ladoga and ordered that by the twentieth of December 5,000 persons be evacuated from the city daily.[1] An evacuation center was to be established in Tikhvin; it was to be large enough to accommodate 3,000 to 4,000 people at a time. But in the beginning, the truck traffic was too irregular and limited to provide transportation for many people. Only old women, children and those who were too weak to walk traveled on trucks. The others had to cross the ice on foot or on skis. Many died in the attempt. Consequently, the rate of evacuation fell far short of the planned level.[2]

The opportunity to leave the city legally by foot across Lake Ladoga had earlier been the topic of a rumor among the citizens of Leningrad. Some people had responded to the rumor with criticism because they considered it an example of the leadership's inability to provide for the wellbeing of the city's people. Anna Ostroumova-Lebedva expressed this attitude in her diary on December 7:

> The mad idea of sending thousands of people on foot out of Leningrad in the freezing temperatures will probably become a reality! Maybe only ten percent of the entire number of evacuees will survive. . . . It is nothing but suicide! What a genius gesture! History will never forget this gesture.[3]

In January a series of developments made it possible to speed up the evacuation of people across Lake Ladoga. Early in the month, the temperature dropped thus increasing the thickness of the lake's ice and allowing the trucks to be driven faster and carry heavier loads. (The trucks that transported the people across the lake to the eastern shore returned to the western shore carrying cargoes of food and other supplies.) More ice roads were also organized for the trucks. In mid-January transshipment points, feeding stations and other facilities were moved closer to the eastern shore of the lake, to the railway stations of Voibokalo and Zhikharevo, thus reducing the length of the truck route considerably (see Map 5). Earlier, on January 11, the State Defense Committee in Moscow ordered the construction of a railway line linking Voibokalo with Lavrovo near the shore of Lake Ladoga, a distance of thirty-six kilometers (22 miles). The rail link would be completed a month later (see Map 5).

On January 22 the State Defense Committee in Moscow ordered the evacuation of 500,000 Leningraders.[4] It placed Aleksei Kosygin in charge of the operation, and under his direction the transportation of evacuees further improved. A number of buses were sent from Moscow. Special medical aid posts were established along the evacuation route where the evacuees could warm themselves and receive medical assistance. The evacuees were taken by train from Leningrad to the western shore of Lake Ladoga and from there they went by vehicle across the ice-covered lake. Upon arrival on the eastern shore of the lake, the evacuees were served soup and other nourishing foods and then taken by train to the eastern regions of the Soviet Union. Many of them would take up residence in the homes of relatives or friends

Even the best trip was not without great danger. Since there were few buses, most evacuees had to travel in the rear of open trucks in temperatures that went down to 40 degrees below zero. Snowstorms that swept over the lake would often cause the drivers of vehicles to lose their way. Many trucks along with their passengers fell through fissures in the ice caused by temperature changes or through holes made by enemy bombardments. The ice roads as well as the transfer points were frequently shelled and strafed by the enemy resulting in the deaths of many evacuees. Despite the many difficulties, the authorities did succeed in evacuating the planned number of people from the city. In January more than 11,000 left, in February more than 117,000 were evacuated and by the end of April more than 550,000 people had been transported across the ice roads.[5]

Each person who was authorized to leave Leningrad was permitted to take 40 to 60 pounds of baggage which the person was required to bring to the railway station.[6] Since there was a weight limit on the amount of baggage that was allowed, the avacuees were forced to leave behind most of their possessions. Many evacuees had little hope of ever recovering their possessions so they tried to sell, for currency, some or all of their belongings before leaving. This could be done on the black market or at official purchasing centers that had been set up for this purpose. At these centers people would sell clothing, furniture, household goods and other items. Before leaving Leningrad, the evacuees were required to turn in their ration cards. They received in exchange special food rations that were to feed them on the trip.

Many people were happy to escape from the city or to have their families removed to a safer place. They dreaded the starvation that killed so many people during the months of November and December. There were also many people who did not want to be evacuated. Ties to their birthplace, loyalty to their city, the feeling of familiarity with their place of habitation and a host of other reasons caused them to prefer to remain in Leningrad regardless of the consequences. Unauthorized evacuation was both difficult and dangerous since it was tantamount to desertion. It took a person of considerable initiative and daring to risk leaving without proper authorization.

POLINA—ORPHAN EVACUEE

Polina Koroteeva was one of many orphans in Leningrad who were evacuated from the city. She became orphaned when her mother died from a heart attack. Her father, who had been drafted into the military, had died less than two weeks earlier. Polina found herself alone except for a baby sister who was less than a year old. There was no one she could turn to in Leningrad because all of her relatives lived outside of the blockaded city. What was she to do? Polina was eventually evacuated from Leningrad and brought by train to the East. The author was introduced to Polina in 1997 in a small village in the Ural region. At that time she shared with him what she witnessed in Leningrad during the blockade and how she was evacuated from the city:

"It was in June 1941, that fascist Germany invaded the Soviet Union and what Soviet citizens called the Great Patriotic War began. I remember the day when the attack on our country was announced. Mother and I had traveled by tram into the center of the city to do some shopping. As we were walking along Sadovaya Street the loud-speakers along the street were turned on. The low voice of the famous announcer Levitan reported that in several minutes there would be an important government statemen. [Yury Levitan was the voice of the State during the Great Patriotic War. He would read the State approved news on the radio.] At midday we heard that our country was at war. I didn't understand completely the significance of the announcement, but mother did. She turned sheet white and became terribly frightened. Other people in the streets were also frightened.

"Mother told me that we must hurry home and take all the money that my parents had saved and use it to buy food. But when we arrived at our neigh-

Polina Koroteeva and her mother

borhood store, there was already a long line of people standing outside of the store. They were talking about the war and how it would affect them. All of them purchased as much food as they could afford because they expected that in the months to come there would be food shortages. Mother and I bought cereals, noodles and flour.

"Several weeks after the war began, father was drafted into the military. He was appointed the leader of a brigade of construction workers that was assigned to rescue people who were buried under the debris of bombed buildings within the city. By this time the fascists were bombing Leningrad. Mother would visit father periodically at the military barracks where he was stationed within the city. She wanted to see father and bring him food.

"Mother would acquire food from abandoned farms along the outskirts of the city. The city trams were still in operation and mother would ride a tram which would take her to the suburbs. She would walk the remainder of the distance to Leningrad's outlying farms and gather potatoes, carrots and cabbages. Traveling to the outskirts of the city was dangerous because the Germans, who were encircling the city, were nearby. However, mother felt that hunger would kill as well as German shells, and she wanted to avoid the grip of starvation.

"Sometime before September 1941, a commission of people came to our home suggesting that I join a large group of children that was to be sent out of the city. They pointed out that the fascists were encircling Leningrad with the intention of starving the citizens into surrendering. If I joined the group of children to be evacuated, my life would be spared from starvation. Mother began to weep and told the commission that she did not want to let me go. The commission replied that she had no choice in the matter; she was ordered to get me ready for my long journey away from the city. Mother did as she was told and began preparing me. The proposed evacuation was not carried out because shortly after the commission came to our home, the fascists blocked off all ways of escape from Leningrad. The siege of the city had begun; it was September 1941.

"During the siege mother and I took part in the defense of Leningrad. We stitched together sacks made of cloth and filled them with sand. Then we carried the sacks to the attic of our building and to the attics of neighboring buildings. The sand was to be used to fight fires that were started by the incendiary bombs dropped by the German airplanes.

"The Germans also hit the city with high explosive bombs and heavy artillery shells. I remember hearing the German airplanes from a distance; the sound they made was different from that made by a Soviet fighter aircraft. As German bombers approached, the people were urged to go to the nearest bomb shelter. Many people did not seek the safety of a bomb shelter for they had seen people buried alive in the shelters. When a high explosive bomb hit a building, it would destroy a large part of it. Many buildings were destroyed, and many people suffered a slow death under the rubble.

"As winter approached it became more difficult to acquire food. The food was rationed out, and I believe every person was allotted 125 grams of bread daily. There were stores throughout the city where the people were to get the bread. Often mother had me get our daily allowance. On the way to the bread station, I would see many terrible sights. Sometimes an artillery shell would explode nearby, and I would see several people fall down dead because of it. I would walk past people who were pulling small sleds carrying their dead loved ones. Sometimes I would see an abandoned sled with a frozen corpse lying on it. Apparently the owner of the sled had become too weak to pull it to the cemetery and simply abandoned it. When I arrived at the bread station there was usually a long line of people. No one talked; everyone just shuffled along, got their daily allowance of bread and slowly made their way home.

"While I was getting bread mother got our daily supply of water. The artillery shells and the bombs had destroyed Leningrad's water pipes so mother would acquire our water from the Griboyedov Canal. Getting water from the canal was a short walk since our apartment was located along the canal. Our apartment consisted of one large room on the fifth floor of a building located near St. Nicholas Cathedral. The canal water, however, was not as fresh as river water and so sometimes mother would walk to the river to get water. Carrying a bucket of water was hard work especially when a person is weakened physically from hunger. Thus, the water brought home was used only for consumption. We didn't use the water to wash our clothes or ourselves. Washing clothes did not enter our minds. We were concerned with staying alive.

"Death took my father in the winter of 1941. Mother returned home from a visit with father one day and expressed her concern about his failing health. She said that he was so weak from hunger that he did not have the strength to stand up. When mother went to see father several days later she was told that he had died. Two days before, his heart had stopped beating; he fell asleep and never awakened. Father was thirty-six years old at the time of his death. Mother was so upset with father's death that nine days later she died.

"Mother died from a heart attack. When she felt it coming she told me to get some medicine from a pharmacist. I went out but couldn't find the medicine mother needed so I headed home back to our cold apartment. When I entered our room mother said that she had considered getting out of bed while I was gone. She decided against it fearing that she would die trying to stand up. She asked me what I would do if she died. I replied that I would lie down next to her and wait to die as well. Mother then stood up and fell to the floor dead. I was now alone with my sister who was just ten months old.

"When the neighbors heard me crying they brought my baby sister and me into their apartment room. They arranged a bed for us and had us sleep together, probably to keep each other warm. The next morning I discovered that my sister had died during the night. She may have died from hunger or maybe I strangled her accidentally by rolling over her small body in my sleep. I will never know how she died. Nevertheless, the neighbors brought my sister's body to a room that was missing one of its walls due to a bomb that had been dropped on the building. The floor of the room was covered with snow and ice and it was on the floor that the neighbors placed my sister next to the dead body of my mother. Here they would remain until a special brigade came to the building in search of corpses that they were to bring to a city cemetery.

"In early February 1942, the neighbors who were taking care of me told me that I was to leave the city. They had been approached by representatives of the city government who had told them about the evacuation of a large group of children. The escape out of the city would be difficult, and the route to be used would be across the ice of Lake Ladoga. I told them I did not want to leave Leningrad because my parents were buried in the city. They were sympathetic with my desire to stay but pointed out that with the coming spring and warm weather, diseases would move through the city killing many people. They explained that since I was already weak from hunger I would probably become a victim of a disease and die. What they said was true, and I began gathering my things and preparing myself for the journey out of and away from Leningrad.

"The journey began on February 9, 1942. In the evening of that day my neighbors brought me to the Finnish Railway Station in Leningrad. There was a train waiting to take me and many other children out of the city. I was lifted into one of the cars that was full of children, and when night came the train began to move forward slowly. At dawn it stopped near a forest and would remain there the entire day. Toward evening, as daylight turned to darkness, the train moved forward again but very slowly. Lake Ladoga is located some sixty kilometers [37 miles] from Leningrad, but, moving only at night, it took the train five days to get to the lake.

"Most of the children on the train including myself suffered from thirst. I tried to satisfy my thirst by getting out of the car when the train was not moving in order to eat the snow along the railroad tracks. The snow was so cold that my hands became numb. I then used my spoon to scoop up the snow, but the spoon became so icy cold that it stuck to my tongue. As I pulled the spoon from my tongue a large piece of my skin came with it. It was painful.

"We arrived at Lake Ladoga in the morning. In the early daylight I could see the ice that covered the lake. The ice extended from our shoreline to the far distant horizon. There we were, a huge crowd of hungry, thirsty, weak children, waiting for the trucks that were supposed to transport us across the ice-covered lake. When the trucks arrived we clambered onto their uncovered beds and began the forty-kilometer [25–mile] trek across the lake. I was wearing a winter coat and a warm shawl, yet I still felt terribly cold. The trip across the lake was uneventful. We did not see any fascist airplanes fly overhead. I was told later that whenever the Germans did see people or vehicles crossing the ice-covered lake they would bomb them or try to drown them by bombing the ice.

"The trucks brought us to the railway station at Zhikharevo [see Map 5]. At the station we were given food. It was delicious. Then we were told to sleep. It was nighttime, and early the next morning a cargo train was supposed to arrive at the station to take us east.

"I could see the front light of the train in the distance as it approached the station early the next morning. Before it stopped we were told to run to the cargo wagons. As we ran, artillery shells began exploding all around us. Shell splinters flew over my head with a high-pitched whistling sound. Some children were struck and fell down dead. Several children turned around and ran back to the station. I continued running toward one of the wagons and pulled myself up and inside. I don't know how I accomplished this; it must have been fear that gave me the strength to do it.

"In the wagon of the cargo train I felt safe. For a while I could still hear German aircraft above us and bombs exploding around us, but that didn't brother me. We had escaped the siege of Leningrad, and I knew that we were being taken out of harm's way. Inside the cargo wagon there were three levels of makeshift wooden beds each covered with straw, and there was a small iron stove, some wood for the stove and some straw with which to start a fire in the stove. After a while the stove was lighted by the women who had arrived with the train to care of us, and soon the inside of the wagon was warm.

"As we traveled east the train would stop at the communities along the way. Residents of these communities would greet us with wood for our stove and with food. In spite of the warmth of the stove and the good food that we were fed, many children died on the train. At almost every station, the bodies of several dead children were carried out of the wagons. I was astonished by this. I couldn't understand why these children had died. They had survived the train trip out of Leningrad and the trip across Lake Ladoga riding in the uncovered beds of the trucks, but now, while eating good food and riding in the warm shelter of a cargo wagon, their bodies gave up and died. These were the thoughts that were running through my mind. I did not express them to anyone. In fact, I did not talk to anyone. I just laid on my straw-covered bed and let the movement of the train lull me to sleep.

"After several days of travel we arrived at Vologda. Here we were given a good hot meal and were brought to a bathhouse to bathe. Following our bath we were addressed by three people who told us that the train was going to take us to the Ural region. They listed the names of the communities where we would be stopping along the way. They said that if we had relatives that lived near these communities we might want to get off the train and take up residence with those relatives. One of the towns that they listed was Michurinsk. I remembered that my grandfather had brought his wheat to Michurinsk to sell at the local market. I didn't know how far away my grandparents' village, Tarakanovka, was from Michurinsk, but I decided that I would get off the train at the Michurinsk railway station.

"It was night when the train stopped at Michurinsk. I was fast asleep and later, when I awakened, I discovered that the train was approaching Griasy, two railway stations beyond Michurinsk. I had slept through my stop. In Griasy we were fed breakfast, but I was still hungry and decided to walk to the local market to buy some more food. I asked someone at the railway station to look after my suitcase and then headed for the local market. At the market I bought some pickled cucumbers and then walked back to the railway station. By the time I arrived at the station the pickled cucumbers had made me sick and had given me diarrhea. The chief at the railway station advised me to go to the local hospital. I begged him to bring me to the railway station of Izberdei, a community located between Michurinsk and Griasy. I had been told that the train had stopped at Izberdei, and I knew that the station at Izberdei was located near my grandparents' village. The chief of the railway station must have felt sorry for me because he ordered a man who worked at the station to bring me to the railway station at Izberdei. He also gave me some medicine for my diarrhea.

"There were many people at the railway station of Izberdei. When I arrived, a crowd of people gathered around me. I was as thin as a rake and looked wretched and pale, and I must have peaked the curiosity of the people because they asked me many questions. They asked me where I was from. I told them that I had come from Leningrad. People throughout the land knew very little about the siege, and the crowd wanted me to tell them about it. I described the fascist air attacks and the artillery bombardments. I talked about the terrible hunger and the corpses of people in the streets. I told the crowd about my parents' deaths and the death of my baby sister. The stories were heartbreaking, and most of my listeners broke down and wept.

"Suddenly there appeared a man asking who it was that needed to be brought to the village of Tarakanovka. I told him that my grandparents lived there and that I would very much appreciate a ride to my grandparents' house. The man knew my grandfather and told me that he would gladly take me to the village. He lifted me onto his sledge, covered me with a large sheepskin coat and commanded his horse to begin pulling. Tarakanovka was located some forty-five kilometers [28 miles] from the railway station, and on the way the man told me that my grandfather was living with his brother. Just before we arrived in Tarakanovka we stopped at my aunt's house. She was happy to see me but became terribly sad when I told her that my parents had died. She urged me not to tell anyone that my parents had died. She was afraid that if my grandfather learned about my parents' death he would go into shock and die as well.

"Grandfather was happy to see me. When he realized that I was too weak physically to climb the steps of the house porch, he took me in his arms and carried me into the house. He was astonished with how little I weighed. He laid me down on the warm Russian stove and gave me something to eat and

Evacuation of Children drawn by Elena Martilla in 1942

drink; the drink contained a medicinal grass extract. As I ate, grandfather asked me many questions about Leningrad and the siege.

"It was my aunt who would tell my grandfather that my parents were dead. She did this about a month after I arrived in the village. Grandfather was shocked and became upset. He became so upset that he died from sorrow just three months later. He was just sixty-three years old when he died. Once again I was alone. I had lost my parents, and now I lost my grandfather."

TAMARA—EVACUATION BY DECEPTION

Tamara Kouznetzova was given the opportunity to leave Leningrad in the autumn of 1941. The officials responsible for recruiting people for evacuation had contacted Tamara shortly after the blockade had been established. They had told her that since her husband was an officer fighting to defend Leningrad along the front line, she was being offered the opportunity along with her young son and daughter to leave the city. Tamara told the recruiters that she did not want to leave. She was afraid that if they left the city they would lose their apartment and all of the personal possessions that they could not take along. No, she would stay in the city. Tamara would regret the decision she made in the autumn of 1941, and more than sixty years later she would share with the author and a friend how, through deception, she got her children and herself out of Leningrad.

When starvation in the city began to take the lives of thousands of people Tamara decided it was necessary to leave the city. If she did not, her children might die. She began a search for some kind of escape and eventually located a military sub-unit that was going to leave the city using a convoy of trucks. The sergeant major of the sub-unit agreed to help her. He had talked with Tamara for quite some time and during their conversation offered to introduce Tamara to the chief of the convoy the next day. Tamara promised she would return.

The following morning the chief of the convoy, a young lieutenant, agreed to take Tamara across Lake Ladoga. He warned her that they would be leaving soon and that she would have to hurry home and get her documents and luggage. He could not be delayed. Tamara knew that she was beautiful and that she looked young for her age, and she noticed that the young lieutenant was attracted to her. He did not know, however, that she was married and that she was the mother of two children. She decided not to tell him.

The apartment was a distance away and Tamara realized that if she did not find someone to drive her home she would miss her second opportunity to leave the city. She ran from street to street looking for a vehicle until she found a parked truck. The driver inside told her that he was too busy to take her; he could not take her. When Tamara offered to give him her bread ration cards for the remainder of the month and promised to give him her husband's new military uniform, the driver told her to get in.

At the apartment Tamara quickly clothed her children and packed some luggage. Before leaving the apartment she went to visit the neighbor lady who was suffering from tuberculosis. Tamara wanted to say good-bye and give her neighbor the remainder of her firewood. The neighbor was very grateful. After saying good-bye there was a scramble down the staircase to the street below where the truck driver was waiting for Tamara and the new uniform that he had been promised. Tamara told him that they had to hurry; she was afraid that they were going to be late. The driver pushed down hard on the accelerator and through the snowy streets of the city they flew.

Upon their arrival the young lieutenant was waiting for them, and the military trucks were parked and ready to leave. He seemed anxious. He remarked that they had been waiting for her. Tamara could tell, however, that he was happy to see her. He asked her about the two children who were holding her hands. She told him that they were not hers. The mother of the boy and girl, she explained (lied), was supervising the children of an orphanage that were being evacuated and the mother had been denied permission to take her own children. Before leaving, the mother had asked Tamara to take care of her children. Tamara had promised the mother that she would, and she would not break her promise; the children must come along.

The young lieutenant said that Tamara was too young to be taking care of two children. It would be much too difficult for her. Tamara insisted that the children must come along and pointed out that it would be much easier to care for the children on the mainland than in Leningrad. The young lieutenant did not want to discuss the matter any longer; it was time to leave and he told Tamara and the children to get into the cabin of one of the trucks. The evacuation from the city had begun.

Their first stop was along the western shore of Lake Ladoga to refuel the trucks. At that time the young lieutenant approached Tamara to inform her that only a short while ago an entire convoy of trucks had fallen through the ice and sunk to the bottom of the lake. The news was shocking. Tamara could still get out of the truck and take her children back to the city, but she decided that living in Leningrad was more dangerous than crossing the lake. If she returned it would mean that she would have to stand in long lines at the bread store everyday. At any moment an enemy bomb or shell could kill her and cause her children to become orphans. If her children should be killed then she would be alone, and the thought of that possibility made her shudder. It was better to die together.

After they reached the opposite shore of the lake the young lieutenant brought Tamara and her children to the barrack of the military sub-unit located along the shoreline. He informed the men at the barrack that Tamara was from Leningrad and that for the past couple of months she had suffered terribly. The men expressed their sympathy and immediately gathered large amounts of food for her and the children. Tamara had not seen this much food since before the blockade. She was truly grateful. She was also keenly aware that she was living a lie. She guessed that the young lieutenant had brought her with him because he believed that she was unmarried. Tamara assumed that he would want her to become his wife.

In the evening the young lieutenant informed Tamara that the convoy of trucks would be leaving that night, and she should be ready to leave. Tamara told him that she would not be going with him. She explained that her grandmother lived in a village not far from Saratov on the Volga River, and she and the two children would travel to Saratov and live with her granny. Tamara then told the young lieutenant that the children were hers and not somebody else's. The officer looked at Tamara with disbelief. How could this be possible? He turned to the boy and girl and asked them to tell him who their mother was. Both pointed to Tamara. The young lieutenant was dumbfounded. He realized that Tamara had deceived him in order to get her children out of the city and to the mainland. He then turned to Tamara and told her that it did not matter. "I shall take you with your children." Tamara refused. She insisted that she must go and live with her granny. She thanked him for all that he had done for her and assured him that she would never forget how he had helped her in a time of need. It was an awkward situation, but finally the young lieutenant accepted the wishes of Tamara and left. Tamara would not see him again.[7]

NOTES

1. A.V. Karasev, Leningradtsy v gody blokady (Moscow: Izdatelstre Adademii Nauk SSSR, 1959), 199.

2. Leon Goure, The Siege of Leningrad (Stanford, California: Stanford University Press, 1962), 236–37.

3. Nikita Lomagin, The Unknown Blockade (Moscow: Hower Institution on War, Revolution and Peace, 2002), 265.

4. Goure, The Siege of Leningrad, 237.

5. Goure, The Siege of Leningrad, 239.

6. Goure, The Siege of Leningrad, 237.

7. A.V. Vinogradov and A. Pleysier, Bitva za Leningrad v sud bakh zhitelei goroda I oblasti: vospominauiiya zashchitnikov I zhitelei blockadnogo goroda I okkupirovan-nykh territorii (Saint Petersburg, Russia: Saint Petersburg State University Press, 2005), 160–66.

Chapter Fourteen

Increasing the Food Supply

As spring approached, Leningrad's authorities knew that the transport of food and other supplies into the city would soon be interrupted. The sun and warmth would cause the ice covering Lake Ladoga to thaw, and eventually it would not be able to bear the weight of the supply trucks. At the same time the breakup of the ice would create large ice floats which would hinder the use of barges pulled by tugs. The city authorities foresaw this development and so before the warmth of spring weakened the ice of the lake they decided that the railway line that ran from Tikhvin to Voibokalo to Lavrovo should be extended some thirty kilometers (18 miles) to the village of Kabona (see Map 5). The railway was extended and thereafter freight trains coming from the mainland could transport their cargo right up to the lake where the supplies were placed on trucks. By shortening each round trip by sixty kilometers (37 miles) it was possible for a driver to make more round trips in one day, and as a result the deliveries of supplies to Osinovets increased.

The ice covering Lake Ladoga began to melt in the last days of March 1942. Numerous wooden bridges were hastily placed over the widening cracks in the ice. The crumbling of the ice and the flooding of the ice roads caused many accidents. On April 15 heavy trucks were barred from the ice roads and only light trucks with continually decreasing loads of supplies crossed the lake. Six days later, on April 21, the Military Council of the Leningrad Front made the decision that after 12 P.M. on that day trucks were no longer to cross the ice roads. In spite of the order, trucks were used on April 23 to deliver sixty-four tons of onions across the lake. It was to be the last freight of food delivered across the ice roads. After the trucks had traveled five kilometers (3 miles) the drivers were forced to stop for fear that the thinning ice was not thick enough to hold them. The sacks of onions were lifted out of the trucks and placed in carts that were pulled by horses. The horses moved the freight of onions another twenty-six kilometers (16 miles). Thereafter, the sacks of onions were placed on the shoulders of men who carried them the remainder of the way. In the last kilometer, the men walked through water that came up to their waist. By this time there was enough food in Leningrad's warehouses to feed the people until the spring thaw was complete. Thereafter, Lake Ladoga could be used for water transport.

The organization of a water transportation system on Lake Ladoga had been given careful thought by Leningrad's city authorities. A major problem was the shortage of water vessels. To obtain sufficient shipping capacity, the authorities arranged for the transfer to Lake Ladoga from the Gulf of Finland a number of fishing motorboats and river steamers. Most of them were moved to the lake by railroad. Leningrad's shipyards were ordered to build eleven metal barges with a freight capacity of 600 tons each. These were also brought to the lake by railroad. Thirty-one wooden barges with a freight capacity of 385 tons each were built at Syas'stroy. At the same time improvements were made to the harbors at Osinovets and Kabona as well as to the storage facilities at both harbors. Finally, it was decided that the defense of the water transportation system was to be the responsibility of the Ladoga Naval Flotilla. (The defense of the ice roads had been the responsibility of the Red Army.)

Leningrad's leadership planned to transport daily across Lake Ladoga and into the city 4,200 tons of supplies and to evacuate daily from the city 1,000 tons of freight. There were two routes across the lake: the short route from Osinovets to Kabona was twenty-nine kilometers (18 miles) in length and the route from Osinovets to Novaya Ladoga was 150 kilometers (93 miles) long (see Maps 4 and 5).[1] On May 22, 1942, almost a month after the ice roads became inoperative, the first boat with supplies arrived along the west shore of the lake. The initial daily transport of food and supplies fell short of the plan because the ice on the lake was not completely gone. However, the volume of supplies that was moved daily increased from 1,500 tons in May to 3,500 tons by the end of June. The success of the water transportation system helped prepare the city for the upcoming winter.

The Germans tried to stop the flow of transports across Lake Ladoga by subjecting the shipping and harbors to intensive bombardments. On May 28 a large number of German aircraft participated in a massive raid. Five groups of nine to fifteen bombers, each protected by fighters, tried to strike the loading bay at Kabona from various directions. The first group was intercepted by Soviet fighters, and after the Germans lost one of its bombers the group turned back. Thereafter, the other groups of bombers appeared, one after another. Engaging these groups, the Soviet fighters shot down twelve of the enemy aircraft. On the following day the Germans conducted another massive air raid, and in the afternoon there were two more raids.[2]

At the same time, a large proportion of Leningrad's remaining population was being evacuated across Lake Ladoga by boat. On the nineteenth of April the Military Council of the Leningrad Front directed that 3,000 people were to be evacuated daily from the city. Women with two or more children, persons living on pensions, invalids, trade-school students, orphans, students, teachers, artists and other people in similar categories were evacuated on a compulsory basis. From May 27 to July 31 the number of Leningraders evacuated was 338,545.[3] In July it was announced that 1,100,000 people still remained in the city and that the decision had been made to reduce the population to 800,000 by evacuating a further 300,000 nonessential residents. The mass evacuation, it was announced, was to be completed by August 15 and was to proceed at an average rate of 10,000 persons daily. The actual rate of evacuation fell short of the goal; between August 7 and August 15, for example, only 46,000 people were evacuated. Nevertheless, by reducing the size of the city's population, the authorities could increase the daily allotment of food to each of the remaining inhabitants.

Earlier, in January, Leningrad's leaders received a report drafted by P.P. Kuze and V.A. Brizgalov, two professors at the Agricultural University. They had calculated that if potatoes and other vegetables were to be planted in the gardens, parks, backyards and vacant lots within Leningrad and in the suburbs of the city, enough food could be produced to feed 1,500,000 people. The report was taken seriously and the city's leaders set aside more than 17,000 acres of land for vegetable gardens. The city's industries were ordered to produce 35,000 spades, 25,000 hoes and 50,000 rakes. Nearly six tons of seeds were brought into the city and were sold to the people and to the workers in factories and other institutions who decided to participate in the gardening program.[4] People who were unfamiliar with gardening were given lectures on the subject. In time, vegetables could be seen growing throughout the city. There were cabbage beds around the sandbagged Bronze Horseman and garden plots in the Summer Garden. The penalty for stealing vegetables from private garden plots was a five-year prison sentence.[5] Many people who participated in the program failed to grow as much as what they had hoped, yet the vegetables they did grow enriched their diet and provided them with increased vitality.

To further increase the production of food, the city's leadership expanded the cultivation of vegetables and rye on the collective farms in the areas around the city. The cultivation of the farmlands was done by thousands of Komsomol members. The authorities also mobilized thousands of school children and brought them to the farms to work. At harvest time the authorities drafted over

10,000 Leningraders to gather in the food.[6] It was decided that the largest part of the harvest was to be used by the soldiers defending the city and by official organizations. A portion of it was set aside to feed the citizens.

Despite the increase in the quantity and quality of food, the death rate in Leningrad continued to rise. From March through July dystrophy continued to predominate in the city, and many thousands died every day from its effects. According to official figures almost 90,000 people were buried in March and more than 100,000 in April. Of those who were evacuated from the city during these months, many died in route. At the same time a large percentage of the living suffered from complete exhaustion, and many experienced the advanced stages of scurvy.

To help cure and prevent the outbreaks of scurvy, hundreds of women and school children were sent into the forests to gather pine needles. It was believed that pine-needle tea would counteract the effects of a vitamin C deficiency. The pine needles were chopped up in machines that had been used to shred cabbage. Vinegar was added to the infusion and then it was filtered. According to Professor Moshansky, head of the Leningrad Health Department, "there wasn't a factory canteen, a school, a government office — in fact there was hardly a place in Leningrad where there weren't buckets of this liquid, and everybody was urged to drink of it. . . . It didn't taste particularly good, but people drank gallons and gallons of it, as a sort of duty to themselves and to the common cause!" [7] In addition, the people gathered and ate wild sorrel, grass and nettles, all of which helped to counter the effects of scurvy.

NOTES

1. Nikolai Kislitsyn and Vassily Zubakov, Leningrad Does Not Surrender, trans. Barry Jones (Moscow: Progress Publishers, 1989), 152.

2. Kislitsyn and Zubakov, Leningrad Does Not Surrender, 152–53.

3. Leon Goure, The Siege of Leningrad (Stanford, California: Stanford University Press, 1962), 285.

4. Kislitsyn and Zubakov, Leningrad Does Not Surrender, 136.

5. Goure, The Siege of Leningrad, 261.

6. Goure, The Siege of Leningrad, 261.

7. Alexander Werth, Leningrad (London: Hamish Hamilton, 1944), 163.

Chapter Fifteen

Indomitable Leningraders

There was an attitude in the city that while the battle for Leningrad was just one of many battles being fought by the Soviet people, Leningrad's struggle was unique. Like all survivors of a battle or a disaster, the Leningraders felt that what they had shared in the preceding winter set them apart from other people. They were proud that they had survived the winter siege and saw their deeds in a heroic light. They believed that their city continued to survive because they, its people, had demonstrated an unwillingness to surrender. Having survived the winter, the Leningraders were determined to further safeguard themselves and secure their city.

The citizens' indomitable attitude was expressed by a sixteen-year-old girl named Valentina Solovyova in an essay written for her teacher during the blockade. She wrote:

June 22 [1941]! How much that date means to us now! But then it just seemed an ordinary summer day. . . . By September the city was encircled. Food supplies from outside had stopped. The last evacuee trains had departed. The people of Leningrad tightened their belts. The streets began to bristle with barricades and anti-tank hedgehogs. Dugouts and firing points—a whole network of them—were springing up around the city.

As in 1919, so now, the great question arose: "Shall Leningrad remain a Soviet city or not?" Leningrad was in danger. But its workers had risen like one man for its defense. Tanks were thundering down the streets. Everywhere men of the civil guard were joining up. . . . A cold and terrible winter was approaching. Together with their bombs, enemy airplanes were dropping leaflets. They [the Germans] said they would raze Leningrad to the ground. They said we would all die from hunger. They thought they would frighten us, but they filled us with renewed strength. . . . Leningrad did not let the enemy through its gates! The city was starving, but it lived and worked, and kept on sending to the front more of its sons and daughters. Though knocking at the knees with hunger, our workers went to work in their factories, with the air-raid sirens filling the air with their screams. . .[1]

The arrival of spring would bring new challenges for the people of Leningrad. It was feared, for example, that the warm-weather temperatures would produce an outbreak of diseases. One Leningrad woman had expressed this fear in a letter that she addressed to her husband earlier in February. The woman was convinced that she would not survive the plagues that she believed would stalk the city. She wrote:

Dear Pavlick,

How are you and how is your health? In your last letter you wrote that you are getting horsemeat. Well, that is not bad at all—we envy you. . . . Things are worse for us, but they have promised us that the situation will be better shortly. We shall wait. A small glimmering is noticeable. We already receive 300 grams of bread. I have already written you that mother died. . . . Pavlick, I sometimes feel so hopeless that at night when I go to sleep I ask myself whether I will be able to get up the next morning. I am very weak. You cannot imagine how I look—only skin and bones, a living skeleton. I think now that we are going to receive food that we might not die of hunger after all, but the organism is so weak that it is susceptible to every illness, and I therefore expect various plagues such as cholera and typhus in spring and I am sure I shall be among the first to fall ill from something. It would be best therefore to leave Leningrad now. . . . Pavlick, can't you arrange this for me? Pavlick, it seems to me now that I would give anything just not to be here. It's true that there is no knowing in advance whether the food situation might not be worse where one is sent than here, but I think that there one can buy—at least for a lot of money—lots of potatoes. . . .

These are all dreams. I think I will soon join mama.[2]

Hoping to avoid an epidemic, the city authorities issued a decree ordering the mobilization of every able bodied person to work on the city's clean up. All men between the ages of fifteen and sixty and all women between fifteen and fifty-five were ordered to clean the city. People who worked a full-day shift were required to extend each of their workdays with two hours of clean up work. People who worked short-hour days were expected to contribute eight hours a day toward the clean up effort. Housewives and students were ordered to contribute six hours of labor a day toward cleaning up the city. Everyone had to carry papers certifying that they had completed their daily required contribution. Newspapers, posters and public-address announcements warned that persons who avoided doing their civic duty violated the rules of socialist community life and were parasites that were helping the enemy. A person who was found guilty of being a parasite in a civil court was forced to pay a fine. People who could prove that they had done more than what was required of them were rewarded with a visit to a public steam bath. More than twenty bathhouses were reopened in March and were available only to people who were medically certified as being dangerously dirty. The massive clean up which began at the end of March would last until the middle of April. More than a million tons of snow, ice and refuse were removed on sheets of plywood, in baskets, on sledges and in trolleys from the city's streets, alleys, yards, squares, staircases, cellars and sewer wells. All of this was done with the simplest of hand tools and by people who were weak from starvation.[3]

The fuel needs of Leningrad's industrial enterprises, hospitals, schools and citizens for the upcoming winter were also addressed. A peat digging campaign was organized. It was hoped that a daily quota of 8,500 tons of peat would be harvested from the peat bogs around the city. Wood gathering parties were recruited and organized and sent to the wooded areas around Leningrad to cut down trees for firewood. Each enterprise and factory sent a lumber-cutting crew composed of its own employees. The task of cutting down trees was very difficult especially since most of the workers were weak from starvation. Aleksei Kuznetsov, Secretary of the Leningrad Regional Party Committee and a member of the Military Council of the Leningrad Front, reported: "Three thousand Leningrad workers, the overwhelming majority of them women, took up saws and axes and went off to cut firewood. Under difficult conditions, with insufficient housing and food, the workers stubbornly learned the profession of lumberjack." [4]

When it became evident that the supplies of firewood and peat were insufficient, it was decided that additional fuel would be acquired by tearing down wooden buildings within the city. The undertaking would require the mobilization of all able-bodied people for an entire month. People who were employed were expected to work on this endeavor during their free time and on their days of rest. The unemployed were to be organized into work brigades by the administrators of housing buildings. Each person was supposed to gather no less than four cubic meters (5.2 cubic yards) of firewood of which two cubic meters (2.6 cubic yards) were to be kept by the person for private use. The wooden houses that were to be torn down would be identified, marked and listed by the authorities. The wood was to be transported by hand and later by freight trams which went into operation in March. In the end, some 9,000 wooden structures were demolished and cut up for firewood, but the results fell far short of the total needs.

Electric power was gradually restored. In February the Military Council of the Leningrad Front decided to organize the importation of coal into the city by way of Lake Ladoga. Some 200 trucks were sent from Moscow and Gorki for the sole purpose of carrying coal to Leningrad. In two months 25,000 tons of coal were brought into the city to fuel the city's electric power stations.[5] One of the immediate results was the partial revival of streetcar service. The Volkhov hydroelectric station was rebuilt to provide Leningrad with power. After the Germans were pushed back from Volkhov, earlier in December 1941, it became possible to rebuild the Volkhov hydroelectric station, which had been dismantled in October 1941 (see Map 5). Toward the end of January 1942 the Elektrosila Works in Leningrad received orders to assist in the reconstruction of the station and to send to Volkhov a number of skilled workers and engineers. The generators that had been removed to the east in October of 1941 were brought back in February 1942. However, the station did not begin to provide electric power to Leningrad until the fall. An underwater cable across Lake Ladoga brought the electricity from the Volkhov hydroelectric plant to Leningrad.[6]

On April 2, 1942, plans were approved in Moscow for the construction of a fuel pipeline across the bottom of Lake Ladoga. Eighteen days later steel pipes that were 101 mm (3.9 inches) in diameter were found in the warehouses of the Izhorsky Works. Hundreds of persons, both military people and civilians, worked on the construction of the pipeline which was completed on June 14. Four days later the pipeline went into service and would provide Leningrad with 300 to 350 tons of liquid fuel daily. By November the pipeline had brought into Leningrad 47,000 tons of liquid fuel which included aviation kerosene for Soviet aircraft, gasoline for trucks and other vehicles and diesel fuel for tanks.

Intensive efforts were made to get the sewage and water systems operational again. As the warm weather thawed out the frozen sewage and water pipes, it was discovered that numerous pipes in both systems were broken due to enemy bombardment and freezing temperatures. The sewage pipes had to be repaired or replaced so that the people's refuse would no longer have to be thrown into the streets or yards as had been done during the winter. Repairs were made to numerous water pipes, and with the availability of electric power the water-pumping stations resumed their operations. The plan was to create enough water pressure to provide running water up to the third floor of the city's apartment houses. If that could be achieved then the Leningraders would no longer have to obtain their water from the city's rivers and canals. The supply of water to the population did improve slowly throughout the summer.

Repairs to housing in preparation for another winter of siege began in the summer. Damage to houses caused by enemy bombardment and artillery shelling was extensive. The majority of the houses had damaged roofs and broken windows. Many buildings that were still in use had shell holes.

Leningrad's dwelling places needed to be winterized. On August 11 the city's leadership published in the local press a lengthy article which gave detailed and technical instructions to the readers on how to prepare their houses for the winter. It said that windows should be boarded up, and it suggested that newspapers be wrapped around water pipes. The city's inhabitants were ordered to keep their kitchens heated to prevent the freezing of water pipes. All tenants living in the upper floors of apartment houses were required to move into empty apartments on the lowest three floors. This was done to prevent the freezing of water and sewage pipes in the bottom three floors. No temporary stoves were to be installed in apartments without the inspection and approval of the fire department. The homemade stoves of the preceding year had been responsible for many fires. In October 1942, it was announced that the campaign to winterize the city's houses had been a success: 872,900 square feet of roofing and 48,064 stoves had been repaired, 220,000 chimneys had been cleaned, nearly 6,000,000 square feet of windows had been glassed or covered with plywood and 490 kilometers (304 miles) of water pipes had been insulated. In all 6,131 buildings had been completely prepared for winter. The authorities had ordered industry within the city to assist the population in this undertaking by providing tools, manufactured goods and skilled labor.[7]

Leningrad's industries would continue producing following the winter of starvation, but their output was limited. Officially, fifty factories that had been closed were reopened in April, seven more in May and eighteen in June. Shortages of raw material and fuel were so severe that production could be conducted only on a small scale. Due to evacuations and deaths many factories had only a few hundred workers instead of the thousands who had worked there earlier. The Kirov Works, which began its operations in April, was very representative. Prior to the war it had manufactured tanks, turbines, guns and tractors. Now it repaired tanks and the diesel engines for both tanks and airplanes. Its main production was munitions, small arms, shells and mortar mines. Practically all the equipment used to make the tanks and turbines was moved east in the summer of 1942, and most of the skilled workers had been evacuated earlier by air to organize the production of tanks in Cheliabinsk. The evacuations, the enlistment of thousands of its workers in the People's Volunteer Army and the loss of workers due to death by starvation and enemy bombardment reduced the Kirov work force from more than 30,000 to about 2,000. Of these workers 69 percent were women and most had not worked at the plant before the war.[8]

Alexander Fadeyev, a Soviet author, visited the Kirov Works after he was flown into Leningrad in April. During the visit, Fadeyev was given a tour of the shop where mortar mines were being produced. He would later describe how he observed with great admiration the female employees who worked in the shop:

> In one of the bays of the shop a group of women were standing at enormous milling machines, milling mines, scattering sparks in all directions. There were stacks of mines, still hot from the moulds, on the floor near them. I stopped next to one of the women. Her face was visible only in profile. A dark kerchief was drawn low over her brow, and I could not guess her age. With her hands, protected by huge gauntlets, she picked up a mine from the heap and then, using the whole weight of her body, held it against the rapidly revolving wheel of the machine. A sheaf of sparks flew around her . . . she picked up mine after mine and pressed them with all the force of her body against the wheel. . . . to do this involved a very considerable physical strain, for the woman's whole body quivered with the effort.
>
> I wanted to see the woman's face and I remained where I was until she turned toward me. She seemed to be a woman of about forty. Her face had a strange beauty. Delicate and stern of feature, it was the face of a saint.
>
> "Is it hard work?" I asked.
>
> "Yes, at first it was very hard," she said, picking up a mine and holding it against the revolving wheel, making the sparks fly once more.
>
> "Where is your husband?" I asked after a brief interval, during which she put the mine down and picked up another.
>
> "He died last winter."
>
> I did not ask of what he had died. I had no need to.[9]

On the day of his tour of the Kirov Works, Fadeyev was invited to arrange a literary evening for the workers of the factory. The readings were to be held in the basement room of one of the buildings. It was a room that was designed to hold seven hundred people, but that evening when Nikolai Tikhonov began his reading there were more than seven hundred workers seated and standing in the room. Everybody knew Tikhonov. He was a native of Leningrad, and month after month since the beginning of the war he had reported to the national press the daily life of Leningrad. Tikhonov read *Kirov is with Us*, a poem that he had written in the confines of a freezing room that was lit by a tiny oil lamp during the winter of starvation.

The main character in the poem is Sergei Kirov. He was much loved by the people at the Kirov Works. Before his assassination, on December 1, 1934, he was the chief of the Leningrad Communist Party. He was widely considered the Soviet Union's second most influential man politically; he was Stalin's right-hand man and many believed that he would be Stalin's successor. He was energetic, good natured and approachable, and he enjoyed immense popularity. For years following Kirov's assassination, many people in Leningrad observed December 1 as a day of mourning, and several buildings and places in Leningrad were given the name Kirov in his memory.

In Tikhonov's poem Kirov walks throughout the blockaded city of Leningrad making sure that his city is safe and secure. It is nighttime and it is bitter cold:

> Broken are the walls of the houses,
> Gaping wide are the ruined arches;
> In the iron nights of Leningrad
> Kirov walks the city.
> The warrior spirit, dark and frowning,
> Silently walks the city.
> The hour is late, the skies foreboding and frozen;
> Grim like a fortress frowns the factory.

The poem continues with Kirov entering the factory that bears his name:

> Here men work without ceasing,
> Rest and sleep forgotten;
> Burdened and laboring with dread,
> They wipe the sweat from their brows.
> Let the scarlet flag of a shell
> Blaze as it will in our factory –
> We shall work for conscience' sake
> Fear and weariness banished.
> Let a moment's fear hold us spellbound –
> Always a greybeard will arise and speak to us.
> Hear what this grandsire says,
> Listen to his matchless words:
> Let our soup be no more than mere water,
> Let our bread be of more worth than gold;
> Like men of steel we will hold out.
> Afterwards, afterwards we will be tired.
> The enemy seeks to conquer by force,
> To take us by hunger,
> To take Leningrad from Russia,
> To lead the people of Leningrad into captivity.
> Never in centuries will that come to pass
> On the sacred banks of Neva.
> Rather the toiling people of Russia will perish
> Than yield to the enemy.
> With hammer-blows we will forge the front anew,
> We will break the enemy's iron ring,
> Not for nothing does our stern factory
> Proudly bear the name of Kirov.

As Tikhonov read the lines that he had penned, tears trickled down the faces of the workers, both men and women. At the end of the reading

Tikhonov was given a great ovation and the poet was called upon to read again and again.[10]

Outside, in the entrance courtyard to the Kirov Works stood a huge memorial to Sergei Kirov. When Fadeyev left the factory after the evening of readings he walked past the free standing statue and later would describe it with these words:

> Wearing a leather cap, he stood in a firm pose on powerful legs, one hand freely drawn away from his body in an orator's wide gesture, a manly, confident smile on his strong, broad, Russian face. The wide-flung skirts of his coat had been pitted by shell fragments which had also left their marks over his mighty frame. But he stood there with outstretched arm, his gesture was a summons to battle, with the confident and fascinating smile of a strong and simple being. He would not be killed now, as he was on December 1, 1934, because Kirov, like the work for which he fought, is immortal.[11]

During Fadeyev's visit to Leningrad the Germans attempted to destroy the ships of the Soviet Baltic Fleet that were iced up in the mouth of the Neva River. Earlier, in November 1941, the ships were brought here to strengthen Leningrad's internal defenses. German aircraft had tried frequently to get through to the city from the direction of the Gulf of Finland but the anti-aircraft guns on the Soviet ships had forced them back. The Germans wanted to quiet these guns with what they called Operation "Eistoss" (Iceroar). The Germans made their first attack on April 4. One hundred bombers escorted by German fighters tried to get through to the Soviet Baltic Fleet ships. They were met by Soviet fighters and an intense barrage of fire from anti-aircraft artillery. Fewer than sixty bombers were able to get through and drop their loads, and only one ship was damaged. The Germans lost on this failed raid more than twenty aircraft. A second attempt was made that night by eighteen German bombers. Only three of the airplanes succeeded in getting past the curtain of fire coming from the anti-aircraft defense forces, and the bombs that were dropped did not hit their targets. Late in April, four more air raids were conducted against the ships. Two cruisers and two destroyers suffered damage, but during the raids the Germans lost another sixty airplanes. Thereafter, Operation "Eistoss" was ended.[12]

In April the Germans also intensified their shelling bombardment of Leningrad. Fadeyev, while walking along the streets of the city, witnessed the artillery shelling of a residential section. In his writings he described the results of the bombardment:

> I saw that the shells had fallen in the depth of [Proletarian Victory] Prospect, not in the street itself but somewhere in the neighborhood of the Eleventh Line. . . .

Something was burning thereabouts, and black smoke was rising to the sky. Along the Prospect movement had ceased. But the people had not hidden themselves; they simply stood against the walls of the houses or under porches or in gateways, waiting until the gunfire should cease.

From the gate of one of the nearby buildings came a group of girls in white overalls and kerchiefs, carrying bags marked with a red cross. Two of them bore an empty stretcher. I went along with the girls.

We passed fresh traces of destruction. One shell had fallen on the Prospect itself in the district of the Eleventh Line, shattering the pavement. Shell fragments had burst the windows and struck the wall of a building on one side of the Prospect, but since there were no signs of activity inside the building or close by it, it must have been empty.

We went on a little farther, and . . . saw a group of people clustered around something on the pavement. The girls ran in that direction, and I ran after them. A heavy-caliber shell had fallen here, shattering the pavement and the lower part of a building. The pavement was strewn with fragments of stone and brick and mortar.

A shell fragment gleamed amidst a pile of rubble. I picked it up; it was still warm.

On the pavement lay an elderly, gaunt woman. Her hand grasped very tightly a string bag in which a loaf of bread, the tail of a herring protruding from a piece of newspaper and some white paper bags were visible. There were bloodstains on her coat near the hip and shoulder. But she had been killed by a fragment of shell which struck her in the head. A crimson pool of blood, dazzling in the sunlight, had formed on the asphalt.

"There is nothing we can do here that is any good," one of the first aid girls said quickly.

"All the same we will have to take her away," said the senior girl.

She quickly bent over the woman and, taking care not to get stained with blood, began to examine the pocket of the woman's coat.

"Here is her passport and money. Zina, find her address and take the food there and tell the people in the house. . . . Where are her ration cards?" she said to herself. She unbuttoned the woman's blouse, slipped a finger into the bodice and drew out a soiled bread card and a provisions card. "Well, here they are, thank heaven. We will return the cards. Just imagine how dreadful it would be if the family had to go without their ration cards."[13]

A lost or stolen ration card meant almost certain death to its owner. Before the authorities would agree to replace a lost card, an investigation was conducted. It was usually a lengthy procedure, and during this time the owner of the lost card did not receive the daily ration of bread. Lydia Okhapkina found herself in this situation. She was a mother of two children and her husband was a soldier along Leningrad's front line. Two of the three ration cards that had been issued to Lydia and her children were lost one morning, and Lydia knew that without them she and her children would starve to death. She wrote: "Oppressive thoughts of death kept pursuing me. I was almost driven crazy by grief and the thoughts going through my head. . . . I got out of bed and throwing myself down on my knees started to pray, praying and crying at the same time. I hadn't any icons, and I didn't know any prayers anyhow. My children hadn't been christened, and I didn't believe in God myself. True, I would repeat to myself: 'Save us, God, don't let us die during an air raid.' But this time I had a different appeal to God, different words to say. I fervently whispered: 'God, you can see how I'm suffering, how hungry my little children and I are. I can't go on anymore. God, I'm asking you for death, but for us all to die together. I can't live anymore. You can see how I'm suffering. Have mercy, God, on these innocent children — and suchlike phrases."

"The next day I heard someone banging on the front door. . . . I rushed to ask who it was. A male voice inquired if Lydia Okhapkina lived here. I let him in. He had come from the front, from my husband. He handed me a small package and a letter. Vasya [Lydia's husband] wrote 'Dearest Lida.' Having read just those two words, I burst into tears and said: 'If he could only see what had become of his Lida!' He went on to write that he was sending us a kilogram of semolina, a kilogram of rice and two packets of biscuits. For some reason I was reading aloud. After the word 'rice' Tolya [Lydia's son] cried pleadingly: 'Mummy, make some porridge, only make it thick. . . .' The soldier, he was a lieutenant, suddenly began blowing his nose . . . and wiping away the tears which he could not hold back at the sight of us."[14]

Under extreme circumstances people discovered their strengths and weaknesses and their inner character. Lydia Okhapkina learned that she would never place her own welfare before the well-being of her children. Yet, there were others who would suffer moral defeat. The latter happened to the mother of a young boy named Igor who for several days at the beginning of the war had been placed under the care of Maria Mashkova. Igor's mother was an employee at the Leningrad State Library, and Maria knew her to be a caring individual who loved her young son very much.

In an interview conducted by Ales Adamovich and Daniil Granin, two excellent chroniclers, Maria Mashkova related that she would not see Igor again until April 1942. She noticed him sitting by a shop. He had the appearance of a skeleton, yet he was bloated. "'Igor, what has happened to you?' 'My mother has thrown me out. She said she would not give me another crust of bread.' 'How did that happen? It can't be!' Igor was in an awful state. I barely managed to get home with him to my fourth floor flat; I could hardly drag him up. . . . He was so frightful to look at, so pitiful! And all the time he kept saying: 'I don't blame Mummy. She's right. I am the guilty one, it was I who lost the ration card.'" Maria fed Igor and then brought him to his mother's place.

Upon their arrival, Maria witnessed the following: "A ragged woman was lying there, already wasted with hunger. The moment she saw her son, she shouted: 'Igor, I won't give you a crust of bread! Get out!' The room was stinking, filthy and dark. I exclaimed: 'What are you doing? After all, it's only three to four days and he [Igor] will go to school, he will be better.' 'No matter! There you are, on your feet, and I can't stand up. I won't give him a thing! I'm lying here starving. . . . ' What a transformation from a tender mother to such a wild beast! But Igor would not leave her. He stayed with her, and later on I heard that he had died."[15]

The renewed intense shelling by the enemy in the spring of 1942 caused the authorities to revive rapidly Leningrad's civil defense, much of which had ceased to exist during the winter months. There was a genuine fear that the Germans would use poison gas against Leningrad. Air-raid and chemical warfare shelters were repaired and rehabilitated. It was also decided that everybody within the city was to become a member of a civil defense organization. Thus, the city's leadership, acting on the instructions of the Military Council of the Leningrad Front, issued the following order:

1. To draft the entire population between the ages of fourteen and sixty to carry out civil defense duties and to participate in an obligatory manner in defending the city from fires and the results of air attacks and artillery bombardment by the enemy. In view of the above, all citizens capable of performing civil defense duties are to be listed in the membership of the civil defense groups of the civil defense house organizations.
2. To direct the civil defense groups to carry the full responsibility for civil defense and fire fighting resulting from aerial bombardment or artillery fire, which they are to combat with their own strength and means. . . .
3. To give to the command posts of the block civil defense organizations the right to enlist during working hours a part of the workers and employees of small enterprises and institutions located within the block for civil defense duty and fire prevention on homes and public buildings upon the sounding of the alert.[16]

Maria Dmitrieva was chief of civil defense under the housing office of the Kirov district, and she witnessed the results of many bombardments. She said in an interview that early one morning two housing complexes on Shvetsov Street were hit by enemy shells. At one complex a shell had gone through a window and exploded in the apartment. "It had killed a girl. . . . She was kneeling in the middle of the room wearing only a slip. She must have jumped up to run somewhere but did not make it in time. It blew her head off. Only her hair was lying on the floor. She must have been eighteen." After examining the damage done by the explosion, Maria made her way to the other housing complex that had been hit. "I got there and started shouting but I couldn't hear anyone anywhere. A window was lit but there was no light on the stairs. . . . I went upstairs to the first floor. I shouted again—there didn't seem to be anyone there. Then I opened the first door that I came to on that floor. . . . As I opened it I saw Katy Dyomina, a young woman, sitting on the sofa by the stove (there was a kind of round stove there). She was holding a baby, about three months old or less, in one arm and [she] had another child, a little boy of about four, across her knees. I went closer and started talking to her—the light was so bad! Then I shone my torch [flashlight] at her and I saw that half of her head had been torn off by a shell splinter—that's how it was! She was dead. But the two or three-month old baby—I don't exactly know his age—was alive! How had he survived? The one on her knees, the three or four-year-old boy was dead. His back and his legs were broken."[17]

There were occasions when shells would enter buildings but did not explode. They remained dormant. Such a situation was witnessed by a civil defense man who also worked in the Kirov district. His name was Ivan Kalyagin and he recalled receiving "a report that . . . there was an unexploded shell in a flat. So I sent an explosives expert [to the flat]. Off he went. He arrived there and then rang me up to say that he could not get the shell away. 'What do you mean you can't get it away?' 'I just can't. Come around and see for yourself.' I went there and walked into the room. There was a woman lying on the floor cuddling the shell—she had wrapped it in a shawl (it was still warm)—and she would not let us have it. She would not let go of it! We tried to find out what was the matter. It turned out that her young baby had been taken away. In a panic a relative had snatched up the baby and gone off as she saw the shell. But the mother had been left behind. She saw this shell and got it in her head that it was her baby. Well, she was already out of her mind. . . ."[18]

One organization that contributed to the defense of the city was the MPVO (Local Anti-Aircraft Defense). It was the job of the MPVO volunteers to fight fires, to rescue people from the rubble of buildings that had been destroyed and to provide medical care to the injured. Each of Leningrad's seventeen districts had two MPVO battalions, and most of the volunteers were women between the ages of eighteen and thirty-two. The women who were assigned to the reconnaissance platoon within a battalion were stationed in various parts of a neighborhood, day and night, to watch for fires started by a bomb or by an artillery shell. Lookout booths were placed on the tallest buildings and each booth had windows on all four sides so that the woman inside could see in all directions. She had in the booth a telephone, and whenever she witnessed a point of destruction she would report to the MPVO headquarters the address of the building. She would also advise her associates on the kind of assistance that was needed.

Operation "Eistoss" and the enemy's increased bombardments of Leningrad in the spring were viewed by the city's leaders as the beginnings of a major military offensive against Leningrad. In response they decided to further transform the city into a military fortress. A compulsory military training program, instituted in July 1941, was to be resumed. It had been largely discontinued during the winter months. Under the program citizens were taught how to shoot a gun, fight with a bayonet, throw grenades and Molotov cocktails, attack tanks, dig in and camouflage themselves. It was made clear in the local press that at any moment the population could be called upon to fight the invading Germans. In August 1942, the city's leadership ordered all Party, Komsomol and administrative personnel, male and female, to pass a 110 hour training program in street fighting.[19] Some Leningraders who underwent the military training were subsequently sent into the armed forces, but the majority remained as part of the city's interior defense forces.

The fortifications inside the city that had been built so hastily the year before were insufficient. Work to strengthen the city's fortifications and add to them began in July. Windows in cellars and in the lower floors of buildings were walled up. New tank traps, pillboxes, gun emplacements and street barricades were constructed. In the southern part of the city almost every house was turned into a fortress harboring a machine gun nest. In other parts of the city the houses at strategically vital street corners were turned into fortresses. Several streets were lined with anti-tank hedgehogs which, when necessary, could be put in a solid mass across the streets. Most of the defense work was done by women who were guided in their activities by military personnel. When the work was completed, Leningrad was far better prepared to resist an attack than a year earlier.

Outside of Leningrad proper to the south was the city's military front that had been established earlier in September 1941. It continued to be an irregular crescent that extended from the German foothold east of Petergof on the Gulf of Finland to a point on the Neva River west of Schlusselburg. It consisted of numerous lines of spaced trenches with mine fields and masses of barbed wire entanglements in between the lines of trenches. The trenches were dotted with dugouts which were the homes of the soldiers manning Leningrad's front line. The dugouts were made with steel girders and wooden walls that were twelve logs thick on the side facing the enemy and almost just as thick on the other sides. To enter a dugout, one had to go down some wooden steps. Inside, the main room was furnished with bunks on each side, a table, a food storage cabinet, a first aid outfit and a large gun that was directed toward the enemy. The wall that faced Leningrad included a small window which helped bring light into the dugout. From these dugouts the soldiers of the Leningrad Front with their large guns were expected to hold back the enemy.

NOTES

1. Alexander Werth, Leningrad (London: Hamish Hamilton, 1944), 90–91.

2. Leon Goure, The Siege of Leningrad (Stanford, California: Stanford University Press, 1962), 248–49.

3. Goure, The Siege of Leningrad, 266–68.

4. Goure, The Siege of Leningrad, 228.

5. Nikolai Kislitsyn and Vassily Zubakov, Leningrad Does Not Surrender, trans. Barry Jones (Moscow: Progress Publishers, 1989), 115.

6. Goure, The Siege of Leningrad, 228–229.

7. Goure, The Siege of Leningrad, 273–274.

8. Werth, Leningrad, 107–114.

9. Alexander Fadeyev, Leningrad in the Days of the Blockade, trans. R.D. Charques (Wesport, Connecticut: Greenwood Press, Publishers, 1971), 61–62.

10. Fadeyev, Leningrad in the Days of the Blockade, 65–66.

11. Fadeyev, Leningrad in the Days of the Blockade, 66–67.

12. Kislitsyn and Zubakov, Leningrad Does Not Surrender, 146–47.

13. Fadeyev, Leningrad in the Days of the Blockade, 20–21.

14. Ales Adamovich and Daniil Granin, a book of the Blockade, trans. Hilda Perham (Moscow: Raduga Publishers, 1983), 371–72.

15. Adamovich and Granin, A Book of the Blockade, 162–63.

16. Goure, The Siege of Leningrad, 279.

17. Adamovich and Granin, A Book of the Blockade, 186–87.

18. Adamovich and Granin, A Book of the Blockade, 190.

19. Kislitsyn and Zubakov, Leningrad Does Not Surrender, 139.

Chapter Sixteen

Breach in the Blockade

In the fall of 1942 the military situation for Leningrad continued to be grave. German forces were still shelling the city from the south and Finnish forces threatened the city from the north. The city was still cut off by land from the rest of mainland Russia and the Soviet Baltic Fleet was bottled up in the eastern Gulf of Finland. The chief commander of the Leningrad Front was Army General Leonid Govorov; he had been assigned to this position in April 1942. To the east, Army General Kirill Meretskov was the chief commander of the Soviet forces that made up the Volkhov Front. They defended the vital supply and communication lines to Lake Ladoga's eastern shore and the wide sector between Lake Ladoga and Lake Il'men.

In April, 1942, Hitler had issued a directive ordering renewed military offensives against the Soviet forces in the northern and southern sectors of the Soviet Union. The directive stated:

> . . . as soon as the weather and terrain become favorable, the German High Command and the German armed forces must again seize the initiative in their hands in order to impose our will upon the enemy.

It continued:

> The objective is to destroy the remaining Soviet defense potential and to cut them off as much as possible from their most important sources of supply. To achieve this, it is planned to maintain our positions in the central sector; in the north, to bring about the fall of Leningrad . . . and on the southern flank to force a breakthrough into the Caucasus. . . . At the beginning of the campaign all available forces must be united for the main operations in the southern sector, whose objective it is to destroy the enemy on this side of the Don [River] in order to reach the oil regions of the Caucasus and cross the Caucasus Mountains . . . we must try to reach Stalingrad or at least bring it under fire from our heavy artillery to such an

extent that it will henceforth be destroyed as a production center for arms and as a transportation center.[1]

The military offensive that was planned against Leningrad was code-named Operation "Nordlicht" (Northlight) and was conditional on Germany's successes in the Crimea and the Caucasus. It was decided that the Eighteenth Army of German Army Group North would be reinforced by five divisions from the Eleventh Army, commanded by General Erich von Manstein, as soon as it had completed the capture of Sebastopol in the Crimea. Then Operation "Nordlicht" was to go into effect. Its objective was for the Germans to cross the Neva River and effect contact with the Finns west of Lake Ladoga, thereby establishing a closed ring around Leningrad. This was to be followed by an assault on the city. At the same time Hitler still hoped to achieve the surrender of the city by intensive aerial bombardment and artillery shelling. Some 800 heavy artillery pieces were to be concentrated around Leningrad. The offensive was scheduled to begin on September 14, 1942.

Preparations for Operation "Nordlicht" were started but would be interrupted. After the Germans captured Sebastopol and all of the Crimea in July 1942, troops of General Field Marshal Erich von Manstein (he had been made a Field Marshal for his part in taking Sebastopol) and vast quantities of heavy siege artillery used against Sebastopol were transported by train to the Leningrad region. At the same time Germany's Eighth Air Corps was assigned to support the forthcoming operation against Leningrad. But the German plans were interrupted. The Soviet command, aware of the enemy's build-up in the Leningrad region and anxious to lift the blockade of Leningrad, launched its own offensives on August 27 in the Sinyavino Hieghts and Mga sector and at Tosno and Uritsk. During the following month the Germans had to fight hard to keep their positions against Leningrad, especially near Lake Ladoga where the Soviet forces achieved deep penetrations. The Soviet penetrations were contained and eventually pushed back with heavy losses to the Soviet forces. However, the fighting absorbed all of the resources of Germany's Eighteenth Army and the five divisions of Manstein's Eleventh Army. Thus, Operation "Nordlicht" against Leningrad was abandoned.[2]

A subsequent crisis in the Caucasus forced the Germans to transfer divisions of the Eleventh Army away from the Leningrad region to support Germany's military operations in the southern sector. In accordance with the directive that Hitler had issued in April 1942, German Army Group South launched an offensive toward the Caucasus. The offensive began on June 28, 1942, and by the end of July German forces had pushed the Soviet forces eastward across the Don River and were advancing onto the industrial city of Stalingrad situated on the banks of the Volga River. In November, after three months of slow but costly advance, the Germans finally reached the banks of the Volga River to the north and south of Stalingrad. They also controlled large areas within

Stalingrad, a city that had been reduced to rubble. As the battle for Stalingrad continued the German High Command brought more divisions to the Caucasus from other areas including the Leningrad region. Even so the Germans were unable to take the city that bore Stalin's name. In the period from the middle of November to the beginning of December large numbers of Soviet forces, brought from the East, encircled the city. The trapped German troops rapidly ran short on food, heating fuel and medical supplies, and thousands started dying from malnutrition, frostbite and disease.

The Soviet High Command decided to take advantage of the enemy's difficulties in the Caucasus. In late November and early December plans were drawn up to end the German blockade of Leningrad. The soldiers of Govorov's Leningrad Front were to cross the ice covered Neva River along a twelve kilometer (8 mile) stretch from Nevskaya Dubrovka to Schlusselburg and then advance east against the German forces who controlled a wide strip of land just south of Lake Ladoga. The troops of Meretskov's Volkhov Front were to attack simultaneously the Germans from the opposite side. The forces of the two fronts were to meet and then turn south driving the enemy before them. The planned offensive was officially approved on December 2, 1942, and it was code-named Operation "Iskra" (Spark). It was further decided that Operation "Iskra" should be launched in January 1943. If it succeeded the Soviet forces would control a corridor of land south of Lake Ladoga, and Germany's land blockade of Leningrad would be breached.

Operation "Iskra" would begin on January 12, 1943. Before it was launched, Army General Zhukov arrived in Leningrad to coordinate the operation. During the offensives the Soviet forces on both fronts made slow but steady progress, and on January 18 the soldiers of the Leningrad Front and the Volkhov Front joined hands. At the same time the Soviet forces gained control over the town of Schlusselburg. The enemy's land blockade of Leningrad was broken, and a narrow corridor of land between eight to ten kilometers (5 to 6 miles) wide along the southern shore of Lake Ladoga was now occupied by Soviet troops (see Map 6). It was known as the Schlusselburg corridor. Further Soviet attempts to widen the Schlusselburg corridor failed and the enemy's blockade of Leningrad to the south was not fully lifted. The city, as a consequence, would remain under German bombardment for another year. However, the success of Operation "Iskra" vastly improved Leningrad's strategic situation by reducing the possibility of a German-Finnish link-up and by improving military cooperation between the Leningrad and Volkhov fronts. Most importantly, control of the Schlusselburg corridor permitted the Soviets to establish between Leningrad and mainland Russia a railway link which would be named "The Road of Victory." [3]

At 10:45 P.M. on January 18 the loud-speakers in Leningrad's squares and parks and at the street corners and railroad stations announced that the blockade against the city had been broken. Family members, relatives, friends, co-workers and acquaintances congratulated each other over and over and re-joiced. On the streets the people wept for joy and strangers fell around each other's necks. Neighbors gathered to celebrate and everyone brought their share of food and drinks. In the factories, managers spoke about the success of the Red Army and urged an even greater increase in production now that the block-ade had been breached. The speeches were usually concise, and the workers im-mediately returned to their job posts. That night, flags were displayed through-out the city and on the morning of January 19 nearly every large building was draped in red. The people, however, were under no illusions. The war was not over. Yet, the breach in the blockade did uplift the people's spirits, and there was a growing assurance that victory over the enemy was forthcoming.

The construction of a railway line through the Schlusselburg corridor to supply Leningrad's military and civilian needs began on the twenty-first of January.The work was done by railroad and construction troops in severe winter conditions and under constant enemy artillery fire and air attacks. In just eighteen days a railway line was laid along the southern shore of Lake Ladoga from Schlusselburg to Poliana. It was thirty-three kilometers (20.6 miles) long and crossed the Neva River at Schlusselburg on a pile bridge erected on the ice (see Map 6). The railway line was opened on February 6, and on the following day the first trainload of food and other supplies arrived in Leningrad. The Germans on the Sinyavino Heights had full view of the railway and with their heavy guns would disrupt and halt the rail movement through the corridor causing many casualties. The Schlusselburg corridor quickly became known as "The Corridor of Death." Less than eighty trains managed to slip through the corridor in February, and the record was not much better in March. Usually passage was attempted at night with the trains running blacked out and without signal lights. In time the supply route through the Schlusselburg corridor would improve. On March 18 a new rail-road bridge across the Neva River was opened up. A second railway line run-ning parallel to the first and closer to the Lake Ladoga shoreline was built in May 1943. By the end of 1943, in terms of capacity, the railway lines through the Schlusselburg corridor had become an important supply route for Leningrad. In addition to food, large quantities of coal, munitions, metal and other raw materials were brought into Leningrad on "The Road of Victory."

NOTES

1. Dmitri V. Pavlov, Leningrad 1941, trans. John Clinton Adams (Chicago, Illinois: The University of Chicago Press, 1965), 169–170.

2. David M. Glantz, The Siege of Leningrad 1941–1944 (Osceola, Wisconsin: MBI Publishing Company, 2001), 98–107.

3. Glantz, The Siege of Leningrad 1941–1944, 128–139.

Chapter Seventeen

Summer of 1943

Living conditions in Leningrad continued to improve in 1943. Food became more plentiful. The vegetable growing campaign produced a harvest of 60,000 tons from individual gardens, and the farms along the outskirts of the city grew an additional 75,000 tons of food. People received their full food rations, and occasionally children received chocolate. Some much needed consumer goods, such as toothbrushes, soap, sewing needles and other items became available in the city's stores. Firewood was brought in from the suburbs where it was cut by a work force of some 10,000 Leningrad women. The electric and water services were almost completely restored.

Shortly after the breach of the blockade, the actors and actresses of the Bolshoi Drama Theater returned to the city of Leningrad from their evacuation. The return of this famous theater troupe was uplifting, and their first performance was given in March 1943. A month later they revived the production of ten plays, and whenever they performed the auditorium was full. Many people would stand for hours at the entrance of the theater with the hope of getting a ticket.[1]

By the summer of 1943 most of the people in Leningrad had gotten used to the daily shelling. Alexander Werth, the British journalist, noticed this when he attended the Dramatic Theater located along the Fontanka River. Outside of the theater he joined a small crowd of people that had gathered to see Gorki's Petit-Bourgeois. They were mostly soldiers all wearing the pale green ribboned Leningrad Defense Medal (see Glossary—Leningrad Defense Medal). There were some young girls dressed in khaki, and several of them were also wearing the Leningrad medal. Standing in line too were some Soviet Baltic Fleet sailors wearing their blue and white striped shirts along with their sailor hats. In the distance, Werth could hear explosions. The shelling of the district had begun and a nearby loud-speaker began to announce: "Attention! Attention! This district is being subjected to artillery shelling. Traffic on the streets is to be stopped and people are to take shelter immediately." [2] The crowd in front of the theater seemed unperturbed by the announcement that was made every few minutes, and when a militiaman finally came up and invited the people to take cover, they refused to leave. When the Soviet batteries along the military front responded in the direction from which the enemy shells were coming, the shelling ended. Shortly thereafter, the loudspeaker announced: "Citizens, the artillery shelling of the district has ceased." [3]

A certain disregard toward enemy shelling was also expressed to Werth during his interview with a young female worker at the Kirov Works. When Werth asked the young lady if her father was employed at the factory, she replied, "No, father died in the hungry year, died on the seventh of January." When she was asked why she had received the Leningrad medal, she answered, "I've worked at the Kirov Works since I was fourteen, so I suppose that is why they gave me the medal." When the young lady was asked if it was frightening to work in a factory which was a major enemy target, she said, "No, not really. One gets used to it. When a shell whistles, it means its high up; it's only when it begins to sizzle that you know there's going to be trouble. Accidents do happen, of course. . . . Only last week we had an accident; a shell landed in my workshop and many were wounded, and two Stakhanov girls were burned to death." (see Glossary—Stakhanovite) When she was asked if she would like to be transferred to another factory where it was less dangerous, she responded by shaking her head: "No, I am a Kirov girl, and my father was a Putilov man [the Kirov Works was formerly the Putilov Plant], and really the worst is over now, so we may as well stick it to the end." After inquiry was made about the other members of her family, the young lady replied that her mother had "died before the war" and that her brother was in the army along the military front.[4]

An increasing number of Leningraders felt confident that the enemy would soon be driven from Leningrad and that what remained of the blockade would be removed. It was an attitude voiced by Vera Alexandrova Karatygina who headed a newly formed department in the Leningrad State Library. Vera was a specialist in the history of Leningrad, and she and fourteen other women were building an extensive record of the defense of Leningrad and of life within the city during the blockade. Nothing was to be discarded. "Everything that seems of the slightest historical value for the reconstruction of the history of our defense of Leningrad, we keep and catalogue and classify," Vera said. "Brochures and invitation tickets of every kind, pamphlets, leaflets, membership cards—everything is important. Theater tickets, concert tickets, programs, concert bills . . . documents relating to our industrial, scientific and literary life; ration cards of the different periods of the blockade . . . all these we are collecting and classifying. We are also compiling large files of newspaper cuttings on every conceivable subject concerning the defense of Leningrad. And just now several of us are here compiling an album of the [breach] of the Leningrad blockade. . . . " [5]

Life had become valuable again. During the days of starvation people had their feelings blunted toward death. They did not weep at the burials of relatives and friends. It was all done in complete silence without any display of emotion. They were unable to weep; the horrific circumstances had frozen their tears. But by 1943 life had regained its importance. Women began to apply rouge and wear lipstick, and men began to shave. At an intersection just across from the Leningrad State Library an old man would sit each day with a set of scales. Before him stood a long line of children, women and men, and all were waiting to be weighed. They were curious to find out if they had regained some weight now that they were eating more and better food.[6]

By mid-1943 the factories that still remained in Leningrad had made an extraordinary recovery. They produced a major part, if not all, of the ammunition requirements of the soldiers along Leningrad's military fronts. They also manufactured various items for other areas of the Soviet Union. The revival of the city's industries was due in large measure to the recruitment of a new force of industrial workers. On February 13, 1943, the city authorities issued a decree which permitted them to recruit young people from sixteen to eighteen years of age. The recruitment began in the latter part of April, and in many instances the young people were assigned as apprentices in factories or were put to work on railways. They joined a labor force that had already been supplemented by office workers. Earlier, under a decree issued in November 1942, the authorities had transferred many office workers to the production line. When possible, these workers were assigned to factories near their places of residence. Young office workers and those who had experience in factory production, were transferred first. The decree exempted persons with secondary or higher educations, those under sixteen or over fifty years of age and pregnant women. To train the new workers the factories organized technical classes and study circles. Most of the draftees under the decree were women, and in time from 70 to 80 percent of the industrial force in Leningrad was female.[7]

If industrial production was to be reestablished at a high level then strict labor discipline was essential. The authorities informed the workers that, with the improvement in living conditions, the old rules concerning tardiness, absenteeism and failure to fulfill production norms would again be enforced. During the winter of starvation and since that time, these rules had not been enforced; it would have been absurd to punish an employee for being absent when he or she was too exhausted and too weak to work. With the continuing use of factory dormitories and the resumption of public transportation, tardiness was not a major problem. However, in many factories a large percentage of workers were absent from May through July due to illness. Because the authorities insisted on the observance of all the rules, they decided to punish workers who were absent by making them an object lesson to others. The violators were tried and sentenced to several months or years of hard labor. They were then sent to work in the same factory where they had been employed, but for no pay and for prison rations.[8]

Other methods were used to encourage high productivity. The traditional socialist competition was one of the methods. A competition would be organized between shops or shifts in the same plant or between different factories. No factory, shop or worker could avoid participating in a competition. The anniversary of the October Socialist Revolution was traditionally marked by a special competition, and 1943 would be no different (see Glossary — October Socialist Revolution). As usual the most successful competitors were given as a reward a Red Banner. Cash prizes were also awarded to the winners of a socialist competition.

Public praising and shaming were resumed as well. Comments on the performance of individual workers were posted on factory bulletin boards, published in newspapers or mentioned in public meetings and speeches. Often medals were given to leading workers. The following was a warning which was posted on a factory bulletin board: "Shame! Shame that a highly skilled riveter like Comrade Gusev should have failed so miserably in the task which our comrades at the front were expecting him to fulfill without fail. We expect him to pull himself together in the future. The Editorial Board." [9] The public shaming of a delinquent worker could develop into such a harassment campaign that few dared to ignore it.

It was during the summer of 1943 that a number of Leningrad's factories were subjected to the most concentrated bombardments of the war. On May 3 the Krasnyi Neftyanik oil tank yard was hit. Several of the oil tanks were destroyed, and a huge fire broke out. Some four hundred fire fighters, many of them were women and teen aged girls, tried to combat the fire, but the burning oil flowed between their legs, setting fire to their clothes and blinding their eyes with acrid fumes. The situation was made worse when the enemy increased the shelling of the area. With great difficulty the fire was extinguished, but fourteen fire fighters lost their lives and forty were injured.[10]

Life in Leningrad's residential districts also continued to be dangerous. The city was still subjected to frequent air attacks particularly at night and to artillery bombardments during the day. In order to cause the maximum number of deaths, the Germans fired volleys on Leningrad at intervals. The enemy batteries would concentrate on individual targets or they would fire on several districts at once. The Germans often used thermite shells to start fires and when a fire did break out in an area they would intensify the shelling of an adjacent area so as to make it more difficult to extinguish the fire. Hundreds of Leningraders were killed or wounded in their homes or in the streets. In street after street new signs painted in white and blue were posted with the following warning: "Citizens! During artillery fire this side of the street is the more dangerous." In the month of September, the enemy shelling became so intense that the city authorities were forced to close temporarily the motion-picture theaters and schools and to prohibit unnecessary public gatherings.

NOTES

1. Nikolai Kislitsyn and Vassily Zubakov, Leningrad Does Not Surrender, trans. Barry Jones (Moscow: Progress Publishers, 1989), 206.

2. Kislitsyn and Zubakov, Leningrad Does Not Surrender, 204.

3. Alexander Werth, Leningrad (London: Hamish Hamilton, 1944), 53.

4. Werth, Leningrad, 61.

5. Werth, Leningrad, 147–48.

6. Boris Skomorovsky and E.G. Morris, The Siege of Leningrad (New York: E. P. Dutton and Company, Inc. 1944), 115.

7. Leon Goure, The Siege of Leningrad (Stanford California: Stanford University Press, 1962), 282–83.

8. Goure, The Siege of Leningrad, 283–84.

9. Werth, Leningrad, 121.

10. Kislitsyn and Zubakov, Leningrad Does Not Surrender, 208.

Chapter Eighteen

Leningrad's Guerrillas

A growing concern for the German High Command was the Soviet guerrilla movement that had risen up against the Germans in the Leningrad region. The guerrillas, also known as partisans, were especially active in the forests of the areas occupied by the Germans. Their activities included blowing up the bridges, railway tracks and trains used by the enemy. They killed German occupation officials and soldiers, and they punished Russians who collaborated with the invaders. The Soviet government was grateful for the guerrilla forces and often glorified the heroes and heroines of the movement, but it wasn't until 1943 that Moscow was able to supply the guerrillas with substantial assistance including guns and ammunition, food and medicines. Before that most guerrillas would acquire food, medicine and sometimes shelter from the village people. The guerrillas were an effective second military front against the Germans occupying the Leningrad region.

On July 3, 1941, ten days after Germany invaded the Soviet Union, Stalin told the Soviet people in his radio address that a guerrilla war must be initiated against the enemy. He called upon the people in the areas occupied by the enemy to organize into guerrilla units and become an army of partisans:

In areas occupied by the enemy, guerrilla units, mounted and on foot, must be formed, diversionist groups must be organized to combat enemy troops, to foment guerrilla warfare everywhere, to blow up bridges and roads, to damage telephone and telegraph lines and to set fire to forests, stores and transports. In the occupied regions conditions must be made unbearable for the enemy and all his accomplices. They must be hounded and annihilated at every step and all their measures frustrated. This war with fascist Germany cannot be considered an ordinary war. It is not only a war between two armies; it is also a great war of the entire Soviet people against the German fascist forces.[1]

Stalin's call for a guerrilla war against the enemy was appealing to many Russians. Guerrilla fighters had long been glorified through books, motion pictures, theater productions and songs. During The Patriotic War of 1812 guerrilla warfare was conducted against Napoleon's army by Russians who did so voluntarily. The most famous guerrillas were nobles such as Denis Davidov, Ivan Dorokhov and Alexander Seslavin and peasants such as Gerasim Koorin, Y. Chetvertakov and Vasilisa Kozhina. The names of these men were known to every Russian man, woman and child. During The Civil War (1918–1921) guerrilla warfare was conducted by the Reds against the White armies and their foreign supporters.

At first, the guerrilla movement was primarily a spontaneous movement. It combined Soviet soldiers, those who had become separated from their units as the Red Army retreated before the invading Germans, with civilians who had fled to the marshes and forests in search of refuge from the enemy. Omel'chenko was a Soviet soldier who joined a small group of peasants whose village had been destroyed by the Germans. He would become their leader and train them in guerrilla war tactics. His story and the guerrilla activities of his group were later told in a Soviet newspaper. The story was typical of how early units of guerrillas were formed in the Leningrad region.

According to the newspaper article, Omel'chenko was taken prisoner by the Germans in August 1941. His captors marched him into a village they had recently taken and stripped him naked. The officer in charge then ordered him to walk to a neighboring village where the Germans, who controlled the area, had established their headquarters. At the German headquarters Omel'chenko was to be taken into custody.

Omel'chenko began his walk on the road that was to bring him to the other village. The road was bordered by open fields that provided no concealment. Omel'chenko was not escorted by a guard; the German officer did not believe that a naked prisoner would try to make a run for it. If he should be so daring, there were German riflemen nearby who could shoot him. When a group of German tanks sped past a cloud of dust hid the Soviet soldier long enough for him to go unnoticed as he dove into a ditch that lined the road. Omel'chenko crawled out on the other side, ran a distance across an open field, dove to the ground and crept on his stomach to some thick shrubbery. There he remained hidden until nightfall. When it turned dark he made his way through the brush and entered a forest. He would continue his escape for the next five days until he collapsed due to hunger and exhaustion.

On the morning of the sixth day, Omel'chenko was awakened by an old peasant. "Where are you from and what has happened to your clothes?" the old man asked. Omel'chenko explained what had happened and then asked the old man to take him to his troops. "The Germans," the old man replied, "burned down our village, and we want revenge for what they have done. There are six of us—me, two old women and three boys. We need both an instructor and a commander. We want to get our hands on a machine gun, but we do not know how to shoot one. You are in no condition to walk very far. Why don't you stay with us?" Omel'chenko agreed to come with the old man but planned to stay with the group only long enough to recover from his ordeal. Then he would try to find his way back to the Red Army.

When Omel'chenko and the old man reached the forest glade where the others were hiding they discovered that two more people had joined the group. On the following day the number had risen to eleven. The women in the group nursed Omel'chenko's wounds, and they returned to their destroyed village to get the milk and eggs that he would need to recover. When he became strong enough, he began teaching the group the art of guerrilla warfare.

Within several weeks Omel'chenko and his group of guerrillas had carried out several successful attacks on the Germans that occupied the area. Their first operation was an attack on three Germans who were sleeping in an abandoned and secluded farm house. Until then the small group had only two rifles that they had found in the fields. After this first operation they had three more rifles and some hand grenades. A week later they captured a machine gun for which the old man had yearned. A week after that Omel'chenko's group of guerrillas stopped an enemy truck that was carrying explosives and with these they were able to blow up two bridges.

Each day Omel'chenko renewed his decision to leave his guerrillas and return to the Red Army. However, there was always a new operation that needed to be carried out and a new attack to be planned. New recruits joined the small detachment, and they had to be trained. New information was also gathered and that needed to be exploited. By the end of September 1941, Omel'chenko decided that he should not leave his detachment of guerrillas before the war was over. Together, they were fighting an effective war against the enemy.[2]

The Germans preferred to capture the guerrillas, extract from them information and then use the information to round up still more guerrillas. They would also arrest anyone who they suspected of giving aid to the guerrillas. These victims were interrogated, and if they did not cooperate with the Germans they would suffer the consequences. A young woman whose name was Panya was one of many civilians living in the Leningrad region who was accused by the enemy of giving assistance to guerrillas. She was in charge of the supplies on a collective farm, and the Germans suspected that she was supplying the guerrillas in the area with food and other necessities.

Upon her arrest, Panya was brought into a small dwelling and questioned by a German military officer. At first the officer tried to cajole Panya, but when it became apparent that her answers were vague and worthless he became impatient. "Tell me where those partisan swine are hidden," he shouted, "or you will wish that you never had been born." Panya did not answer but looked at each soldier within the room. At the command of the officer one of the soldiers stepped forward and swung a fist at Panya's face. Panya jerked back, but the soldier's second fist struck her in the head causing her to fall to the floor. Two others grabbed Panya's shoulders and brought her to her feet. Panya still refused to answer the questions.

The German officer decided to show the people within the village what would happen to a person who refused to cooperate. Two of the soldiers took hold of Panya's arms, carried her out of the building and dragged her to the end of the village road. Panya's face was like a ragged sponge that had been dipped in red paint. Her eyes were open and there was defiance in her gaze. At the end of the road the soldiers stood Panya up against a rickety fence next to an old house, but as soon as the soldiers loosed their grip she slipped to the ground like a rag doll. Her feet stuck out at a grotesque angle, and the blood from her face ran down the front of her dress. The German officer again approached his victim and demanded that she tell him where the guerrillas in the area were hiding. Panya did not answer.

The officer then ordered his men to build a fire. Pieces of wood were gathered into a pile and lighted. Meanwhile a small group of village people gathered. They were about to witness the execution of Panya. The execution began when two soldiers carried Panya's limp body to the fire and pushed it on the burning wood. The flames quickly ignited her dress. A murmur rose from the village people as they stood motionless watching one of their own being burned to death, but no sound came from Panya. When it was over the people drifted away. Toward evening Panya's father walked to the execution site to bring the charred corpse of his daughter home. He had made a wooden coffin that he had placed on the table in his house. He had decided that he would bury her the next day.

In the morning the Germans arrived at the father's house. They demanded the charred body of Panya. They had decided to make the destruction of Panya's body complete. A fire was built on the village road, and again Panya's body was burned until only her ashes remained.

Panya's behavior under interrogation and her execution that followed would become well- known throughout the area. The guerrillas considered her actions heroic, and eventually delegates representing the guerrilla movement from the area brought her story into the besieged city of Leningrad. It was one of many that exemplified the guerrilla war that was being conducted by civilians outside of Leningrad. Stories such as these bolstered the morale of the Leningraders. It was uplifting and reassuring that others outside of the city, young women such as Panya and the guerrillas whose lives she had protected, were fighting against the enemy that was trying to destroy Leningrad and its people.[3]

At one time during the blockade guerrilla delegates from two districts within the Leningrad region arrived in the besieged city with a pledge to fight against the Germans until they were removed from the region. The delegates had made their way through enemy lines and were carrying with them two blue-covered notebooks such as were used by school children. The first few pages of one of the notebooks contained a letter addressed to Comrade Stalin. The letter told how in one week the Germans occupying the two districts had destroyed thirty-nine villages, had burned two hospitals and ten schools and had shot more than one hundred collective farmers, old men, women and children. It expressed the guerrillas' determination to destroy the enemy, and it listed their accomplishments. The guerrillas had, the letter reported, killed some twenty thousand Wehrmacht officers and men, caused eight train wrecks, blew up twenty-seven bridges and destroyed more than two hundred motor vehicles and tanks. The letter ended with a pledge that none of the signers would stop fighting so long as a single German remained in Russia. It closed with the following words: "The bloodthirsty fascists want to break our spirit, our will. They forget that they deal with a Russian people who never were and never will be at their knees."

The remainder of the first notebook and all of the second notebook was filled with signatures of guerrillas who had read the contents of the letter and wanted to tell Stalin about their determination to fight the enemy. There were more than three thousand signatures in both notebooks. They had been obtained by carrying the letter over a vast territory across rivers, fields and hills from one guerrilla camp to another where each signature was penned near carefully screened fires in forests or in caves.[4]

The guerrilla movement also included diversionary groups whose activities were highly secretive. The members of these groups participated in intelligence gathering and acts of sabotage. They were often taken by airplane from Leningrad and dropped behind the enemy's military front line in an area within the Leningrad region that was occupied by the enemy. After they completed a mission they would report back to headquarters in Leningrad and wait for further orders. These guerrillas would try to avoid a confrontation with the enemy. Many of the members were able to speak German, and often they would wear German military dress.

Vasily Klyuyev was a member of a diversionary group. He was working in Leningrad as an electrician when the war broke out. Shortly thereafter, he was assigned by the military recruiting office to take a course on sending messages using Morse code. He took the course in the evening after work and mastered quickly what he was taught. One evening two military officers called him into a room away from the others and approached him with an offer. He agreed to join them and was brought to an intelligence gathering training school. Here he learned to work with a machine that was used to send code, to operate a radio receiving and transmitting set, to read maps of the Leningrad region, to use a parachute and different kinds of weapons and to become skilled in hand to hand combat. After Vasily completed his training, he was assigned as the signaler for an intelligence gathering group.[5]

All guerrillas before they were sent from Leningrad and into occupied territory behind German lines were required to take an oath. It was an oath taken by Vasily and it read as follows:

I, son of the great Soviet people, voluntarily join the ranks of the guerrillas of the Leningrad region at the call of our leader and teacher, Comrade Stalin, and take the sacred and inviolable oath of the partisan before my Fatherland, to shoulder arms until the last fascist invader is destroyed on the land of my forefathers and fathers. My motto is: When you see the enemy, kill him!

I vow sacredly to preserve the revolutionary and fighting traditions of the Leningraders and always to be a brave and disciplined guerrilla scorning danger and death. I vow with all my might, ability and thoughts to help self-sacrificingly and courageously the Red Army free the city of Lenin from enemy blockade, to rid all towns and villages of the Leningrad region of German invaders.

I vow to take ruthless, tireless revenge on the enemy for the burnt towns and villages, for the death of our women and children, for the tortures, violence and outrages perpetrated against our people. Blood for blood! Death for death!

I shall not surrender my native Leningrad to be outraged by fascism. If by my faintheartedness and cowardice I betray the interests of the working people of the city of Lenin, then my retribution for this will be the hatred and contempt of the people, the curses of my relatives, and an ignominious death at the hands of my comrades.[6]

One of Vasily's most memorable missions began in July 1943, when he and four comrades were dropped at night behind German lines within the Leningrad region. Five biplanes were used; each carried a pilot and one of the members of the group. Two of the members were young women. Biplanes were used because they could fly low and thus the drop would be more accurate. When flying over enemy lines the engines of the biplanes were shut off, and the biplanes continued gliding quietly without being noticed. Vasily was sitting in the rear seat of one of the biplanes. He had on his right side a radio transmitter, on his left he had several batteries and on his lap a bag filled with food and ammunition. When he reached his destination the pilot circled and waved for Vasily to get out and jump. Vasily got out of his seat, climbed onto the bottom wing of the biplane and from there jumped. As he looked down he saw only darkness. He fell free for several seconds then he pulled the cord of the parachute. He felt a jerk as the parachute opened, and he could hear the engine of the biplane fade away in the distance as it was returning to Leningrad. Meanwhile the other biplanes had dropped Vasily's comrades, and all had been dropped north of the town of Oredezh. Their assignment was to gather intelligence about the enemy's activities on the Vitebsk Railroad which connected the city of Vitebsk in Belorussia with Leningrad. They were to determine the number of troops and what kind and how many supplies the Germans were transporting on the railroad line. Vasily was supposed to report all this information to headquarters in Leningrad.

The group established their base camp in a forest a distance from the railway line. The camp consisted of a dugout, and the soil that they had dug out with their knives and hands they had placed in one of their parachutes and removed to other areas in the forest. From different areas of the forest they had gathered small dead trees and used them to cover the dugout. They then covered the roof with moss and planted on top of the roof a small tree. After they carefully covered the entrance, the dugout was unnoticeable. It was to be their dwelling place during the days when they watched the Vitebsk Railroad and gathered information.

After a few days, Vasily could report to headquarters in Leningrad that the Germans had established zones running along both sides of the railroad and that the zones were carefully patrolled by soldiers and dogs. It was impossible for Soviet guerrillas to get near the railway line. At the same time the group discovered that there was an unusual amount of German activity going on in the village of Siverskaya, a railway station through which the Vitebsk Railroad ran. Every day one of the group members would make his or her way to the village and from a distance watch the activity within the village. Vasily was required to stay at the campsite. If something should happen to him the group would lose their communication with headquarters.

When the group was given permission from headquarters to gather information from within Siverskaya, it was decided that Zhenya, one of the young women within the group, should try to penetrate the ring of security the Germans had established around the village. Zhenya could speak German fluently. She was to dress in civilian clothes and pretend that she was on her way to Siverskaya in order to barter some of her clothes for food. If she should succeed at getting into the village she was to contact, within the village, a Soviet female liaison named Galya.

The day that Zhenya entered Siverskaya would be an eventful one. Dressed in civilian clothes, Zhenya walked up to the road that led to the village. When she saw an enemy truck approaching, she hailed the driver and asked him in

German to give her a ride into the village. She explained to him that she needed food and would try to barter for some. The driver told her to get in and brought her into Siverskaya past the German control post. Zhenya contacted Galya and learned that Siverskaya had become the military headquarters for the Eighteenth Army of German Army Group North. The village and the surrounding area were being heavily fortified, and the Germans were in the process of establishing telephone lines to the area. She also learned that in Galya's house there lived two German officers. Zhenya returned to base camp safely and reported all that she had learned, and Vasily in turn informed headquarters in Leningrad about the group's discoveries. Headquarters responded by ordering the group to capture one of the German officers living in Galya's house, bring him back to the camp and gather from him information.

The capture of one of the German officers took place in the evening. As the officer approached Galya's house he took the key from its place, unlocked the door and entered. He then took off his overcoat and hung it up. It was dark so he proceeded to light the lamp, but suddenly there appeared before him two strong young men holding pistols. They ordered him to raise his hands. The German officer raised his hands. The two young men then took his pistol from its holster, removed his belt and cut the buttons from his slacks. They then gagged his mouth, placed a sack of potatoes on his back and shoved the German out the door. With one hand the German held the sack of potatoes, and with his other hand he held up his slacks. In this way the German officer was forced by his two captors to walk before them out of the village and into the nearby forest.

Vasily and his comrades discovered that the German officer had a wealth of information. His name was Fritz Hippel, and he was the chief of radio and telephone censorship for the Eighteenth Army. Fritz confirmed to the group that Hitler had given the order to destroy Leningrad by bombing, shelling and starvation. He told them that Hitler wanted to transport the young people of the Soviet Union to Germany. He also imparted to the group a great deal of information about the Eighteenth Army. For ten days Vasily transmitted to headquarters in Leningrad the information that his comrades extracted from Fritz. Thereafter, the group received orders from headquarters to hand Fritz over to a local guerrilla detachment. This was done.[7]

NOTES

1. Neil Mishalov, Radio Address of 3 July 1941, by Joseph Stalin, Chairman of the Council of People's Commissars of the U.S.S.R. (transcribed and translated by Soviet Russia Today, August 1941), <http://www.mishalov. com/Stalin-3 July 41. html> (30 May 2007).

2. Boris Skomorovsky and E.G. Morris, The Siege of Leningrad (New York: E.P. Dutton and Company, Inc., 1944), 174–76.

3. Skomorovsky and Morris, The Siege of Leningrad, 158–160.

4. Skomorovsky and Morris, The Siege of Leningrad, 161–62.

5. A. Losev, On the Firing Line (Luga: Luga Publishers, 2005), 68–69.

6. Skomorovsky and Morris, The Siege of Leningrad, 152–53.

7. Losev, On the Firing Line, 72–81.

Chapter Nineteen

The Blockade Ends

In early September 1943 the German High Command decided that German Army Group North should make preparations for a retreat. A defense line, the so-called Panther Line, was to be built toward the west many kilometers behind the positions held by the German forces in the Leningrad region. Construction on Panther Line began on September 7, and the defense line was finished by the end of the year. It extended from Pushkinskiye-Gori, east of the city of Pskov, toward the southern tip of Lake Pskov and from there along the western shores of Lake Pskov and Lake Peipus and then up to the Narva River and along the western bank of that river up to Narva near the southern shore of the Gulf of Finland. The total length of Panther Line was 425 kilometers (264 miles) of which 215 kilometers (133 miles) were land fronts and 210 kilometers (130 miles) were water fronts. Panther Line included tank obstacles, wire entanglements, emplacements for machine guns and anti-tank guns, concrete shelters, steel shelters, roads and road bridges. Most of the construction was done by the 30,000 workers who were recruited from the Soviet civilian population in the area and by 17,000 German soldiers and 7,000 German civilians who were brought to the area. The building materials used to construct the fortifications were transported to the defense line in railroad cars and on boats.[1]

In addition, the Germans constructed a series of intermediate defense lines within the Leningrad region. The intermediate lines would permit the German forces to withdraw westward to Panther Line in an orderly fashion. The most important of these intermediate lines was the Luga Line, extending along the Luga River and southwards to Novgorod.

If a withdrawal to the Panther Line should become necessary, it would create a serious dilemma for the Germans. There were approximately 900,000

Soviet civilians living in the area between the southern outskirts of Leningrad and Panther Line. It was believed by General Field Marshal George von Kuchler (Kuchler replaced General Field Marshal von Leeb as commander of German Army Group North in January 1942) that as his troops retreated westward to Panther Line the Soviet forces would follow in pursuit, and the Soviet commanders would conscript thousands of civilians living in the area. Faced with this dilemma, the Germans, in October 1943, began to evacuate a large percentage of the civilian population who inhabited the areas of the Leningrad region occupied by the Germans. Many villagers were transported to the Baltic States.

On November 17, 1943, Russian soldiers fighting for Andrei Vlasov entered Chashchah and ordered the villagers to get together their things and be prepared to leave the village that evening. (Vlasov had been a Lieutenant General in the Red Army but was captured by the Germans in June of 1943. He then changed sides and led Soviet soldiers who were German prisoners of war against Stalin.) Among the villagers in Chashchah were Vera Vinokurova and her daughter and mother. They believed that to refuse to leave would be useless. They knew that if they did not obey, Vlasov's men, who had betrayed the Motherland, would burn down their house and force them to leave anyway. After Vera and her mother gathered together some clothes, spoons and cups they waited to be driven from their home. The remainder of their possessions would have to be left behind.

By evening Vlasov's men had arrived at Chashchah to round up the villagers and drive them to a railway station where they would board a train that would transport them to the Baltic region. Before the villagers were taken away, Vlasov's men torched each of the houses in the village. As the flames lighted the darkened sky, the villagers watched their homes burn. Vera and her family were brought to Latvia and were placed in the home of a poor farming family. Later on, when the Soviet forces began pushing toward the Baltic States, Vera and her family were transported to Austria and placed in a concentration camp. There they would live until they were liberated by the Soviet forces who took control of the camp.[2]

It was in the fall of 1943 when the Soviet High Command began making new preparations to drive German Army Group North from the Leningrad region. According to their operational plan the forces of the Volkhov Front, still commanded by Army General Meretskov, were to carry out two major offensives. The forces to the south were to liberate Novgorod. One group was to approach Novgorod from the north and another was to approach the city by crossing the northern point of Lake Il'men south of Novgorod. The two groups were to converge west of Novgorod and capture the encircled enemy forces within the city (see Map 1). Simultaneously, General Meretskov's forces to the north stationed just east of Tosno, Liuban' and Chudovo were to drive the German forces from those three towns and continue westward toward Luga (see Map 1). At the same time, the operation required Army General Govorov, commander of the Leningrad Front, to transfer tanks, artillery guns, tons of ammunition and one of his armies under cover of night to Oranienbaum, the Soviet bridgehead located west of Leningrad on the south shore of the Gulf of Finland. General Govorov was to conduct two concentric assaults, one from Leningrad and the other from the Oranienbaum bridgehead, and to encircle the enemy forces in the Petergof and Strel'na districts (see Map 2). Subsequently, they were to advance toward Narva and Pskov (see Map 1). The attack date for the military operation was scheduled for early January. In preparation for the operation the Soviet High Command supplied both fronts with reinforcements and military hardware. In the end the Leningrad and Volkhov fronts combined had more than 1,200,000 officers and men. The soldiers of the two fronts and the soldiers at the Oranienbaum bridgehead were provided with more than 21,000 guns, more than 1,400 tanks and self propelled guns, 600 anti-aircraft guns, 1,500 rocket guns and 1,500 airplanes.

The military operation was launched on January 14, 1944. In the Novgorod region Meretskov's forces initiated a two-pronged attack toward Novgorod. South of Novgorod the Soviet forces crossed the northern point of Lake Il'men, and at the same time a second group approached the city from the north. The fighting was fierce and the casualties were high on both sides, but Meretskov's forces pushed forward. Before Novgorod was encircled, the Germans evacuated the city and withdrew westward to Panther Line. When the Soviet forces entered Novgorod on the twentieth of January they discovered that more than half of the city's buildings had been destroyed. Less than one hundred of its inhabitants were in the city; most of the other civilians had been transported to Germany to work in labor camps. At the Oranienbaum bridgehead the Soviet forces commanded by the veteran Lieutenant General Ivan Fedyuninsky launched their attack against the enemy during the early hours of January 15. More specifically the attack was launched in the area around Gostilitzi, twenty-two kilometers (13.6 miles) southwest of Petergof. Simultaneously, the forces of the Leningrad Front commanded by Govorov began an attack along their entire front. After fierce fighting, Govorov's forces captured Krasnoe Selo on January 19, then Pushkin, Pavlovsk, Mga, and Gatchina on January 26. Elsewhere, Meretskov's forces stationed in the northeast launched their offensive and captured Tosno, Liuban' and Chudovo. As the enemy retreated westward, they left behind the numerous artillery pieces with which they had bombarded Leningrad.[3]

On January 27, General Govorov, Andrei Zhdanov and other members of the Military Council of the Leningrad Front made a long hoped for announcement that was broadcast over the city's loud-speakers:

Comrade Red Army men, sergeants and officers of the Leningrad Front! Sailors of the Baltic Fleet! The working people of Leningrad!

In the course of twelve days of heavy fighting the troops of the Leningrad Front broke through and surmounted the strong, deeply echeloned enemy defenses along the whole length of the front at Leningrad, took by storm the most important enemy resistance centers and strong points outside Leningrad, including the towns of Krasnoye Selo, Ropsha, Uritsk, Pushkin, Pavlosvsk, Mga, Ulyanovsk and Gatchina,. . . .

As a result of the battles a historically important task has been accomplished—Leningrad has been completely liberated from enemy blockade and from the barbaric shelling.

To mark this victory and the complete liberation of Leningrad from enemy blockade today, January 27, at 20:00 hours the city of Leningrad will salute the valiant troops of the Leningrad Front with twenty-four volleys of 324 guns. . .

Glory to the fighting men of the Leningrad Front!

Glory to the working people of Lenin's city!

Eternal glory to the heroes who fell in the struggle for Lenin's city and for the freedom and independence of our Motherland. . .[4]

Immediately following the gun salute, a female worker from a local factory spoke over the radio broadcast network. She expressed the people's gratitude to the soldiers of the Leningrad and Volkhov fronts and to the sailors of the Soviet Baltic Fleet:

Dear brothers, fathers and fighting men! I am addressing these warm words of greeting and profound gratitude to you on behalf of the people of Leningrad. It was in honor of your heroic feats that the artillery salute was fired today. It was victory over Hitler's beasts that Leningrad celebrated. And it was not the bursts of enemy shells, but the victorious salute of our own guns that Leningrad heard today. Today it is bright and festive in our streets. And this is all due to you, our dear fighting men. The children of this great city are blessing you. Smash the bloodthirsty Nazis, drive them farther to the west, don't let them leave the soil of Leningrad alive. Tomorrow we will get down with new strength to the joyous work of restoring our city. Glory to our valiant fighting men![5]

In less than three weeks of fighting the Soviet forces had driven the Germans one hundred kilometers (62.5 miles) south and southwest of Leningrad and eighty kilometers (50 miles) west from Novgorod. Plus the Germans had been cleared from the main railroad line between Leningrad and Moscow. By the end of February the Germans had been driven to Panther Line.

To the north of Leningrad the Finish forces still occupied positions only thirty kilometers (18 miles) from the city. Their presence behind their strong defenses represented a threat to Leningrad. After the Soviet government failed to drive Finland from the war by diplomatic means in the spring of 1944, the Soviet forces did so militarily in June of that year. On June 10, the troops of General Govorov's Leningrad Front began the Vyborg operation to drive the Finnish forces from the Karelian Isthmus. On June 20 they succeeded in seizing Vyborg but were then rebuffed in their attempts to penetrate deeper into Finland between June 23 and July 13 (see Map 1). At the same time, the Soviet forces of the Karelian Front commanded by General Meretskov carried out the Svir-Petrozavodsk offensive. (General Meretskov was assigned to command the Karelian Front after the Volkhov Front was disbanded in February 1944.) The offensive was designed to clear Finnish forces from the area east of Lake Ladoga (see Map 1). The offensive lasted until August 9 during which time General Meretskov's troops liberated the territory between Lake Ladoga and Lake Onega. By August 10, 1944, the battle for Leningrad had come to an end. All the German and Finnish forces had been driven from the Leningrad region.

Leningrad had suffered enormously from the blockade and during its battle of defense. More than one thousand factory buildings and almost ten thousand apartment houses were destroyed or severely damaged due to enemy shelling and aerial bombardments. The total number of civilian deaths in Leningrad from starvation and bombardment is not known. An official Soviet commission, which investigated the German atrocities committed in the Leningrad region, placed the number of civilian deaths for the entire period of the siege at 632,253.[6] The statistic is low. Recent studies place civilian losses at between one and a half million and two million. The military casualties were just as appalling. By the war's end, according to a conservative official count, the Soviet forces fighting in the Leningrad region lost more than one million killed, captured or missing. No city in the history of humankind had suffered a siege that was this destructive to human life.

NOTES

1. Steven H. Newton, Retreat from Leningrad: Army Group North 1944/1945 (Atglen, Pennsylvania: Schiffer Publishing Ltd., 1995), 27–28.

2. A.V. Vinogradov and A. Pleysier, Bitva za Leningrad v sud bakh zhitelei garoda I oblasti: vospominaniiya zashchitnikov I zhitelei blockadnogo goroda I okkupirovannykh

territorii (Saint Petersburg, Russia: Saint Petersburg State University Press, 2005), 360–61.

3. David M. Glantz, The Siege of Leningrad 1941–1944 (Osceola, Wisconsin: MBI Publishing Company, 2001), 153–166.

4. Nikolai Kislitsyn and Vassily Zubakov, Leningrad Does Not Surrender, trans. Barry Jones (Moscow: Progress Publishers, 1989), 252–53.

5. Kislitsyn and Zubakov, Leningrad Does Not Surrender, 255.

6. A.V. Karasev, Leningradtsy v gody blokady (Moscow: Izdatelstre Adademii Nauk SSSR, 1959), 185.

Glossary of Names, Titles, and Abbreviations

GREAT PATRIOTIC WAR

Citizens of the Union of Soviet Socialist Republics (USSR) called World War Two, the Great Patriotic War.

KOMSOMOL

Membership in the Komsomol (The Young Communist League) was made up of young people between the ages of fifteen and twenty-eight. Komsomol membership among students in institutions of higher learning was usually high because membership would help a person gain admission into these institutions. Although the age limit for membership was twenty-eight, provision was made in the Komsomol statutes for officers to remain in the organization beyond that age.

Komsomol members were exposed to intense ideological indoctrination and were expected to participate in all aspects of Soviet society. Members would offer their services to the armed forces if the State called for recruits in an emergency situation. They were also expected to work in a factory or on a collective farm whenever there was a shortage of labor.

Members who entered the military or who joined an industrial or agricultural force were responsible for the political education of their co-workers who were of the same age group. Komsomols had been trained for this responsibility during Komsomol meetings which were mainly discussions and lectures on Marxist-Leninist ideology.

Komsomol members performed an important surveillance function in society. They frequently inspected enterprises and did this usually without prior warning. They sought to expose corruption, waste and inefficiency in management and laziness and tardiness among workers. The surveillance function of the Komsomol was even more extensive in institutions of higher learning. The activities of students who were members were carefully observed. Failure to meet the Komsomol standards of behavior could result in expulsion from the organization. Komsomol members with a university education were an important source for recruitment for the Communist Party

LENINGRAD DEFENSE MEDAL

On December 22, 1942, a decree of the Supreme Soviet of the Union of Soviet Socialist Republics (USSR) instituted a medal "For the Defense of Leningrad." It was awarded to everyone who was taking part in the defense of Leningrad. On the obverse of the medal, portrayed in bas-relief, are a soldier and sailor together with a male and female worker both armed with rifles. On one side of the medal are the words "For the Defense of Leningrad" and on the other side "For Our Soviet Motherland."

MOLOTOV COCKTAIL

The name "Molotov cocktail" is derived from Vyacheslav Molotov, the People's Commissar for Foreign Affairs. When Finland refused to cede to the Soviet Union in 1939 some parcels of territory and strategic ports, the Soviet forces attacked Finland by land, sea and air. Molotov claimed in radio broadcasts that the Soviet Union was not dropping bombs on Finland but rather food to the starving Finns. The Finns called the air bombs "Molotov bread baskets." Soon thereafter, the Finns responded by attacking Soviet tanks with "Molotov cocktails." The original design of the Molotov cocktail was a mixture of ethanol, tar and gasoline in a bottle. The bottle had a pyrophoric Bengal fire stick attached on its side. Before the bottle was thrown the Bengal stick was lit, and when the bottle broke on impact the mixture inside ignited.

NKVD

The Narodnyy Konissariat Vnutrennikh Del (People's Commissariat of Internal Affairs) was better known as the NKVD. Its origin was in Cheka (Extraordinary Commission) established in December 1917 as a temporary police force empowered to investigate counterrevolutionary activities and was to be abolished once Vladimir Lenin and the Bolsheviks had consolidated their power in Russia. It conducted a campaign of terror against the propertied classes and enemies of Bolshevism. Cheka's functions were transferred, in 1922, to the State Political Administration, or GPU, which was less powerful than its predecessor. In 1923, the United Political Administration, or OGPU, was created, and during its tenure, which ended in 1934, repression against the people lessened. The secret police again acquired vast punitive powers when they became, in 1934, the People's Commissariat for Internal Affairs, or NKVD. The NKVD was not subject to the control of the Communist Party nor was it restricted by law. It was the instrument that Joseph Stalin used in the 1930s against the people he wanted removed from the Party and arrested in the country. The NKVD remained one of the most powerful and feared Soviet institutions throughout the Stalinist period.

OCTOBER SOCIALIST REVOLUTION

Vladimir Lenin and his Bolsheviks removed from power the Provisional Government in Russia on November 7, 1917, according to the Gregorian calendar. The removal was called the October Socialist Revolution. In Russia the Gregorian calendar was adopted after the October Socialist Revolution (so named because it took place in October 1917 in the Julian calendar). On January 24, 1918, the Council of People's Commissars decreed that January 31, 1918, was to be followed by February 14, 1918.

STAKHANOVITE

On August 31, 1935, Alexey Stakhanov, a thirty-year-old miner working at the Central Irmino Mine in the Donetsk Basin, was reported to have dug 102 tons of coal in a single six-hour shift. It was many times more than a miner was expected to cut. Stakhanov was rewarded and praised, and the Soviet workers were told to model themselves on Stakhanov. It brought about the Stakhanovite movement. The title Stakhanovite was conferred on workers who had set production records by working harder or through reorganizing the way things were done in their places of employment. They were rewarded with better pay and with praise and publicity.

Bibliography

Adamovich, Ales, and Daniil Granin. A Book of the Blockade. Translated by Hilda Perham. Moscow: Raduga Publishers, 1983.

Fedeyev, Alexander. Leningrad in the Days of the Blockade. Translated by R. D. Charques. Wesport, Connecticut: Greenwood Press, Publishers, 1971.

Fischer, Louis, ed. Thirteen Who Fled. New York: Harper and Brothers, 1949.

Glantz, David M. The Siege of Leningrad 1941–1944. Osceola, Wisconsin: MBI Publishing Company, 2001.

Goure, Leon. The Siege of Leningrad. Stanford, California: Stanford University Press, 1962.

Karasev, A.V. Leningradtsy v gody blokady. Moscow: Izdatelstvo Adademii Nauk USSR, 1959.

Kislitsyn, Nikolai, and Vassily Zubakov. Leningrad Does Not Surrender. Translated by Barry Jones. Moscow: Progress Publishers, 1989.

Lomagin, Nikita. The Unknown Blockade. Moscow: Hower Institution on War, Revolution and Peace, 2002. (In Russian).

Losev, A. On the Firing Line. Luga: Luga Publication, 2005. (In Russian).

Mannerheim, Marshal. The Memoirs of Marshal Mannerheim. Translated by Count Eric Levenhaupt. London: Cassell and Co., Ltd., 1953.

Meisel, James H., and Edward S. Kozera. Materials for the Study of the Soviet System. Ann Arbor, Michigan: George Wahr Publishing Co., 1950.

Mishalov, Neil. Radio Address of 3 July 1941 by Joseph Stalin, Chairman of the Council of People's Commissars of the U.S.S.R. Transcribed and translated by Soviet Russia Today, August, 1941. http://www.mishalov.com/Stalin-3July41.html (29 May 2007).

Mishalov, Neil. Radio Address of 22 June 1941 by Vyacheslav Molotov, Assistant Chairman of the Council of the People's Commissars of the USSR, and the People's Commissar for Foreign Affairs. Transcribed and translated by Novosti Press Agency, June, 1941. http://www.mishalov.com/Molotov-22 June 41. html (29 May 2007).

Newton, Steven H. Retreat from Leningrad: Army Group North 1944/1945. Atglen, Pennsylvania: Schiffer Publishing Ltd., 1995.

Pavlov, Dmitri V. Leningrad 1941. Translated by John Clinton Adams. Chicago, Illinois: The University of Chicago Press, 1965.

Salisbury, Harrison E. The 900 Days: The Siege of Leningrad. New York: Avon Books, 1970.

Skomorovsky, Boris, and E.G. Morris. The Siege of Leningrad. New York: E.P. Dutton and Company, Inc., 1944.

Skrjabina, Elena. Siege and Survival. Translated by Norman Luxenburg. New York: Pinnacle Books, Inc., 1973.

Tikhonov, Nikolai. The Defense of Leningrad. London: Hutchinson and Co.,Ltd., no date.

Vinogradov, A.V., and A. Pleysier. Bitva za Leningrad v sud' bakh zhitelel goroda I oblasti: vospominahiiy a zashchitnikov I zhitelei blokadnogo goroda I okkupirovannykh territorii. Saint Petersburg, Russia: Saint Petersburg State University Press, 2005.

Werth, Alexander. Leningrad. London: Hamish Hamilton, 1944.

White, William L. Report on the Russians. New York: Harcourt, Brace and Co., 1945.

Index

Books by the Author

Bitva za Leningrad v sud' bakh zhitelel goroda I oblasti:
vospominahiiy a zashchitnikov I zhitelei blokadnogo goroda I okkupirovan-
nykh territorii. (The Battle of Leningrad: Memories of its Citizens and People
in the Occupied Surrounding Areas)
Saint Petersburg State University Press, 2005

Surviving the Blockade of Leningrad
University Press of America, 2006

The Women of Izmaelovka: A Soviet Union Collective Farm in Siberia
University Press of America, 2007